LIFE BEYOND WASTE

LIFE BEYOND WASTE

Work and Infrastructure in Urban Pakistan

WAQAS H. BUTT

STANFORD UNIVERSITY PRESS

STANFORD, CALIFORNIA

Stanford University Press
Stanford, California

© 2023 by Waqas Hameed Butt. All rights reserved.

Printed and bound by CPI Group (UK) Ltd, Croydon, CR0 4YY

Library of Congress Cataloging-in-Publication Data

Names: Butt, Waqas H. (Waqas Hameed), author.
Title: Life beyond waste : work and infrastructure in urban Pakistan / Waqas H. Butt.
Other titles: South Asia in motion.
Description: Stanford, California : Stanford University Press, 2023. | Series: South Asia in motion | Includes bibliographical references and index.
Identifiers: LCCN 2022041080 (print) | LCCN 2022041081 (ebook) | ISBN 9781503634770 (cloth) | ISBN 9781503635722 (paperback) | ISBN 9781503635739 (ebook)
Subjects: LCSH: Refuse collectors—Pakistan—Lahore. | Refuse and refuse Disposal—Social aspects—Pakistan—Lahore. | Caste—Pakistan—Lahore. | Lahore (Pakistan)—Social conditions.
Classification: LCC HD8039.R462 B88 2023 (print) | LCC HD8039.R462 (ebook) | DDC 363.72/8209549143—dc23/eng/20230224
LC record available at https://lccn.loc.gov/2022041080
LC ebook record available at https://lccn.loc.gov/2022041081

Cover design by Daniel Benneworth-Gray

Photography courtesy of the author

Typeset by Newgen in Adobe Caslon Pro 10.75/15 pt

*For
my Nano,
Saeeda Bagum*

CONTENTS

ACKNOWLEDGMENTS

Even before its inception, this book has been shaped by the thought, insights, effort, concern, and care of any number of people. Over the course of several years, a handful of individuals, for whom I use pseudonyms in this book, have exhibited a generosity when sharing much about their lives and worlds, as well as that of many others. That generosity has molded my thinking and writing in important ways. Most obviously, I would not have been able to get a sense of how waste work and processes of urbanization have transformed the city of Lahore without their words, observations, and explanations. They made clear how life in Lahore—of individuals and communities—is inextricably linked to their own lives and that of their kin. Aside from such empirical observations, however, their generosity demanded I make certain decisions about what to include and not in my writing. In making those decisions, one confronts the ethical substance of intellectual work. My hope is that the words appearing across the pages of this book honor the generosity that these individuals have repeatedly shown me over the years.

There were also many others—workers, supervisors, attendance checkers, drivers, junkyard owners, intermediaries, and managers—who showed and explained to me the everyday workings of Pakistan's waste infrastructures. They let me accompany them on numerous occasions, responded to my questions, and tried their best to clarify what seemed so obvious to them. Many others did not show any interest in my research, or, as was the case with Pashtun workers, did not speak to me due to surveillance and policing by the Pakistani state. Ethnography must recognize not only those who are active participants but also, those who are present even if they are unwilling or unable to participate, since their lives, too, are part of the worlds about which we write.

Several people in Lahore were instrumental to starting and completing the research that went into this book. After an outdoor lunch in FC College, where he listened to my initial frustrations conducting fieldwork, Imdad Hussain not only explained the intricacies of local government and its relationship to waste management but also put me in touch with an alumnus of FC College who was a manager at Lahore Waste Management Company. That alumnus, Sohail Anwar Malik, allowed me to spend time with a field staff of supervisors, drivers, and municipal workers. Later, Shazia Khan in Lahore arranged a meeting with informal workers when they were being prevented from collecting household waste. This initial meeting was an introduction as much to these workers as to the politics of waste in urban Pakistan. Those politics have not diminished in any way. All these initial connections made possible the bulk of my fieldwork and thus, the materials comprising this book.

Rafay Alam, at the time but also more recently, has always created time for conversations about Lahore—its history, politics, and landscapes. I would also like to thank Jatoi Sahb at the Solid Waste Management Department who gave me a broad historical overview of waste disposal and management in Lahore, as well as the office staffs at the SWM Department, the Lahore Waste Management Company, OzPak, and AlBayrak who explained the intricacies of these institutions. Conversations with representatives of the Jharu Kash Mazdoor Union also helped situate waste work within Pakistan's labor politics. Conversations about research with Hassaan Sipra, Adila Batool, and Muhammad Nawaz Chaudhary increased the breadth of my knowledge about waste throughout Pakistan.

The staff at the archives in the Punjab Civil Secretariat, Punjab Government Library, National College of Arts, and National Institute of Historical and Cultural Research (Quaid-e-Azam University) were all forthcoming and helpful as I conducted archival research. In particular, Abbas Chughtai Sahb and Madam Shamim Jaffri created a space for me over several weeks in the Punjab government archives so I could patiently work through materials related to Lahore, sanitation and public health, architecture, and related topics from the colonial period. I would be remiss not to mention William Glover, who over email gave me initial leads about what archival resources to pursue. Also, Rabia Nadir shared with me a treasure trove of knowledge about history, migration, labor, and spatial dynamics in Lahore over several illuminating conversations at her home and office.

For nearly two decades now, I have returned to Lahore and always found support among friends and family there. I cannot begin to express my gratitude to Sher Ali Khan, Sarah Eleazar, and Zahid Ali for their friendship. Ammar Ali Jan, Tabitha Spence, Abdul Aijaz, Nida Kirmani, and Ali Usman Qasmi have supported this project in their own ways. Zehra Hashmi, Sardar Hussain, Anila Daulatzai, and Muntasir Sattar all helped me figure out how to do fieldwork over the course of many months. Though I have relied upon numerous family members in Lahore and across Pakistan, Imtiaz Mamu, Diddi Baji, and Taya Ammi have created homes for me over the years.

Numerous people in San Diego contributed to this research and writing. Joseph Hankins has been a cornerstone of steadfast support, always ready to have a conversation about any topic or concern popping into my head. Lilly Irani and the Feminist Labor Lab shaped the writing of this book in countless ways, while key interventions of this book would not have been possible without the guidance of Kalindi Vora at a formative moment. I have also found myself returning to courses and conversations with David Pedersen, Joel Robbins, and Steve Parish. Whether in the seminar rooms and hallways of SSB, nearby at Regents Pizza, or out somewhere in North Park, the friendships that grew during my years in San Diego were as much about intellectual companionship as they were about mutual support and care. Michael Berman, Amrita Kurian, Tadeusz Skotnicki, David Pinzur, Allen Tran, Raquel Pacheco, Corinna Most, and Andrew Somerville each in their own way provided the necessary companionship to overcome challenges and grow during my years in San Diego. Also, special thanks to Gary Lee, with whom I shared lengthy discussions over innumerable meals that kept us both nourished in multiple ways.

Various parts of the book have benefited from the contributions of colleagues at conferences, colloquiums, and workshops. Talat Ahmed, Kaveri Qureshi, Ayaz Qureshi, Barbara Harris-White, and Geeta Patel at the University of Edinburgh debated my materials with a rigor that pushed the work in unexpected ways. Radhika Govindrajan and several others at the University of Washington gave me an opportunity to present materials that were developed into the final chapter of the book. I want to thank Ifthikar Dadi for allowing me to share my work with a large and diverse audience at a colloquium at Cornell University. The engagement of Natasha Raheja at the colloquium, as well as at earlier moments when the manuscript was in an embryonic phase, has proven invaluable. I would also like to thank audiences at South Asian University, Lahore University of Management Sciences, and Binghamton University for valuable feedback on various chapters. Sharika Thiranagama, Kamran Asdar Ali, and Michelle Murphy took part in a vibrant book workshop organized by the Centre for Ethnography at UTSC that improved the quality of the manuscript, while furnishing me with the confidence to make clear the stakes of my work. I would also like to express my gratitude to others who have engaged with my work in different venues and at different moments: Nikhil Anand, Naveeda Khan, Surinder Jhodka, Jacob Doherty, Patrick O'Hare, Catherine Alexander, Ayyaz Malick, Amy Zhang, Mythri Jegathesan, Sarah Besky, Josh Reno, Ishita Dey, Nida Rehman, Kavita Philip, Maura Finkelstein, Sophia Stamatopoulou-Robbins, Eli Elinoff, Kasim Trimezy, and Ashveer Pal Singh.

Over the past few years, the colleagues and friends I have made in Toronto have been proven supportive. Shiho Satsuka, Zoe Wool, Firat Bozcali, and Cassandra Hartblay gave insightful comments on various parts of the book. In addition to their intellectual engagements, Katie Kilroy-Marac and Alejandro Paz have been reliable sources of support as I transitioned to life at the UofT. Ajay Rao at the Centre for South Asian Civilization gave me a space to present my work. Naisargi Dave, Francis Cody, and Sumayya Kassamali, in addition to being some of the most careful readers, have been friends who I can also rely upon as colleagues. Conversations with Bradley Dunseith and Alaa Mitwaly are always refreshing and allow me to remain open to the possibilities of academic work. Michael Lambek ensured my transition to Toronto went as smoothly as I could have hoped for, and his support for the book workshop allowed me to finalize a draft of the manuscript that could be submitted for review. The Doug-Ford-mandated friendship of Raheel

Khursheed (and Sumayya) ensured we all remained nourished and supported during the COVID-19 lockdown. Despite my long-winded explanations, Pahull Bains did her best to provide support and advice as this project entered its last stages.

I would also like to thank Thomas Blom Hansen for advocating for this project and demonstrating a keen interest in having this book brought into the world. Despite taking up his position at Stanford University Press after I had just submitted my manuscript, Dylan Kyung-lim White has been an editorial beacon, being attentive and guiding the book smoothly at every stage of the process. Having such editorial guidance has allowed me to concentrate my own efforts on honing and finalizing the manuscript itself. Finally, I would like to thank the anonymous reviewers for their detailed, extensive, and thoughtful feedback.

Numerous friends, old and new, have heard about this work over way too many years. In particular, Dilveer Vahali, Mina Vahali, Jan Schotte, Anthony Ngo, Katherine Juhasz, Ondrej Juhasz, Chandani Patel, and Pradeep Ghosh have been sources of relaxation and joy. My family in New Jersey, New York, and Switzerland have kept me in grounded in ways I cannot express. I relish the opportunities to spend time with Tahir, Roz, Sisi, and now Zahid in their home, enjoying some of the best pizza in the tristate area. Watching movies and ordering takeout with Ahmad has always been a blast. The visits of Salman, Erica, Sofia, and Kira during winter holidays are equally rambunctious and lovely affairs. Despite not always appreciating the intricacies of my work, my parents Abdul and Riffat Butt have prioritized care over anything else, which has over the years given way to genuine curiosity and openness. This is unsurprising, as they always taught their children, not to mention many others, to pursue knowledge and be thoughtful about the world around them. I have tried to mirror that approach in the pages of this book: to pursue knowledge about the world that originates from a place of care.

ILLUSTRATIONS

In 1952, several thousand migrants from those areas of Punjab that became part of India, many of whom had been displaced by the violence of Partition and belonged to the Dalit, group known as Gagare, found themselves on what was then Lahore's agrarian peripheries. A member of the Municipal Corporation of Lahore (MCL) at the time, Mehnga Lal Sapoochvi observed these displaced migrants "had no source of livelihood," as the MCL had criminalized begging and robbed them of a possible means of supporting themselves. He then went on to note, despite a policy to have them employed within governmental departments, "no possible arrangements have been made to assist" them. That same year, in Punjab's urban centers, sanitation and public health was noted to be deteriorating since "conservancy" staff and labor had been replaced by "inexperienced" hands, just as urban populations ballooned due to an influx of refugees and a fall in municipal revenues (Government of Punjab 1952, 45). When confronted by the deteriorating state of sanitation and public health in urban centers, on the one hand, and the arrival of several thousand Dalit migrants onto Lahore's peripheries on the other, it was self-evident to members of the MCL what was to be done with such migrants: they were to be "employed as sweepers."[1]

Over the next several decades, low- or noncaste (Dalit) groups,[2] from the Punjab have migrated across Pakistan for a variety reasons—from the violence of Partition to changes in agrarian livelihoods to expanding urban economies—and consistently found themselves toiling away in the country's waste infrastructures, whether employed as municipal sanitation workers or laboring under informalized work relations.[3] During this time, Lahore's geographic boundaries have expanded from its traditional center of the Inner City (Andarūn-i-Shehr) and pushed in a southeasterly direction, away from the River Ravi that now abuts its northern and western boundary (see Figure 1.3). As the city expanded in a southeasterly direction, residential and commercial development oriented toward a politically ascendant middle and upper class has taken place on its previously agrarian peripheries, just as the urban poor and working-class communities have been excluded and their settlements within this unevenly urbanizing landscape rendered precarious. Forms of life, ones that have arisen across Pakistan's rapidly and unevenly urbanizing landscapes, have emerged enmeshed in a world of waste, one in which all kinds of trash, detritus, refuse, discards, and other material things have proliferated from commodities consumed and disposed of on a mass scale.

Today, Lahore's population produces more waste that at any other point in its history.[4] Dirt, ash, construction sand, unused cement, broken bricks, paper notebooks, household plastics, metal wiring, animal feces, glass bottles, rotting food, dried-out rotis, human hair—these are just some of the materials produced every day by the city's estimated 11 million inhabitants. Each day, this collective detritus and refuse is collected, transported, and disposed of by either several thousand workers from the City District Government of Lahore (CDGL) or an equally large number of workers laboring under informalized work relations. Although municipal sanitation workers are almost entirely Christian and informal workers are predominantly Muslim, both classes of workers are assumed to come from low- or noncaste backgrounds. These workers, along with residents, shopkeepers, junkyard owners, intermediaries, suppliers, and countless others, perform an essential form of work in Lahore's waste infrastructures: they take away waste materials from certain places in the urban landscape and transform them into something else that is then present elsewhere.[5]

It is undeniable that, despite Pakistani cities being often described as veritable "wastelands," overwhelmed by their own collective detritus, an enormous amount of work and labor is marshalled on a daily basis to dispose of these materials, so that life in a city like Lahore can go on and be reproduced. Sanitation workers use municipal handcarts to gather waste materials, either by sweeping "public" spaces with a *jhāṛu* (handheld broom) or taking them away from "private" ones for an extra fee. When handcarts reach capacity, workers place a soiled sheet on the ground, tip it over so a portion of the waste falls, and then, usually with the help of another worker, pick up the sheet by its ends and hurl the materials into containers or directly into compactors. Many of these workers make sure to separate potentially valuable items (*bachat*) from the trash (*kachrā* or *korā*) to sell to junkyard owners. Simultaneously, informal workers, many of whom reside in *jhuggīān* (clusters of huts) settlements on Lahore's urbanizing peripheries, traverse its landscape to collect waste materials from a variety of spaces, both public and private. These workers similarly deposit useless trash onto the back of a donkey cart or refitted motorbike and use soiled sheets to make layers of waste materials. Then, once having made several layers this way, they go over to those same municipal containers or machinery, stand on top of their carts, pick one layer up at a time, and, with the help of another worker, dispose of the materials. Also receiving minimal service fees, informal workers separate from the trash those materials that can be sold forward, but, unlike most municipal workers, these materials are brought back to their households, where they are sorted, accumulated, and eventually sold to junkyard owners and/or intermediaries, who then supply these materials to manufacturing and industrial units where waste materials will be remade into commodities.

Regardless of who collects them, waste materials, having been deemed to no longer be of use or worth, are deposited into municipal containers and then transported through a combination of machinery and human labor to a series of dumping grounds and a landfill site on the city's outskirts. Other materials enter the city's waste infrastructures but are directed into other spaces, such as junkyards, warehouses, and industrial units, where they will be remade into commodities. Whether waste materials are disposed of or remade into commodities, much of the everyday work surrounding these materials takes them from one place and makes them present elsewhere, while also transforming those same materials into something else of use again.

The texture of urban life across Pakistan has been transformed by a series of related but distinct processes—from unevenly and rapidly urbanizing landscapes to interlinked spatial, economic, and infrastructural dynamics to entwined levels of proliferating consumption and waste generation. This particular form of work—waste work—reveals the intimate and unexpected connections—social, economic, spatial—between forms of lives and the worlds of waste in urban Pakistan as they have taken shape in recent decades. The account that unfolds across the proceeding pages, in which such connections are unpacked and examined, foregrounds the lives and labors of waste workers and their kin, which have been and continue to be central to the everyday life of Pakistani cities. It is only by being attentive to waste work as a social and political relationship that we can then discern not only how lives and worlds in urban Pakistan have come to be reworked and transformed over the course of several decades but also what possibilities for life have been made available to those whose effort and toil reproduces life—whether of individuals or collectives—in a city like Lahore.

LIFE BEYOND WASTE

INTRODUCTION

IN OCTOBER 2017, I spoke on the phone to Rameez, who is a sanitation worker employed by the municipality in Lahore. I asked him about the neighborhood and home where the family lives, while he casually told me about upcoming plans for his eldest son's wedding. Before hanging up, we agreed to meet. A few days later, in the early afternoon, I saw him standing outside the railway ticketing booth that has been converted into a field office for the Solid Waste Management Department. Outside the office, a garbage compactor was parked, awaiting instructions, while a dozen or so sanitation workers were streaming out after having their attendance taken. Inside, the *dāroghah* (sanitary supervisor) and a couple of workers still lounged about after their shift had ended—I waved and gave them my salaam. After greeting them, I returned to Rameez, who was holding a carton of mangled wood pieces. Though his responsibilities as a municipal sanitation worker are predominantly focused on sweeping and collecting waste materials from public spaces, for which he is paid a wage, Rameez also takes away waste materials from households, for which he gets paid a minimal service fee and keeps some materials that he will deposit at a nearby junkyard and eventually cash in for money (Fig. 0.1). This time, Rameez explained, he was taking the wood pieces home where they would be used for cooking purposes when gas supplies drop.

FIGURE 0.1. *Municipal handcart containing waste. Note, in front of image, netted bag hanging, where potentially valuable waste is temporarily stored. Source: Author.*

We then sat in one of the many *qingqi* rickshaws that run dedicated routes between where Rameez lives and where he works. We passed by areas like Quaid-e-Azam Industrial Estate and Township before entering working-class settlements situated on Lahore's southwestern periphery. For the past decade or so, Rameez, along with his immediate family, has resided in one such settlement named Bāgrīāṉ (see Map 0.2). In the elapsing two years, the locality's main road had been incrementally built up, with greater commercial activity, and it is now considerably more *pakkā*,[1] though still uncomfortably uneven from a spattering of potholes. We eventually reached the *galī* (alley) that leads to Rameez's *mohallā* (neighborhood). In 2015 the alley was made of dirt and rocks. It, too, had been flattened and became somewhat more paved. Houses stand mostly one next to the other, though one or two empty plots of land are sandwiched between them, while agricultural fields growing animal fodder stand just beyond these houses. Though residents of Bāgrīāṉ perform all

MAP 0.1. *Map of Pakistan*

kinds of work across Lahore, many municipal workers I came to know reside here and in another nearby area known as Green Town—where Rameez previously resided with his natal family after they migrated to Lahore from more agrarian areas of Punjab.

It is not just the locality of Bāgrīā̠n that has changed during this time; so has the home in which Rameez and his family reside. The front gate has been made more robust. The area just inside the gate, previously used as a kitchen, now has a rickshaw parked there. Beyond another entryway, a compact kitchen has been built, and the two rooms on the first floor have filled out with electronics and furniture. An upper portion, which was under construction at the time of my visit, has an open balcony, with

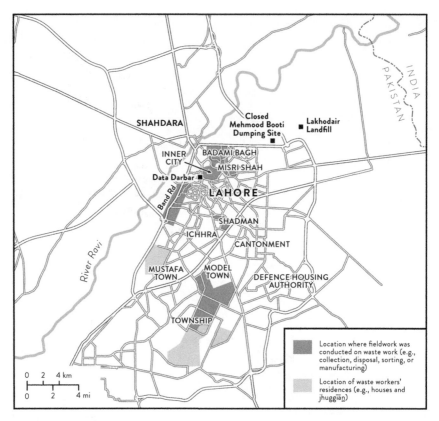

MAP 0.2. *Map of Lahore*

a screen in the floor through which light filters to illuminate the seating area below. As the home has no windows, Rameez told me how the family relishes moments when the first floor gets bathed in sunlight. As Rameez pointed out other incremental changes, an earlier conversation we had in May 2014 flashes through my mind: we discussed household finances, for which Rameez uses the English word "circuit," when he turned to me and said, "Butt Sahb, in Punjabi, it is said, 'A home should be one's own, even if it's a straw hut (ghar āpṇā hove, bhaven kakhā̱n dī kullī hove).'"

Indeed, homes were constant matters of concern for waste workers and their kin. Residing in a *jhuggīā̱n* (huts) settlement located along Multan Road, just before Thokar Niaz Baig, Manzoor and his kin, for the past several decades, have been taking away and collecting waste materials from a couple hundred households in two different localities across Lahore. Though also receiving a service fee like Rameez, most of the income generated out of their toil comes from those materials that can be separated and sold forward to junkyard owners and intermediaries who supply industrial and manufacturing units across Pakistan with these materials for production purposes. In order to do so, potentially valuable waste materials are brought back to the *jhuggīā̠n* settlement where Manzoor and his family reside (see Fig. 0.2). Importantly, mostly male kin collect waste from localities under Manzoor's control, though female kin also at times engage in that labor, while much of the work of sorting and dissembling done within the home is performed by female kin, though here too male daily laborers are at times brought in. For several decades now, like many other informal workers, Manzoor and his extended kin network have utilized this form of work to generate a relatively stable source of income.

During this same time, however, cycles of dispossession and re-settlement have rendered their settlement precarious and uncertain.

FIGURE 0.2. *Settlement of* jhuggīā̠n *(huts) in Lahore where some waste workers reside. Source: Author.*

Explaining why their homes have been subject to repeated and violent acts of destruction, another waste worker who resided in a *jhuggī* was prone to say, "These *jhuggīān̲* might be garbage for housing societies, but for us it is a home." Since we first met in 2014, Manzoor and his immediate family have been forced to shift their homes at least three times. In 2017, they had just been settled in a locality (Jatt Chowk) adjacent to where we had met previously in 2014, after a housing society near their previous settlement had made a complaint to the Lahore Development Authority (LDA) that then cleared their *jhuggī*, as well as that of many others. The area where he came to reside has just recently been settled, with a spattering of built homes and a few other *jhuggīān̲*. This time, the *jhuggī* was placed on a plot of land owned by someone else that shared a wall with a nearby shop. Upon entering, I noted quilts hanging to dry on the brick wall and asked Manzoor about them. They were ralli quilts they had acquired many years ago, he told me (see Fig. 0.3). Having been removed only a couple of months ago, I was surprised by how quickly the *jhuggī*, inside and out, had been rebuilt, so the lives of Manzoor and his kin could go on—its wooden structure had been secured; beds, storage

FIGURE 0.3. *Quilts drying inside a* jhuggī. *Source: Author.*

bins, appliances, and any number of other items were protected by its roof remade from second-hand materials; and donkeys, carts, and motorbikes used for all kinds of purposes were arranged against the wall of the neighboring shop.

As their work involves collecting, transporting, and sorting waste materials, the lives and homes of Rameez, Manzoor, and any number of others have been undeniably shaped by a world increasingly saturated by waste. Yet, it is not just these lives and homes that have been shaped by such a world, so have the lives found in those aforementioned housing societies populated by Lahore's ascendant middle and upper classes. These middle- and upper-class households consume commodities of all kinds that then generate waste materials that must be disposed of—a form of work or labor performed by those like Rameez and Manzoor across urban Pakistan. Indeed, this act of disposal is essential not only to maintaining the cleanliness but also to reproducing the status of such households and the lives contained within them. In that sense, waste work holds together lives and worlds across Lahore's unevenly urbanizing landscape. As an expansive social and political relationship, it is a form of work that connects, with each other, any number of lives across Pakistan, ones that have arisen in a world awash with waste.

The central concern of this book is that particular form of work or labor—waste work—that comprises differentiated kinds of effort exercised on a world in which waste materials have proliferated through the consumption of disposable commodities taking place on a mass scale.[2] This form of work has been organized at a similarly collective scale, such that waste materials are taken away on a regular basis from certain spaces, whether households, shops, or plazas, and made present elsewhere and transformed into something else, whether through containers, dumping grounds, landfills or junkyards, warehouses, or industrial units. For this reason, waste work constitutes an infrastructure aimed at reproducing forms of life in Lahore and beyond that have been organized along the lines of caste, class, and religion. Moreover, as an infrastructure, it is embedded in a complex field of social and political relationships, ones that extend from and connect the workings of the bureaucratic state and informal economies to the uneven trajectory of urbanization across the country. Approaching waste work from this perspective—as an infra-structure materializing wider transformations of life—a series of questions appears before us: What set of processes, both past and ongoing, have converged around waste materials and work? How does this form of work, organized as an infrastructure, move and transform waste materials, while concurrently stitching together individual and collective life across urban Pakistan? And what forms of life are reproduced through these variegated and distinct processes?

Caste, Class, Religion

Pakistan was founded as a nation-state for the Muslim minority of the Indian subcontinent. After its creation, this Muslim minority became Pakistan's majority, while non-Muslims (Christians, Hindus, and others) became the new country's religious minorities. Along with Bengal, the partitioning of the Punjab saw Hindus and Sikhs depart those areas that became part of Pakistan for India, while Muslims left those areas of the Punjab (as well as other regions of the subcontinent) that became part of India for Pakistan. Despite these geographic and demographic reworkings, Muslim nationalism, with its unifying imaginings of community, that took shape in British India and sustained the demand for Pakistan has had varying degrees of success in encompassing the ethnic, linguistic, caste, and sectarian identities of Muslim groups across Pakistan.[3] The question then becomes, How has the project of the Pakistani state, animated as it has been by the contested hegemony of Muslim nationalism,[4] shaped forms of life, especially along the lines of caste, class, and religion, in a city like Lahore as urbanization has unfolded? This book responds to such a query by delineating those forms of life as they have been organized and transformed across Pakistan over the past several decades.

Many of the waste workers with whom I conducted fieldwork had some connection to the region situated in the Bari Doab, between the rivers Ravi and Sutlej, that is known as Maajha Punjab. Forms of life in this region have historically been built upon and shifted alongside caste-based relations of work, exchange, settlement, and marriage in which both low- or noncaste groups and those of upper-caste backgrounds have been embedded. As many have noted (Ali 1988; Harding 2008; Barrier 1967), those caste groups who were considered "agriculturalists," either because they owned lands or were seen to be "cultivators" or "agriculturalists" by the colonial state, have been dominant across both agrarian and urban settings in the Punjab, while low- or noncaste groups have fallen into a number of designations as "menials" or *kammis* (village servants) that have had varying and distinct connections to agrarian labor.[5] Relatedly, prior to Partition, castes, such as Khatris, Aroras, and Banias who were predominantly Hindu, were prominent actors in urban centers and commercial activity across the Punjab, becoming connected to the agrarian economy through indebtedness. As I explain in greater detail in chapter 1, many of these low- or noncaste groups, especially those who were directly involved in agriculture, were embedded in a complex set of relations with "cultivators" or "agriculturalists" that involved work, exchange, land, settlement, and marriage, and would be recruited by municipal government as "sweepers."

Caste-based relations in the Punjab were not just a division of labor; they were also a division of laborers (Ambedkar 2014). An assumption existed across Punjab's agrarian landscapes that certain kinds of persons were disposed to perform certain kinds of work. The status of land-owning groups presumed to be from upper-caste backgrounds was premised upon a connection between landedness and cultivation, which positioned these groups as a landed peasantry valorized and protected by colonial and postcolonial regimes. Their positioning, at once material and ideological, was in contrast to the status of low- or noncaste groups, which was derived from a lack of landownership and performing other kinds of noncultivating (or "services") work, even if they did engage in cultivation as nonlandowners. As limitations existed to undoing such hierarchical relations that could then shift the status of persons from distinct caste backgrounds, conversion to Sikhism, Christianity, or Islam, as well as the emergence of reform movements like the Arya Samaj, attempted to undo caste hierarchies by repositioning individuals from these caste groups within another social category (i.e., Muslim or Sikh) or reworking categories themselves (i.e., Hindu), which is why conversion or reform was accompanied by the taking on of different names. For instance, Chūṛās (noncaste Hindus) that converted to Islam, Christianity, and Sikhism came to be known as, respectively, Musalis, Masihis, and Mazhabi Sikhs, while others became adherents of Balmiki/Valimiki sects (taking on that name) or entered "upliftment" projects of Hindu reform movements.

Concurrently, these forms of life have shifted through repeated and prominent interventions by successive colonial and postcolonial regimes. Accompanying the growth of the colonial state and its techno-legal apparatus following the Rebellion of 1857 and direct Crown rule a year later, revenue and land settlement in the Punjab, as well much of British India, sought to make the agrarian economy more productive and rational, such that revenue could be extracted more efficiently. This intervention subsequently had the effect of stabilizing what was then understood to be its social structure, especially with regards to the "customs," "rights," "obligations," and "services" enjoyed by the various groups, especially the "tribes" and "castes" that populated Punjab's agrarian landscape.

Also commencing in 1881 and continuing until the final decades of British rule, a large-scale system of canals was constructed in central and western Punjab. This system of canals, as well as the colonies that accompanied them, were built on tracts of land situated between Punjab's primary rivers. Not receiving water, these lands had gone uncultivated, and they were often described as barren, being referred to as "wastelands" throughout this period (Ali 1988; Fox 1985; Gilmartin 2020; see also Gidwani 2008, 93–113). Not only would land grants be given to those who remained loyal during the Rebellion of 1857 and were designated "agriculturalists," the Punjab Land Alienation Act of 1900 prevented those belonging to "nonagricultural tribes" from acquiring property rights,[6] just as other "agriculturalists" were taken from more densely populated eastern parts of the Punjab and settled, along with "nomadic" populations, in those areas opened by land and revenue settlement, canal colonization, and eventually, other infrastructures like the railways. These "agriculturalists" were oftentimes accompanied by low- or noncaste groups who were landless laborers, considered "nonagriculturalists," and who worked under a variety of "customary" relations with "agriculturalists" (see Ali 1988; Harding 2008; Barrier 1967). Many of these interventions by the colonial state at once stabilized caste-based relations surrounding work, settlement, and exchange, just as they pushed landless agrarian labor into wage labor, and certain low- or noncaste groups, who were already considered "menials" or "artisans," became involved in artisanal and other kinds of trades. Urbanization throughout this period also provided opportunities for work and settlement in cities like Lahore, as well other urban centers across the Punjab and North India.

Following the formation of Pakistan, those groups considered "agriculturalist" and seen to be of upper-caste backgrounds have been able to reproduce their position across generations, especially by utilizing their control over and access to land in the Punjabi countryside to gain access to other sources of power, wealth, and status, whether through patron-client relationships, political parties, industrial development, informal markets, urban settlement, education, and/or employment. On the other hand, those who would be considered of low- or noncaste, or "nonagriculturalists," have historically performed various kinds of work and labor in the countryside but lacked control over and ownership of land. While many have acquired land and experienced upward mobility, access to those same sources of power, wealth, and status enjoyed by upper-caste groups considered "agriculturalists" has been closed off to or severely limited to low- or noncaste groups considered "nonagriculturalists," especially waste workers like those with whom I conducted fieldwork. Just as the hierarchies characteristic of caste-based relations in Punjab have diminished or been undone over the years, other kinds of relations and forms of life have emerged in urban centers across Pakistan that draw upon these historical inequalities and interdependencies.

Caste as a social category has intersected with and at times, been eclipsed by other categories, specifically religion and class, within social and political life. As a putatively egalitarian religion, Islam was presumed to not recognize arbitrary distinctions and the ascriptive status characteristic of caste, while other secularized and egalitarian discourses have charted out a liberal framework for caste equality.[7] When caste practices such as prohibitions against touch and commensality erupt into public life, they are deemed illegitimate, as they are viewed to be contravening both egalitarian ideals within Islamic traditions and liberal models of equal citizenship. Moreover, because of large-scale conversions to

Christianity and the hegemony of Muslim nationalism, Christianity as a minority religion (similar to Hinduism) rather than caste has become the historical basis for social and political identity among Christians in Pakistan, which at times has made Christian status synonymous with being low- or noncaste (Walbridge 2003).[8] Additionally, as Christians have faced violence after accusations of blasphemy, greater emphasis has been placed on Christians as a religious minority, especially in light of a global human rights discourse on religious freedom and persecution. As religion has become a prominent marker for one's social and political identity in Pakistan, renewed associations between religion and caste have been created as social life has been reorganized across the country, which I explore in chapter 4.

Along with religion, another point of convergence has been between caste and class, specifically the dominant role played by *ashrāf* groups among Muslims across the Indian subcontinent, or what some have recently described as "*ashraafiya* hegemony."[9] The term *ashrāf*[10] was used by the colonial apparatus as a category for conducting censuses and ethnographic description, where it would reference higher status patrilineal descent groups among Muslims, akin to twice-born caste Hindus, but with the added quality of having presumed "foreign" ancestry, whether descent was reckoned through presumed Arab, Afghan, Persian, or Central Asian lineages.[11] On the other hand, *ajlāf*[12] referred to those who belong to groups that could not claim such "noble" descent and ancestry and engaged in occupations similar to ones described earlier for low- or noncaste groups—on both accounts (i.e., descent and labor), *ajlāf* groups being associated with Hindus of "lower" caste background. The distinction between *ashrāf* and *ajlāf* became critical to the ways in which the colonial state negotiated social, legal, and political relationships with Muslim groups, while *ashrāf* elites, as a privileged class of Muslims, sought to legitimize themselves as the representatives of Muslims as a unified community in British India.[13]

Additionally, the cultural and political hegemony that Urdu language and Urdu-speaking populations attained in the early years of Pakistan's independence tended to be inflected by the higher status accorded to *ashraafiya*, especially ideals of respectability (*sharāfat*) attached to the inheritances from Mughal courts of manners, dress, literature, aesthetic norms, and Islamic ethical traditions (*akhlāq*). Not only would those considered or claiming the status of being *ashrāf* come to constitute a powerful component of Pakistan's class formation,[14] kinship among Punjabi Muslims tended to incorporate status distinctions between *ashrāf* and *ajlāf*, not to mention the hegemony the *ashraafiya* and Urdu language enjoyed among urban elites in Punjab. The status of *ashrāf* groups, as well as higher-status *ajlāf* ones, across Punjab, as well as Sindh,[15] was implicated in, though distinct from, the control of land and differentiated forms of work and labor.[16]

Such distinctions—*ashrāf* and *ajlāf*, "agriculturalist" and "non-agriculturalists"—have been central to forms of life in Punjab and across Pakistan because they are points of convergence between caste and class: they index status attributions arising from differing relationships that groups had to state institutions and the ownership of and control over land, the kinds of work and labor those relationships entailed, and the ensuing accumulation of power, wealth, and status (i.e., forms of capital). Yet, even in the most contemporary accounts, class as a category of analysis has tended to eclipse caste when scrutinizing the country's sociopolitical landscape,[17] just as caste has been increasingly recognized to have significance in organizing social, economic, and political life across Pakistan's history.[18] The question then becomes how have such categories—caste, class, religion—converged in a city like Lahore and what does that reveal about Pakistan's social and political landscape.

In Lahore, as Ammara Maqsood (2017) described in her recent monograph, an older middle class that had coalesced in the city under the colonial regime expanded in the immediate postcolonial moment by virtue of their ownership of land, access to education, and state employment, while an emergent middle class has arisen since the 1980s, migrating from smaller towns in the Punjab or residing in older parts of the city and finding employment in "significant [numbers] in mid-level positions in the private sector or run[ning] small businesses" (2017, 7). Both sections of Lahore's middle classes are drawn heavily from what have been considered *ashrāf* groups, as well as higher status *ajlāf* ones, and many of whom have historically controlled land in the countryside and/or maintained access to sources of power and status in terms of education, the bureaucracy, and employment. Even though caste is not a category explored in Maqsood's account, we can see how the convergence of caste, class, and religion has shaped the texture of urbanization across the city of Lahore. The final two chapters of this book extend these insights by analyzing the set of relations—affective, spatial, material—that have sutured together Lahore's urbanizing landscapes, while other chapters examine how such categories and relations are also embedded in the workings of the bureaucratic state and its techno-legal apparatus and informalized relations of work and exchange organized around commodity production and consumption. The forms of life we see being reproduced in a transformed state across Pakistan arise from how deeply historical inequalities and interdependencies have been woven into the fibrous relations assembling and sustaining social and political life across the country.

Forms of Life

As a way of proceeding, let me pose a pressing set of questions, ones that will be unpacked across the pages of this book and returned explicitly to in the Coda: How do particular forms of life emerge entangled with the worlds of waste in contemporary Pakistan? What historical processes are implicated in and materialized through this convergence of waste and life? What are the stakes—intellectual, political, ethical—of accounting for waste and life together? And how should these stakes imbue our narration of the lives and worlds of those who toil with waste materials? Not only are these questions of significance on their own terms, but they have also been at the forefront of surging interest in waste among scholarly and popular audiences.

Recent accounts have foregrounded transformations in capitalism, labor, and ecologies to identify the forces—political, economic, social—that inhere within contemporary worlds of waste across any number of settings.[19] In a fascinating and detailed account of Brazilian *catadores* ("scavengers") who return to work at Jardin Gramacho garbage dump in Brazil, Kathleen Millar utilizes "forms of living" to reference "both livelihood and way of life," such that we can delineate "everyday efforts to construct the good" as well as "to the ways that different materials, relations, and practices in economic life *take shape*" (Millar 2018, 11–14, emphasis in original). Although I share many of these concerns, especially how to speak about waste work and waste workers jointly without falling into the trope of waste-as-abjection, such accounts tend to limit forms of life to specific relationships to waste materials organized around economic, ecological, or moral concerns. Moreover, when narrativizing those forms of life as they have become attached to the worlds of waste, certain assumptions are made about what processes or events, whether past or ongoing, take on significance, while treating these lives and worlds as if they are transparent in nature, simply appearing before us as the materialization of world-historical forces (e.g., capitalist exploitation or anthropogenic climate change). In fact, minimal attention is given to exploring such questions as the historical identities upon which these forms of living have come to depend, the extensive nature of life-making projects and historical processes implicated in waste infrastructures, or the intimate relationship between waste work and the reproduction of life. Put slightly differently, such approaches are apt to move too hastily between what is deemed structure and what is deemed an (quasi-) event, as well as why, and in what particular ways, such events are actualized in some lives and not others (see Das 2015, 16). Then, we must account for both—forms of life and worlds of waste—without subsuming either to a larger set of structural relations, processes, or transformations, thereby not severing them from lives as they are actually lived.

In his rendering of "form-of-life,"[20] Giorgio Agamben draws out the implications and risks to our notions of life if we sever life as lived from its forms: "A life that cannot be separate from its form is a life for which what is at stake in its way of living is living itself" (2000, 4). He goes onto to clarify, "[This formulation] defines a life—human life—in which the single ways, acts, and processes are never simply *facts* but always and above *possibilities* of life, always and above all power (Agamben 2000, 4, emphasis in original). Not only does this approach remain attentive to the possibilities inherent within life, in its myriad forms, that are in excess of the sanctioned order and dispensation of things and persons,[21] but it also establishes enduring connections between life itself (i.e., ones that are often rendered as biological or natural) and forms of life (i.e., ones that are often rendered as social). Relatedly, Veena Das (1998) has highlighted the fact that forms of life are, on the one hand, organized along horizontal lines of differences, where agreements embedded in institutions like marriage, property, or labor fashion the shape any particular life might take within a society. On the other hand, such forms, she argues, are also operating orthogonally with vertical lines of differences in life itself, where the parameters of the human are contested and made discernible. Drawing on these insights, my own utilization of forms of life is a way of illustrating that much more is at stake in these lives and worlds than waste materials themselves, how they are worked with and transformed through labor and techno-infrastructural entities, or even perhaps the drudgery and precarity that comes with toiling away in those infrastructures. It becomes a technique for foregrounding the subtle shifts in and repeated contestations taking place over life when the particular forms of life that have emerged in the worlds of waste are traced out across urban Pakistan.

What counts as a life, especially a human one, was a point of contestation among waste workers and many others. Waste workers were apt to describe their treatment as akin to what is meted out to machinery or animals (*jānwar*), which can be exploited without much concern for their well-being; at other times, they chalked up their everyday experiences of discrimination and disrespect to being viewed as not or less-than-human by a host of others; or they emphasized how they demonstrated humanity when forgiving those who abuse them or cooperating rather competing with others from their *birādarī* (patrilineal descent group). These contestations over humanity—one's own and that of others—are inseparable from extant social orders and hierarchies organized around caste-based relations and codes of conduct, while also being entrenched in contemporary worlds of waste in Pakistan and elsewhere. To account for these shifts in and contestations over life requires a more nuanced and expansive notion of life—and I would add, its reproduction—that does not sever links between life as lived and the forms of life. So, the task of accounting for life and waste in the contemporary world demands a patience when tracing the contours of lives as they are actually lived in myriad forms, being embedded in multiple life-making projects unfolding across discrete scales of activity.

This book maintains that there are intellectual, political, and ethical stakes when we account for life and waste in the world today. As such, the account found in its pages remains attentive to any number of life-making projects and historical processes—both of which operate at distinct spatiotemporal scales—when narrativizing forms of life that emerged within the worlds of waste in urban Pakistan. The forms of life organized around caste-based relations of concern to me are not simply part of some past form to be considered; rather, this book argues that those forms, and the identities and relations upon which they were built, have organized and canalized many of the distributive processes through which capitalism, urbanization, ecologies, and the worlds of waste materialize themselves in Pakistan today. Yet, the book keeps open spaces for possibilities, in which forms of life emerge in ways that cannot be reduced to reified forces (i.e., capitalist production and urbanization), categories (i.e., caste and class), or divisions (i.e., the natural and the social). Across its lines the book traces any number of historical processes to discern the possibilities as they actualize themselves within these forms of life, especially for those whose lives and livelihoods have come to be ensnared within this world of waste. Let me now turn to unpack how waste infrastructures have sustained such lives and worlds, and how they come to be reproduced through and beyond these infrastructures.

Infrastructures between Disposality and Circulation

Waste is usually conceptualized as an entity that has been exhausted, is lacking, deformed, or reduced in its usefulness or worth. Such conceptualizations, however insightful, tend to disentangle waste as a material and conceptual entity from the materialities, histories, and knowledges that constitute it. Though the term *waste*, not to mention others such as *infrastructure*, were largely absent from the colonial lexicon, with most of the concern being with dirt, rubbish, filth, stagnant water, and cesspools,[22] the colonial moment was a formative one for waste infrastructures. It was a moment in which a regime of colonial sanitation and public health intersected with a central category of governance—the public—to put into place infrastructures of urban life. As I demonstrate in the first chapter, not only did distinctions between public and private reorganize spatial concepts and practices across Lahore's landscape, but also related notions of custom and contract sought to incorporate relations of work and exchange surrounding different materialities into the techno-legal apparatus of the bureaucratic state, such that caste-based relations and codes of conduct were incorporated into urban infrastructures. Moreover, the elementary act of disposal, in which the public is to be protected by the bureaucratic state from certain dangers, risks, and harms attached to waste materials, has been and continues to be formative in shaping forms of life as they have emerged within worlds of waste, both in Pakistan and globally.

In urban centers across the world today, waste materials have been proliferating from the consumption of disposal commodities occurring at a mass scale. Increasing levels of consumption and waste generation are intertwined as disposable commodities, being made from materials easily used and discarded (e.g., single-use plastics), are now produced and consumed at scales and frequencies with no historical precedent. As such, disposability refers as much to the material qualities and amount of things that comprise life across the world today as it does to specific kinds of social relations, in which the relation between people and things facilitates value being realized from the consumption and discarding of commodities at unprecedently rapid rates. In other words, disposability is a pervasive ideology that crosscuts numerous social, political, and economic relations structuring contemporary life. Infrastructures accompanying disposability[23] unsurprisingly approach waste as mass waste, with its anonymizing, abstracting, and generalizing character—something that aligns with articulations of the public (Chalfin 2014, 2017; Hird et al. 2014). Imbuing waste as a material and conceptual entity, disposability not only shapes the kinds of work surrounding waste materials but also permeates the technical, infrastructural, and institutional entities assembled around those materials. As the first two chapters make clear, disposability has been elementary to how the bureaucratic state and its techno-legal apparatus has approached waste as an object of governance and management, as well as the labor and techno-infrastructural entities organized around such an object.

A large mass of discarded materials—what were previously commodities to be consumed—will be remade into commodities to be consumed yet once again. Much of the work performed in spaces such as streets, junkyards, warehouses, and manufacturing units transforms these materials by remaking them, such that they can be brought back into circulation. That work or labor would be considered part of the 73.3 percent of nonagricultural labor in Pakistan that is employed informally (International Labor Organization 2018), while the diverse activities— categorizing, dismantling, weighing, buying, selling—taking place within them would be a component of the 30–35 percent of economic output, as measured through gross domestic product, produced in the informal economy (see Shehryar 2014). The forms of work and exchange described throughout this book are part of Pakistan's changing political economy, which has been described by S. Akbar Zaidi as being marked by the informalization of "relations of production and exchange" (2014: 52). The informalization of livelihoods, especially of "surplus populations," have become increasingly and precariously tied to working with the material excess (i.e., waste) of contemporary capitalism in Pakistan.

The proliferation of disposable commodities and waste materials has created situations in which individuals and groups have found sources of livelihood through the recovery and sale of potentially valuable discarded materials, something accompanied by informalized relations of work and exchange. As I show in chapters 3 and 5, these relations of work and exchange have been organized to provision waste materials as resources for commodity production, even if those who perform this work are excluded from and enjoy an autonomy within the labor process while coming to be settled on the Lahore's urbanizing peripheries. Although waste workers, junkyard owners, intermediaries, and many others are "salvaging" materials for capitalist accumulation happening elsewhere (Tsing 2015), informal economies must be understood as internally differentiated in ways that enable a variety of actors in Lahore's waste infrastructures to access these materials and work, such that they materialize value out of them, maintain a source of livelihood, and, ultimately, reproduce their own life and that of others (see Sanyal 2007). These livelihoods are thus embedded in infrastructures of circulation, in which waste materials, commodities, and money are kept in motion at multiple, intersecting spatiotemporal scales. Here, too, waste work is constituted into an infrastructure of urban life, in which materials, work, and related techno-infrastructural entities are meant to facilitate circulation.[24] The discussion of informality is meant to demonstrate how infrastructures of circulation enact a constitutive connection between the uneven forms of life that have emerged across urban Pakistan and the production and consumption of disposable commodities organized at a mass scale.

Waste infrastructures in Pakistan combine infrastructures of disposability and circulation around the particular materialities of waste materials. These infrastructures have grown to comprise differentiated kinds of work and labor and expansive techno-infrastructural entities, while also being organized in relation to the techno-legal apparatus of the bureaucratic state, networks of circulation, and processes of uneven urbanization.[25] Institutions at the municipal level have been historically endowed with the power and authority to oversee, manage, and calibrate the movement of materialities of all kinds across Lahore as an administratively and geographically bounded entity.[26] In exercising this power and authority, there have been investments, both financial and affective, in techno-infrastructural entities (piping, drains, streets, machinery, and equipment). These investments—when hinged, formally, to a bureaucratically organized workforce and functioning, informally, alongside other workers, intermediaries, and junkyard owners—will provision waste disposal and management as a public good or service. The movement of waste materials simultaneously happens within and beyond the parameters of the bureaucratic state, as informalized relations of work and exchange are just as constitutive of Pakistan's waste infrastructures. This is why, as I have suggested previously (Butt 2020a), access to waste infrastructures, the materials that are disposed and circulated through them, and the goods or services they enable are differentiated across actors—from workers, supervisors, and managers to junkyard owners, intermediaries, and citizens.

It must also be kept in mind that waste work—a constitutive component of these infrastructures—removes waste materials from *spaces* like a household, shop, or industrial unit where they are produced, which concurrently makes those same materials present elsewhere in any other number of spaces across Lahore and beyond. So, on the one hand, infrastructures of disposability bring together municipal and informal workers, supervisors, containers, and any number of techno-infrastructural entities, such that waste materials can be taken away and deposited into other spaces (i.e., dumping grounds). On the other hand, infrastructures of circulation implicate many of these same figures, especially informal workers residing in *jhuggīā̱n* on the urban peripheries, but also bring into their spatial ambit the seemingly endless number of junkyards, warehouses, foundries, mills, and wholesale markets dotting Lahore's unevenly urbanizing landscape and extending across many other regions of Pakistan. It is in these spaces that waste materials are further sorted, disassembled, and exchanged as they are transformed and remade into commodities. Combining disposability and circulation, waste infrastructures are composed of and enact a series of ordered *and* transformative relations among materials things, bodies, persons, spaces, and forms of work.[27]

Taking a labor-centered approach, this book draws attention to how waste infrastructures[28] are constituted through and implicated in multiple intersecting, yet distinct processes that have unfolded in urban Pakistan over the past several decades. This approach, first, emphasizes how the labor of low- or noncaste groups in Pakistan has been mobilized by both state institutions and informal economies, thereby organizing urban landscapes in ways that reproduce historical inequalities and interdependencies. The livelihoods of waste workers and their kin, not to mention many others further along the value chains of waste, are attached to waste materials. This attachment of livelihoods and waste necessitates the constant flow of waste and money across any number of actors engaging in exchanges at multiple spatiotemporal scales. Second, it details how waste infrastructures are made to happen by coordinating considerable amounts of heterogenous effort—be that formalized, contractual labor, informalized work, and/or any other number of unremunerated acts—alongside many other materials things and techno-infrastructural entities. And last, it underscores the relational nature of waste materials and work, such that we can see the forces—political, social, economic—at play in organizing waste infrastructures, while also allowing us to remain attentive to the contingency of these convergences (see Simone 2004; Cowen 2020) and thus the unexpected possibilities and relationalities inhering within attendant forms of life. Taken together, this approach underscores that waste work does not simply dispose of or circulate waste materials. Rather, constituted as an infrastructure, this form of work is embedded in and emerges out of numerous processes, entangling any number of actors with their own intentions and life-making projects, while participating in reproducing life, in Lahore and beyond, at several interconnected scales.

Life Reproduced

One of the central claims of this book is that a particular form of work, waste work, is elementary to examining how a variegated set of processes have unfolded over the past several decades and shaped the forms of life that have emerged across urban Pakistan. Such a claim only holds weight if we appreciate what work as a category of action makes possible. Though differentiated by the kinds of effort exercised on the world, all forms of work or labor are situated within dispensations of social and political life, such that any particular instantiation of work or labor presupposes and entails historical conditions of working and living. As such, I approach work as a category of action central to the organization and reproduction of life itself.

In making such a claim about the centrality of waste work to the reproduction of life, I take my cue from transnational Marxist feminists who have foregrounded reproduction by drawing attention to the gendered nature of the labor process itself: certain kinds of work, usually those performed by gendered and racialized subjects, are fundamental to capital accumulation through the appropriation of unpaid work or energy, even if that work, energy, and those who exercised them were devalorized and were placed, *only formally*, outside the capital-labor relation[29] (see Fortunati 1995; Murphy 2015; see also Bear et al. 2015; Bhattacharya 2017; Mies 1998; Moore 2017, 2018). What needs to be underscored at this point then is the fact that the reproduction of life, and its potential appropriation for accumulation, is the result of expansive distributive processes that bring into relation any number of material things, bodies, persons, spaces, and forms of work, or what I identified above as waste infrastructures. In other words, there are many processes operating and unfolding beyond these infrastructures, but they are brought into relation to one another as waste work is constituted into an infrastructure of urban life. So, in what ways are such infrastructures caught up in reproducing life?

Waste work has been bureaucratized and coordinated through institutions, infrastructures, and work regimes aimed at sustaining the collective life of cities, while simultaneously being organized around the dynamics of mass waste generation and the production of commodities under capitalist relations. This is how and why waste work has been constituted into an infrastructure of urban life. As such, the activities that go into disposing of and/or circulating waste materials are forms of social cooperation that make possible accumulation, just as they exist outside and at times demonstrate "antagonism" toward that accumulation (Weeks 2011; see also Weeks 2007). This is akin to what Anna Tsing has called "salvage accumulation" as "the process through which lead firms amass capital without controlling the conditions under which commodities are produced" (2015: 62–63). Yet, what Tsing and many others have foregrounded is the fact that those activities that reproduce life—whether that be care work, ecological conditions, biological matter, or metabolic life—exist prior to and are in excess of capitalist production and accumulation, even if the latter seek to appropriate those activities, energies, and relations required for reproducing life.[30] The task then becomes to remain attentive to how processes of reproduction play themselves out in ways that are not circumscribed by the domains of the state and capital, which at once decenters the latter and recognizes their significance in shaping the former (i.e., reproducing life). This act of decentering not only opens up the worlds of those who work to reproduce themselves and their social relations through a particular kind of work but also foregrounds the reproduction of historical interdependencies and inequalities, upon which the state and capital depend but which operate beyond their purview.

Waste work is aimed at reproducing forms of life in Lahore that have been historically organized along the lines of caste, class, and religion. Noting the prominent Dalit leader B. R. Ambedkar's description of caste as "graded inequality," Ajantha Subramanian (2019) has recently unpacked a "stratification of labor" to analyze how specific upper-caste groups have utilized technical forms of knowledge and labor (i.e., engineering) and the language of merit and academic achievement to reproduce and preserve their status in postcolonial India and beyond.[31] Subramanian's approach allows us to apprehend caste as "a form of capital" (Subramanian 2019, 15; see also Bourdieu 1986) in which things such as inherited privileges, academic qualifications, and many other sources of power, wealth, and status come together to reproduce historical inequalities and interdependences. In the present context, we have already seen how much of Lahore's middle and upper classes are drawn heavily from higher-status Muslims groups who have historically had control over land in the countryside and/or maintained access to sources of power, wealth, and status—all of which are forms of capital. On the other hand, those from low- or noncaste backgrounds, who have been historically excluded from control over land and have entered this line of work as they migrated to and settled on Lahore's urbanizing peripheries, have not had access to those same forms of capital availed to the city's middle and upper classes. Approaching waste work as an infrastructure enables us to see how this particular form of work allows collective life in a city like Lahore to go on, while at the same time reproducing the system of graded inequality (i.e., caste-based relations) upon which waste work is premised.[32]

Waste work has been organized into an infrastructure of urban life, such that forms of life at multiple, convergent registers and scales come to be reproduced both in Lahore and across much of Pakistan. Just as this form of work, comprising all kinds of activities, relations, and practices, reproduces forms of life in a city like Lahore, it also facilitates the intergenerational trajectories of waste workers and their kin as they have strived to reproduce themselves within Lahore's urbanizing landscape. The reproduction I describe is a distributed process that unfolds at the following registers and scales: (1) the reproduction of forms of life organized around caste-based relations in Pakistan, even if there has been an overt disavowal of caste by the Muslim nationalist project; (2) the reproduction of urban life, especially through the dependence of upper- and middle-class existence upon the stigmatizing toil of waste workers from low- or noncaste backgrounds; and (3) the reproduction of lives and livelihoods of waste workers, their kin, and many other actors further along the value chains of waste, all of whom discover creatively ordinary ways to generate incomes out of commodity detritus from across Lahore and Pakistan.

Scholars, activists, and many others have drawn attention to waste generation on unprecedented scales to alert us to changing configurations of waste and labor and the techno-infrastructural entities and imaginaries that are at once a symptom of and cure for the excesses of contemporary capitalism and urbanization. On the other hand, by foregrounding reproduction as its central analytic, this book traces how capitalism, urbanization, and their infrastructures in Pakistan build upon forms of life in which caste-based relations and identities have been foundational. As such, it argues that contemporary forms of living and working, whether in South Asia or elsewhere, depend upon the reproduction of historical inequalities and interdependencies, which tend to be obscured by the presentism of contemporary accounts of waste and capitalist urbanization. Being attentive to reproduction gives us insight into not only configurations of waste and labor under contemporary capitalism but also what forms of living and working are actually possible for those who inhabit urbanizing landscapes like Lahore across the world today.

Methods: Possibilities and Limits

A major challenge in writing this book has come from the difficulties that come with studying caste in Pakistan today. A consistent set of objections has been made by scholars, activists, and others, challenging the claim that caste exercises any *significant* force in Pakistan's history, whether past or ongoing. Caste may have a sociological reality among Muslims across the Indian subcontinent, but other bases of identity, whether those be religion, class, ethnicity, language, or gender, are more pertinent when critically understanding the creation of Pakistan or its political and social trajectory since independence. Even when speaking about forms of association like *birādarī* or "tribe," stress has generally been placed upon things like kinship or patronage, which are undeniably important when exercising political power (democratic or authoritarian) in Pakistan. Still others argue that caste does not have the same significance as it does in India as a nation-state with a Hindu majority. Not only is caste a constitutive component of Brahmanical traditions, but caste has also been recognized through a wide variety of legal categories and political techniques in the neighboring country. However, this ends up leading to a comparative approach, most prominently comparing a Sayyid dominance to a Brahmanical one, and these strategies end up reproducing the claim that caste either is not as powerful a force in Pakistan or operates differently than it does in India and under Brahmanical dominance. Whether as recognition or disavowal, such approaches fail to reconcile the fact that, in the words of Suraj Yengde, "caste as a social construct is a deceptive substance, known for its elemental capacity to digress from its primary motive of existence" (2019, 7). The erasure of caste in Pakistan across popular and academic discourses, as well as across a diverse set of political affiliations, results from an inability to interrogate the sociohistorical production of categories, whether they be of caste, nation, religion, class, or gender. Rather than comparing categories, we must trace how such categories are produced under specific sociohistorical conditions, which underlies the methodological approach to studying caste across the pages of this book.

The centrality of waste work in this book may give the impression that its treatment of caste is limited to what are seen as "traditional caste-based occupations." Rather, the book identifies, on a methodological level, how caste is enmeshed in the operations of the bureaucratic state, informal economies, and uneven urbanization. This book approaches caste not as inhering in those who are presumed to be from low or non-caste backgrounds, as that would fall into the fallacy of "castelessness;" rather, it locates caste as a category that is crucial to organizing all kinds of relations—social, political, economic—that cuts across contemporary life in Pakistan.[33] Moreover, the antiquated problem of whether Muslims across South Asia have caste gives way to an assessment of how caste actually operates in Pakistan (and potentially its diaspora) today. Reframing the problem in this way allows us to trace how caste endures, through its transformation, across many domains of social and political life, but with the hope of identifying the necessary work required to undo the historical inequalities and interdependencies that it has upheld.

Caste as a historical category does not exist in a vacuum. This book focuses on its interaction with class, and to a certain extent, religion, precisely because doing so allows us to make clear how access to sources of power, wealth, and status have reproduced caste-based relations, whether through the hegemony of *ashrāf* groups among Muslims across South Asia or through those with control over land in the Punjab. While *ashraafiya* hegemony is undeniable in Pakistan's past and present, we must not remain blind to the regional (or diasporic) histories that imbue caste with social and political force. Moreover, the pervasiveness of caste cannot be fully grasped if it is disentangled from the study of gender and sexuality, especially the control over women's bodies and sexuality. Such control can vary in its coerciveness, from kin-based marriage practices (e.g., endogamy) to sexualized forms of violence.[34] We must remain sensitive to the endurance of caste through its intersection with class, gender, and sexuality in organizing contemporary life across South Asia and its diaspora.

Waste work emerges out of the gendering of the labor process. Not only are women involved at every stage of the process by which waste materials are disposed of and/or circulated, but the feminization of male workers also emerged repeatedly throughout my fieldwork. However, two major limitations of the research that provided the materials for this manuscript arise from a lack of access. First, my access to women, especially outside spaces of work, was notably limited. Part of this had to with the fact that I was often introduced to men by men, and, after entering domestic spaces, I remained in the position of a non-kin male, which limited my conversations with women and their openness to engage with a variety of topics. Aside from formalized interviews with female workers employed by the municipality and conversations with the wives of male informal workers, I rely heavily upon insights and narratives provided to me by men. Additionally, although waste workers from Pashtun backgrounds form a sizable component of Pakistan's waste infrastructures, I chose to not conduct any fieldwork with them. This decision resulted from the fact that Pashtuns have become the site of surveillance by the Pakistani state, especially its military and intelligence agencies. Whenever I was introduced to a Pashtun waste worker or junkyard owner, I was met with suspicion and reticence. Thus, early on in my fieldwork, I decided to avoid interacting with Pashtuns active in this line of work, so as not to draw undue attention to an already vulnerable and surveilled community. It is undeniable that this limited access constrains the arguments unfolding across these pages. My only hope, however, is that readers take these limits and constraints not as marking an end point but rather as a point of departure for pushing my own materials and claims in ways I was unable to do myself.

Overview of the Book

The first chapter returns to a historical moment when infrastructures were being organized to govern urban life in colonial Lahore. This chapter examines how waste materials and work became a site of intervention for a colonial regime of sanitation, public health, and governance. It pays particularly close attention to how the category of the public, as it was embedded in the techno-legal apparatus of the bureaucratic state, connected spatialized practices surrounding different materialities (e.g., sewage, water, night soil, rubbish) with relations of work and exchange. Chapter 1 also traces out the position of the prominent Dalit group known as the Chūṛā that would be recruited as "sweepers" into municipal departments across the Punjab and North India, and how the caste-based relations in which they were embedded were appropriated and integrated, at least partially, into the bureaucratic state and its techno-legal apparatus through the category of the public. As such, this chapter makes clear how forms of life in Punjab have become embedded in infrastructures stretching across the urban landscape, and as the bureaucratic state has expanded and waste work has become further bureaucratized, such forms of life, and caste-based relations upon which they are built, continue to organize spaces, work, and life in Lahore and across much of urban Pakistan.

Chapter 2 examines the relationship that the bureaucratic state has had to waste materials, work, and infrastructures in contemporary Lahore. Since the 1980s, Lahore has been undergoing rapid urbanization, which has involved population growth, higher levels of consumption, and spatial and infrastructural expansion. The nature of democratic politics across Pakistan has also undergone a transformation, where "intermediary classes" have gained prominence through political parties, market and trader associations, and other organizational entities, which has been connected to the changing dynamics of patronage. This chapter details how, within such a context, waste workers have mobilized social and political relationships, both within and outside state institutions, to access waste materials and work. Second, it examines how the bureaucratic state, through the intermediary figure known as the *dāroghah*, provides waste disposal services to the public by exercising limited control over waste workers and contending with the politics of patronage within localities. This chapter argues that the bureaucratic state comes to occupy a managerial role in relation to urban infrastructures, which crosscuts distinctions such as public and private, state and society, and labor and management. Taken together, the first two chapters of this book make clear that categories and distinctions of the bureaucratic state and its techno-legal apparatus exercise an important force in organizing infrastructures of disposability, even if those infrastructures comprise activities, relations, and practices that exceed those categories and distinctions.

Chapter 3 transitions to infrastructures of circulation by trekking through spaces—*jhuggīāṉ*, junkyards, warehouses, furnaces, manufacturing plants—where waste materials are worked with and exchanged, being procured and transformed into resources to be used in remaking commodities. This chapter engages discussions of informality within South Asia that have highlighted the contradictory situation faced by labor: for laborers excluded from formalized sectors of capitalist economies, relations of work and exchange have emerged to generate surpluses that are simultaneously directed at need and accumulation. The chapter examines the highly fragmented and differentiated processes through which surpluses are generated out of waste materials and work. Rather than discussing the exploitation of labor through wages, this chapter demonstrates how forms of exclusion, with their own kinds of remuneration, allow for surpluses generated to be simultaneously directed at meeting need by waste workers and small-scale *kabāṛīān* (junkyard owners) and fostering accumulation by larger-scale *kabāṛīān* and *bīopārīān* (intermediaries). This chapter argues that informality undergirds more formalized sectors of capitalist economies, uneven urbanization across much of Pakistan, and the reproduction of historical inequalities and interdependencies.

Whereas previous chapters explored how waste work, constituted as an infrastructure of urban life, is embedded in social and political relationships stretching across the bureaucratic state and informalized economies, the following chapters mark a shift in the book, where waste materials, work, and infrastructures are situated within the trajectory of urbanization in Lahore and more broadly. Chapter four examines how waste work becomes a site for mediating collective life in urban Pakistan, in which intimacies across caste, class, and religious lines are constantly negotiated. Waste work separates waste materials from those who produce it (e.g., middle- and upper-class households), while at the same time attaching those same materials to those who either live or work in physical proximity to these materials or are presumed to be low- or noncaste by birth. This chapter thus situates waste work within distributive processes in Lahore, whereby waste materials are made absent for some, just as they are made present for others. It first examines the affective and material relationships formed between waste workers and households from which they collect waste, and then analyzes the ways in which others, who may share a world in common with waste workers, distance themselves from these materials and those persons presumed to do this work by birth. This chapter argues that the affective, material, and spatial relationships in which waste workers, *kabāṛīān*, *bīopārīān*, households, and many others are enmeshed create an uneven intimacy that is reflective of wider process of urbanization.

The final substantive chapter examines how waste workers and their kin have experienced shifts in work, settlement, and life as they have migrated to Lahore and reproduced themselves across generations. Low- or noncaste groups in Punjab have historically been landless labor, working under a variety of coercive relations with landowning groups from upper-caste backgrounds, engaging in different kinds of agrarian work and being settled on the land owned by others. This chapter demonstrates how forms of settlement and work have endured through transformation as waste workers have migrated to Lahore's urbanizing peripheries, while indebtedness has been enfolded into the home as a site of social reproduction. Just as reproduction occurs at intergenerational and domestic scales, it unfolds also at the scale of workers' bodies, where their lives and bodies are exhausted through laboring with waste materials. Delineating these spatiotemporal scales highlights how forms of life historically built upon caste-based relations are reproduced on Pakistan's urbanizing peripheries.

Taking inspiration from recent characterizations of the Anthropocene "as the apotheosis of waste" (Hecht 2018), the coda emphasizes the significance that the theoretical framework of reproduction has for discussions of caste, waste, and life in the contemporary world. It returns to a key ethnographic moment in order to reflect upon the theoretical frameworks used to critically examine caste in Pakistan, in which caste is seen as enduring through its transformation and being a site of contestation. Next, the coda makes an argument for studying the forms of life that have emerged alongside and out of worlds of waste in the contemporary moment without flattening them to those processes, specifically an intensifying form of consumptive capitalism and anthropogenic climate change, that saturate our expectations of contemporary life. The reason for doing so, as this book has illustrated, has been to delineate what are the actual possibilities for reproducing life in a world consumed by waste in any numbers of forms.

CHAPTER 1

AN ORDER FOR URBAN LIFE

BY THE 1920S, Lahore had expanded considerably outside its traditional center of the Inner City, and much of this growth was directed in a southernly direction, where the Bari Doab Canal, intersecting the city from northeast to southwest, was constructed in the 1860s and the Civil Lines, Cantonment, and several burgeoning settlements would come to be situated. Despite this proliferating growth, the Lahore Improvement Trust Committee[1] asked Basil Sullivan, who at the time was the consulting architect to the Government of Punjab, to prepare a town planning report focusing almost exclusively on the Inner City. For officials like Sullivan, forms of life encountered in the Inner City were marked by disorder and excess, which limited interventions by the colonial regime into the built environment that were common throughout the late nineteenth and early twentieth centuries in recently constructed and burgeoning localities to its south. What is noteworthy about Sullivan's descriptions are, thus, not the interventions one expects to accompany a planning document such as his; rather, it is the order of urban life that can be seen constructed out of and being imposed upon forms of life across Lahore's changing landscapes.

Despite using the common trope of the "seriously congested" Inner City, Sullivan emphasized, "The paved lanes and streets are swilled down and swept and the bazars [sic] are cleaned," but did locate a problem

elsewhere: "No effort of this nature, however, can cope with house refuse thrown into the street and loose cattle by the thousand, in the lanes,
bazars [*sic*] and chauks. The difficulty is complicated by the existence of
kuchas[2] where it is impossible, for lack of space, for soil carts to go. From
such places all refuse must be carried out by hand" (1929, 6). Sullivan then
went on to draw a contrast between outer and inner spaces: "It is noticeable how clean and swept the insides of the houses are and how squalid
outside. Inside is usually found a court with the building round it. Outside is a dirty wall and a dirtier parnala covered with old kerosene oil tins.
Through this rotting channel is discharged sullage, frequently over the
joints of the water supply pipes" (1929, 6; see Figure 1.1). Sullivan moves
swiftly between the outer spaces of pipes, streets, and electrical wiring
and inner ones of households, *kuchas*, and bazaars. His movement across
spaces took on such salience because so much emphasis was placed upon
the outer domains of "dwelling, pipe, or rain" in sanitation and public
health "that these effectively [became] proxies for the social and subjective" (Hamlin 1998, 215). One image in particular (Figure 1.2) demonstrates how the social, the environmental, and the subjective collapsed so
seamlessly into one another. In a locality known as Rarra Tallian within
the Inner City, a shirtless man with a muscular frame donning a lungi
stands outside a home. Just inside past the entrance, we see half of a cow
tied to an oil press. We do not see the actual press but only the rope that
goes around the cow's neck. Above stands a woman on the terrace with
her head resting on her hand and looking down in the direction from
where the photograph is taken. The image is so striking because, unlike
the others that do not have a human subject, this one is framed almost as
a portrait of life in Lahore.

This report and its accompanying images move between, and thus
link, the outer domains of the built environment and the inner ones
of social life: electrical wiring, projections or encroachments, cattle and
livestock within homes and thoroughfares, the presence of rubbish, "sullage" flowing over water pipes, and grain sitting out in the open or near
drains. These scenes are ones of disorder and excess, of activity and building going unchecked and unregulated—they are imaged indictments
of forms of life to be brought into the ambit of order. Yet, for them to

(17)

HAVELI KABLI MALL.

Sullage discharged down parnala covered with rotting tin.
Waterpipe entering property through sullage drain.

FIGURE 1.1. *Image from Sullivan's Report titled* A Note for the Use of the La-
hore Improvement Committee and of the Lahore Improvement Trust When
Formed, with Special Reference to the City of Lahore inside the Walls. *Source:
Cambridge University Library. Reprinted with permission.*

(**18**)

RABRA TAILLIAN.

Cattle pressing oil on ground floor of dwelling house.

FIGURE 1.2. *Image from Sullivan's Report titled* A Note for the Use of the Lahore Improvement Committee and of the Lahore Improvement Trust When Formed, with Special Reference to the City of Lahore inside the Walls. *Source: Cambridge University Library. Reprinted with permission.*

present life in this way—as excess to be ordered—a series of distinctions must inhere within their frames: inner and outer, internal and external, and private and public. I take Sullivan's report as a point of departure for this reason, as it presents a pressing question about urban infrastructures and the reproduction of life: How did an order of urban life, emerging as it did out of a colonial regime of sanitation, public health, and governance, come to integrate forms of life organized around caste-based relations? Put slightly differently, as infrastructures of all kinds were being assembled across Lahore's urbanizing landscapes, how did caste become embedded into the very order of urban life?

Caste and the Public

An order for urban life emerged in Lahore during this period that effectively brought together spatial practices and relations of work and exchange through the techno-legal apparatus of the bureaucratic state. Not only did the category of the public warrant and legitimize a range of state interventions aimed at bodies, populations, and environments, but this category also concealingly embedded caste into the emerging order for urban life during this period. It did so by drawing upon forms of life in the Punjab, in which distinct caste groups were situated in a complex set of relations of work, exchange, settlement, and marriage. These forms of life, as well as their attendant relations, came to be reworked through a range of processes, from land and revenue settlement and canal colonization across the Punjab to the expansion of infrastructures and urban municipalities like Lahore.

As Dalit groups, especially the group known as the Chūṛā, were recruited into Lahore's sanitation workforce, those caste-based relations, which were understood to be customary in nature, were integrated into the order of urban life through contractual relations. As this chapter illustrates, those relations were not simply ones of work and exchange among the municipality, "sweepers," "scavengers," households, cultivators, and any number of actors; they were also spatial in nature, as they involved the movement of materialities across Lahore's urbanizing landscape. This is why waste infrastructures in Lahore (but also elsewhere) sustain relations between things, bodies, persons, spaces, and kinds of work, thereby repro-ducing historical inequalities and interdependencies.

The category of the public emerged across the imperial world through regimes of sanitation, public health, and governance that cut across di-verse arenas of social, economic, and political life. Following the Rebellion of 1857, as the bureaucratic, legal, and technical apparatus of the colonial regime grew, sanitary legislation and public health reform[3] increasingly focused its attention on institutions (i.e., municipal governments) and infrastructures (i.e., piped water, underground sewerage, and caste-based labor). Invested in theories of disease emerging out of medical and sci-entific knowledge of the time, institutional and infrastructural interven-tions sought to spatially reorganize cities across British India in ways that safeguarded civilian and military institutions and sites from the potential outbreak of illnesses (e.g., cholera, smallpox, typhoid)—the sources of which were regularly attached to native populations and environments (see Oldenburg 1984; Arnold 1993). While fundamentally concerned with securing and legitimizing colonial rule, the regime of sanitation, public health, and governance that took shape in this period consisted of an expansive techno-legal and bureaucratic apparatus that regulated various kinds of activities, especially in streets, thoroughfares, and other "outer" spaces, through "laws of public nuisance."[4]

In a well-known essay on the place of garbage in modernity, Dipesh Chakrabarty emphasizes that "modernist categories of 'public' and 'pri-vate' were constantly challenged by the ways Indians used open space. The street presented, as it were, a total confusion of the 'private' and the 'public' in the many different uses to which it was put. People washed, changed, slept, and even urinated and defecated out in the open" (1991, 16). These ways of using spaces, undergirded as they were with their own concepts, went against these modernist categories, not to mention the regime of sanitation, public health, and governance built upon them. Rather than relying upon the possibilities posed "by the ways Indian used open space," it is important to complicate Chakrabarty's rendering, as others have (see e.g., Kaviraj 1997), by emphasizing how these categories and their atten-dant spatial concepts and practices have shifted across historical moments in relation to changing urban politics, especially along the lines of caste, class, and gender. Moreover, these categories were translated into "local" contexts as subjects, from diverse backgrounds, engaged with them across different arenas of urban life, where "endow[ing]" something "with the status of ... public" consistently raised definitional problems about this category (Glover 2007, 220). Definitional ambiguities surrounding the public allowed it to shift and be applied across diverse contexts, especially vis-à-vis waste materials and work. While one aspect of the public sought to bring spatial practices in line with the techno-legal apparatus of the bureaucratic state, another of its features made relations of work and exchange into sites of legal, technical, and bureaucratic interventions. Before examining such interventions, it will be important to unpack how the order of urban life emerging during this period relied upon specific low- or noncaste groups and their position within forms of life in the Punjab.

Low- or noncaste groups in the Punjab have been historically a class of landless agrarian labor that fell under a variety of names and designations and engaged in different kinds of work across the countryside and urban centers. One of the most populous and significant of these groups was the Chūṛā, which has been recruited into municipal government in the Punjab and across North India (see Prashad 2000; Lee 2017; Streefland 1979). In one of the primary ethnological studies of the Punjab, Denzil Ibbetson, who served as census commissioner for the Punjab in 1881 and then later as its lieutenant-governor, described the "scavenger castes" as one of "the lowest of the low," and "[their] hereditary occupation is scavenging, sweeping the houses and streets, working up, carrying to the field, and distributing manure, and in cities and in village houses [. . .], removing night soil" (Ibbetson 1916, 290). Ibbetson then went on to describe the Chūṛā, which, as mentioned already, converted to Christianity en masse during the colonial period, as a "sweeper or scavenger, and hence the out-caste, par excellence, of the Punjab. ... As a scavenger or rather as a 'sweeper up of dust' the Chuhrá is termed khák-rob" (1916, 293). Ibbetson then detailed all the other names that the Chūṛā was thought to go by (Megh, Mihtar, Dhed, Changar, among others) and their associated occupations (weavers, "domestics," leather

workers) and described the distribution of these occupational group-
ings across various regions of the Punjab. As I explain below, low- or
noncaste groups in Punjab were embedded in myriad relations of work,
exchange, settlement, and marriage with those who were viewed to be
of higher caste backgrounds. So, rather than a reflection of the social
reality of caste in Punjab, the categorical distinction found in Ibbetson's
account must be read critically as a reflection of how colonial forms
of knowledge facilitated practices of governance. Most pertinently, this
connection between knowledge and governance facilitated the inte-
gration of contractual relations with customary ones, as specific caste
groups were recruited into municipal sanitation workforces over the
course of several decades.

As gestured to in the Introduction, the distinction between "agriculturalist" (or cultivator) and "nonagriculturalist" (or noncultivator)
has been constitutive of forms of life in the Punjab, in which individuals and groups from different caste backgrounds have been historically
moored. As such, the Chūṛā, who fell into the latter designation, were
embedded in unequal relations with those who were considered to be
of upper-caste backgrounds, who had control over land in the countryside, either through ownership or cultivation. For instance, the Chūṛā
participated in what at the time was known as the *sepidari* system, in
which low- or noncaste groups provided their labor, services, and in-
struments in exchange for a share of the grain (as well as other kinds of
remuneration).[5] Another related though distinct system of organizing
agricultural labor was known as the *siri*, "where landholding cultivators
would contract with landless laborers to provide various agricultural services for an entire season in exchange for a proportion of the harvest,"
and those laboring as "*siris* resembled constant yet unequal companion
in agricultural operations, working alongside 'cultivators-proper' in every
aspect of cultivation" (Gill 2019, 13; see also Harding 2008). Finally, there
have also been practices of unpaid labor in the Punjab known as *begaar*, in which landlords provided land for agricultural and residential
purposes and tenants (oftentimes from low- or noncaste backgrounds)
"paid half of all they produced" and "contributed *begaar* when this was
demanded" (Ahmad 1970, 61). Like other low- or noncaste groups, the

Chūṛā were moored in forms of life that embedded them in a complex set of relations with those of upper-caste backgrounds for work and shares of grains, harvest, and other forms of remuneration through the *sepidari* system, though other kinds of labor mobilization (i.e., *siri*) were present and these groups exhibited a degree of labor mobility between settlements.[6]

Such relations between landless agrarian labor (predominantly from "lower"-caste backgrounds) and landowning or cultivating groups (predominantly from "upper"-caste backgrounds) were stabilized and reorganized through revenue and land settlement, canal colonization, and the techno-legal apparatus of the bureaucratic state. Concurrently, low- or noncaste groups also moved away from "customary" forms of work and entered into wage labor (though they did circulate between the two); came to find employment in construction work, specifically of canal, rail, and road infrastructures; and became artisans and traders of certain goods, such as skins, leather, and furs. Even if the condition of the Chūṛā residing in urban centers was thought to be defined by working with night soil (making them into "customary sweepers"), unlike the Chūṛā engaging in diverse kinds of work in agrarian settings, the migration of Chūṛās into urban centers across the Punjab and North India involved their recruitment into sanitation workforces by municipal governments, which ensnared them in both customary and contractual relations set up throughout the late nineteenth and early twentieth centuries. We can now return to the question: How did these relations—formulated as "customary" by colonial forms of knowledge and governance—become embedded into an order of urban life through the category of the public?

Ritu Birla (2008) has examined how colonial law, specifically the Indian Companies Act of 1882, was predicated upon categories of public and private that enabled a bifurcation between economy and culture. Kin or family-based firms, consisting of their own relations of work, exchange, and inheritance, were constituted within the domain of Hindu and Muslim personal law, as this was the domain of custom, while the market as a public venture was constituted within the domain of contract (see also Gilmartin 1988). Here, too, categorical distinctions of public and private involve others such as inner and outer and custom and contract, but rather than organizing spatial practices, these distinctions are embedded within the relations of work and exchange that are at once internal and external to capitalistic social relations (Sanyal 2007; Gidwani and Wainwright 2014; see also Chatterjee 1993). The fluctuations between custom and contract described later in this chapter demonstrate how institutions of the bureaucratic state that were emerging under colonial rule were built upon caste-based relations, in which relations of work and exchange surrounding waste materials connected an order of urban life in a city like Lahore and forms of life prevalent across Punjab's diverse landscapes. The contracts implemented under colonial conditions were not simply legal documents; they were social in nature, fundamentally invested in organizing and maintaining historical inequalities and inter-dependences (Viswanath 2014; see also Mills 2014). This is an important point to keep in mind, since it emphasizes that urban life in Pakistan is upheld by the intersection of caste with other social categories such as class, gender, and religion.

As municipal governments were being founded and their powers expanding throughout the colonial period, institutions became increasingly invested in the movement of matter across spaces, specifically from enclosed, inner ones emplaced in the private to open, outer ones emplaced in the public. That spatial movement depended upon relations of work and exchange, in which the labor of low- or noncaste groups was elementary, and those relations were understood to be part of the domain of custom. Municipal institutions, subsequently, enacted a variety of contractual relations to incorporate these customary relations into their own legal, bureaucratic, and technical apparatus. This was done in such a way that ensured custom was constituted as the inner, private domain outside of contract that nevertheless provided the latter with content. The category of the public, as well as its other (the private), were implemented in Lahore across several sites—material things, spaces of the built environment, and relations of work and exchange—and the concern consistently raised across these sites resulted from instability of these categorical distinctions. For that reason, waste materials and work have been and remain a perpetual site of contestation, whether in colonial Lahore or contemporary Pakistan.

Separation and Containment

Almost immediately after the annexation of Punjab in 1849, sanitation and public health interventions in Lahore were directed in the low-lying areas just south of the Inner City, where the Civil Lines, the Cantonment, and several other settlements came to be located. At the time, multiple hollows, excavations, and ditches dotted the urban landscape and were deemed a constant source of threat: stagnant pools of water contained all kinds of "filth" and festered with diseases—this was especially the case for Anarkali as the original location for colonial administrators and the military.[7] The irregularity of the landscape, dotted with the "ruined" remnants of the "Ancient city," were thought to impact sanitary and public health conditions: As "much of this ground having been the site of the Ancient City, is intersected with the ruins of foundations of walls, streets, gardens, enclosures, and tanks which prevent the escape of the rain water, and are receptacles for the filth that is inseparable from the vicinity of a large city."[8] Interventions related to water—a river, a canal, drains, pipes, sewerage—thus sought to rejuvenate a putatively "decaying" and "ruined" landscape.[9]

It should be kept in mind that these low-lying areas took on such salience because they contained spaces inhabited by military and civilian administrators. Transformations of urban landscapes across British India have been described as displaying "an 'enclavist' or 'segregated' character," where the majority of efforts related to medicine, sanitation, and public health prioritized the health of the Indian Army through the Indian Medical Services (a military institution) and those efforts only being extended to the "the masses" after 1918 (Arnold 1993, 63). Thus, one of the most prominent spaces within these urban landscapes were military cantonments. Though initially located in Anarkali just outside the Inner City, the Cantonment in Lahore was a few years later abandoned because of Anarkali's "unhealthiness" and shifted to the village of Mian Mir located further away from the Inner City and Civil Lines and along the Bari Doab Canal. Throughout the latter half of the nineteenth century, a series of epidemics broke out across the Punjab and other parts of India, and, as concerns were raised about their effects on the Indian Army, the Royal Commission on the Sanitary State of the Army in India emphasized that high levels of mortality arose from "inadequate sewerage and water supply, poor drainage, and ill-ventilated and overcrowded barracks" (Harrison 1994, 61; see also Arnold 1993, 74). In 1869 based on letter requests from the principal of Lahore Medical College, the provincial sanitary commissioner called on the secretary to the Government of Punjab and its superintending engineer to present a report on the flushing of drains, which was such a pressing concern as the "great want at present is, security against cholera; and English experience proves that a pure water supply is the greatest preventative of this disease, and that in the absence of such a supply other sanitary improvements afford very little security from this attack."[10]

By this time the Cantonment had been moved to Mian Mir, where a quarter of the troops stationed therein later perished from an outbreak of cholera. Cholera, importantly, was an illness that was seemed to "strike suddenly and unpredictably," drew considerable "administrative concern," and was associated very much with "disorder" (Arnold 1993, 159, 198). This outbreak of cholera and other illnesses initiated a series of inspections across the Punjab that sought to ascertain sanitary conditions in villages within a five miles radius of cantonments. These inspections and the conditions they discovered were meant to impact where military cantonments would be located and the kinds of interventions that were deemed necessary to ensure sanitary conditions within cantonments and the health of the troops stationed therein. During one such inspection, the provincial sanitary commissioner reported:

> In the wells from which the European troops are supplied I found the water about 10 feet from the surface. The wells are boarded over, a trap-door being formed in the cover, through which water is drawn in the usual way by bhistís. As the bhistís in drawing water stand on the cover immediately over the water, the dropping of their feet of course falls back into the well. No matter who comes to draw water, including the sweeper fresh from handling the latrine utensils, the dripping of the people's feet and hands all returns

to the well; and when it is recollected how large a number of people draw from one of these wells in the course of the day, it will be seen that existing arrangement provide effectually for the wholesale contamination of the well water.[11]

This assessment was shaped by various theories of illness circulating at the time (e.g., contagionism and miasma) that motivated investments in improving water supply to cantonments throughout the closing decades of the nineteenth century.[12] As Warwick Anderson (1995, 2006) has noted, colonial sanitation and public health sought to create closed and cordoned-off spaces, through cantonments themselves and practices such as the cordon sanitaire, to separate European bodies and populations from the dangers taking place in open spaces inhabited by native bodies and populations. These interventions into water, directed as they were at the Civil Lines and the Cantonment, must be similarly understood as a way of organizing spatial relationships among things and persons through a logic of separation and containment.

Securing colonial rule was accomplished by spatially separating Europeans and Indians through water supply, drainage and sewerage, and disposal of filth and rubbish. These acts of separation were accompanied by ones of containment, where things like water, dust, and dirt were placed into certain spaces and not others. This ordering logic fundamentally reshaped Lahore's landscapes at the time and would eventually be extended to those spaces of the city inhabited by "native" populations, which were themselves internally differentiated along the lines of caste, class, and religion. Though the rest of the book does not engage with cantonments in Lahore or elsewhere in Pakistan, it is important to emphasize, first, these spaces continue to be highly separated and contained spaces across Pakistani cities, and, second, the logic of separation and containment continues to organize the relationship that persons have to those materials things now known as waste, especially as it moves across spaces within Lahore's landscapes. Moreover, that logic is also discernible in infrastructures of disposability that seek to take away materials elsewhere, one of which is dumping grounds where these materials are to be contained. As the coming chapters elaborate, that logic continues to imbue waste materials and work with different kinds of value, while also organizing social and spatial relations stretching across Lahore and other urban centers in Pakistan.

Watery Matters

Institutions and infrastructures were assembled in Lahore that aimed to govern the movement and circulation of materialities, so certain kinds of progress and reform could be made in subjects and their environments, which would then legitimize interventions by the colonial state.[13] During the late nineteenth and early twentieth centuries, municipal institutions were increasingly being invested with power and authority related to sanitation and public health. A series of municipal acts were passed to reform and expand the scope of municipal institutions during this time, most prominently those enacted under Lord Ripon (1880–1884), which invested "local" government with greater administrative and financial controls.[14] From its establishment in 1862, one of the primary matters taken up by the Lahore Municipal Committee (LMC) was water supply and drainage, and by 1876, it committed itself to provisioning an uncontaminated water supply and the building of "an improved and complete drainage and sewerage system." At the time, a number of wells (estimated to be well over 3,000) were the major sources of water for the burgeoning city but were deemed by the LMC to be on the whole "unfit for use" (Latif 2005 [1892], 298). These representations of contaminated groundwater notwithstanding, "a system of water-works [had] opened" by 1881 that was funded by the Government of India, with the supply being taken from wells located on a "strip of land" that was the bed of the Ravi before it had changed its course (Government of Punjab 2013 [1908], 38).

The other side of supplying "pure" water through piping was its removal through drains and sewers. As public works like filling hollows and ditches, paving roads, and building drains were carried out, early drainage and sewerage infrastructure—simply described as "open rectangular channels built of brick set in mud mortar and plastered"—was laid down around 1852 haphazardly when military officials were attempting to deal with breakouts of illnesses among troops and Europeans. Unlike waterworks, which were constructed and implemented in and around the Civil

Lines and the Cantonment, watery matter circulating through drainage (and sewerage) across the city continually posed infrastructural challenges for municipal institutions. Drains, especially, were seen as posing a "public nuisance," being described as "extremely defective" and "useless," leading to the dire state of Lahore's *mohallās* and "gullies," where the majority of the population resided. The power and authority to oversee sanitation and public health, in fact, arose from the fact that the LMC was given the ability to regulate the construction, maintenance, and improvement of streets and buildings (see Glover 2008, 131; Harrison 1994, 166). Under "offences affecting the Public Health, Safety or Convenience" for instance, fines (20 rupees) were outlined for the nonremoval or unlawful disposal of certain materials either in streets, open areas, or drains and sewers. The kind of problem that drains, streets, and other open or public spaces posed is discernible in discussions of the cholera epidemic that devastated the city for several weeks the same year the waterworks opened.

A report titled "The Sanitation of Lahore" appearing in the *Tribune* highlighted one of the "principal causes" for the outbreak to be the construction of the waterworks themselves, which involved "digging up of the narrow lanes for laying the pipes," "the bursting of the reservoir and the damage done to the neighborhood in consequence thereof, and the upsetting of the whole drainage system of the city." When the "rains set in [. . .] the city became one cesspool of putrid water." "Another powerful cause for the sickness" was identified to be "uncleanliness of the city." The report described how "every lane in the city looks more like a drain than a passage for human beings [. . .]. In the morning, the sweepers by sweeping the drains in the middle of the lanes create such a stench that people find it difficult to pass through laneslanes [. . .]. The scavengers' carts should also not be allowed to stand along with their savoury loads but should be hurried out of the city as fast as possible." In the proposed drainage and sewerage scheme mentioned earlier, the municipal engineer offered a strikingly similar diagnosis of streets, drains, and other open or public spaces:

> In the larger streets they [*drains*] are placed close to the houses, but have no connection with them; in the smaller streets and lanes in the centre of the

road. They are laid down with little regard to the laws which regulate the flow of water in open channels, being merely built on the surface, and rising and falling as the ground does; so long as the fall is constant they work and carry according to the inclination and capacity, but the slightest impediment stops them and the sewerage flows over the road to be absorbed or evaporated. The depressions in the ground and the bends in the gutters are so numerous that a constant flow of sewage is impossible, and very little of the sewage ever reaches the intercepting sewers (Government of Punjab 1876, 2–3).

It was not, in the words of Chakrabarty, the "uses to which [the street] was put" that confounded distinctions between "private" and "public," but street, drains, and sewers comprised a built environment resistant to modernist imaginations of spatial order. To entirely reconstruct streets was viewed as impractical, so they were "to be accepted intact, so far as their general direction and position is concerned," but it would be necessary to have them "opened up and widened" for purposes of "sanitation and convenience," as "fresh air and ventilation" are critical to "the health and comfort of animal existence as pure water" (Government of Punjab 1876, 8–9). The widening of streets had not only sanitary and health benefits. In the 1920s, Ganga Ram (a prominent engineer and patron of Lahore), for instance, called explicitly for the widening of the streets to increase the value of land in the city. The LMC carried forward, in a piecemeal fashion, the widening of a limited number of streets in the Inner City, while, owing to financial costs, only a two-mile outfall sewer and later sanitary improvements, such as "guttering and metaling of roads" and "remodeling intercepting sewers," were constructed to have sewage discharged into a back channel of the River Ravi.

As the city expanded outside the Inner City, the Civil Lines, and Cantonment, the Lahore Improvement Trust (LIT), founded in the 1920s, became responsible for emerging areas such as Misri Shah, Faiz Bagh, Bhaghpanpura, Qila Gujar Singh, Gawal Mandi, and Landa Bazaar (see Government of Punjab 1945, 23). The LIT drew up and implemented various plans related to land use, streets, drainage and sewerage, and infrastructures. For instance, Misri Shah, located north of the Railway Workshop, became the site of a Development Scheme in 1939 (see

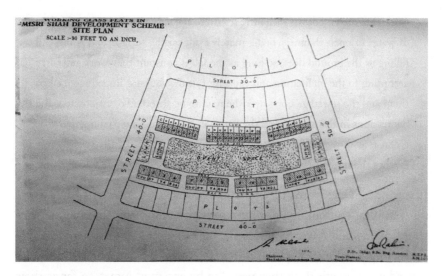

FIGURE 1.3. *Plans for working class flats in Misri Shah area of Lahore.*
Source: *Government of Punjab 1945.*

Figure 1.3), with first an earthen road and brick soiling, the construction
of an approach road, and provisioning of underground sewerage. In the
case of the low-lying area of Gowal Mandi, the growth of which was
"unchecked" and "unplanned," flooding was "inevitable" during and after
the rains (Government of Punjab 1945, 29), and on the northwest of the
city was Mozang, which was a crowded "village" that became the site of
repeated "piecemeal" improvements focusing on water, drainage, and sewerage infrastructure (Glover 2005). By the late 1930s, although a sewerage
system (known as the Howell plan) had been constructed in many burgeoning locales, which would be built upon in the years preceding partition, it was noted that commercial and governmental buildings mostly
were "already ... equipped with water flush appliances," but there was
"little prospect that many house owners will proceed voluntarily to install
water flushed sanitary appliances in their houses, nor is it likely that the
Municipal Committee would compel house owners to do so" (Government of Punjab 1924, ii). It should be underscored that underground sewerage and their technological connections were predominantly found in
those localities inhabited by British and wealthier Indian populations at
this time.

Thus, in lieu of connections to underground drainage and sewerage infrastructure for most of Lahore's population, households had their night soil, kitchen runoff, and other watery matter removed through a combination of built environments and the labor of "sweepers" and "scavengers." William Glover describes how, "Night soil from rooftop latrines was collected in small earthen vessels (*gumlas*) once a day, usually in the morning, by 'sweepers' who customarily received one chapatti (unleavened bread) as payment. Liquid waste from the latrine was channeled to drains in the street through a vertical notch (*parnala*) in the house's outer wall rather than through internal piping" (2008, 113). The following sections analyze the complex relations among low- or noncaste groups (described as "sweepers" or "scavengers" in colonial accounts), households, contractors, and the municipality. Here, what must be underscored is how points of connections between inner spaces (households) and outer ones (streets, drains) took on such salience because they were points where categorical distinctions—between private and public—converged and an order of urban life was to be enacted. Material things, streets, drains, sewers, and persons were emplaced within the public as composing the infrastructures of urban life, just as that emplacement was simultaneously done alongside that of the private, most prominently the household but also, other things, spaces, and activities. These categorical distinctions and the order built upon them were and continue to be ideological in nature, which tends to obscure the unstable and blurry boundaries between private and public, inner and outer, and of course, custom and contract.

Custom and Contract

Rupa Viswanath (2014) has described how the position of low- or noncaste groups, who were largely nonlanded laborers enduring varying degrees of coercion, was reproduced through the colonial regime by its incorporation of "mutual obligations" between these groups and landed elites. Described usually as "sweepers" or "scavengers," those who worked with different kinds of waste materials—night soil, household runoff, rubbish, and other discard—moved across many of the inner and outer spaces described thus far. The taking away of these materials, which were considered polluting and impure for not only caste Hindus but also

Muslims and Sikhs, was part of complex relations of work and exchange that brought together "hereditary" or "customary sweepers," contractors, municipal institutions, landowners, households, and many other actors. Sweepers and scavengers were remunerated with money (e.g., a few annas), chapattis, and other kinds of things in exchange mostly for taking away night soil from household latrines, though they also engaged in the removal of materials from other spaces as well, such as *kuchas*, streets, and drains. Some of this material would be sold to cultivators or landowners (zamindars) from Lahore's agrarian hinterlands, while other materials could be repurposed or sold to *kabāṛīāṇ* (junkyard owners) (see Prashad 1995, 8–10). From the perspective of municipal institutions and colonial officials, the intricate relations of work and exchange among workers, households, localities, cultivators, or landowners were customary ones.[15] As the sanitation workforce expanded and investments were made into filth depots, carts, and other techno-infrastructural entities throughout the late nineteenth and first half of the twentieth centuries, customary relations of work and exchange were kept in a delicate balance and integrated with contractual ones.[16]

The Punjab Municipal Act "[recognized] the customary rights of sweepers and stat[ed] that under no circumstances could the municipality take over the conservancy of private houses as this was the domain of the customary sweeper" (Khalid 2012, 62; see also Johnson and Khalid 2012). Concurrently, the various materials sweepers or scavengers worked with fell under the purview of municipal power and authority. The Punjab Municipal Act also affirmed that "all dust, dirt, dung, ashes, dung, animal-matter or filth or rubbish of any kind collected by the committee from the streets, houses, privies, sewers, cesspools else-where" will "be vested in and belong to the committee" (Government of Punjab 1884, 40–41). Being vested property, this material's "direction, management, and control" fell under the municipality's legal power and authority (1884, 40). This vested asset contained value in itself—in the form of manure—but also took on value through monetized and nonmonetized exchanges taking place among scavengers, sweepers, households, landowners, cultivators, and the municipality. Thus, as the LMC could not intervene into the customary or hereditary rights of sweepers, it did have power and authority to regulate the movements of different materials things, for which it deployed contractors.

The LMC repeatedly offered contracts either to have wards of the city cleaned or to allow cultivators or landowners to take away these materials to Lahore's agricultural hinterlands for use as manure. Auctions for these contracts would be held in which individuals, sometimes coming from different caste groups that were "rich sweepers" organized as "cliques," made bids to win contracts for various wards.[17] These auctions were not ones in which individuals paid the municipality for the contract, but rather these individuals offered a competitive rate to be paid to them by the municipality in exchange for their organization of labor and other resources to remove material things from a specified ward. In the case of cultivators and landowners, it was recognized these groups had prescriptive rights to the materials, but eventually a contract system was instituted to exercise municipal control and realize monetary value of those materials and work. The municipality thus had direct contractual relations with the individual who won the bid (contractors), not those who carried out the work of waste removal (sweepers or those who conveyed these materials to agrarian hinterlands), although there was often overlap between contractors and workers. This mixture of customary and contractual work was the mechanism by which attempts were made to formalize and bureaucratize customary relations. Yet, that arrangement between custom and contract, along with formal and informal and bureaucratic and extra-bureaucratic, like other distinctions discussed above, were unstable, with the distinct relations of work and exchange being linked across them.

In fact, there was a constant fluctuation between custom and contact in Lahore that arose out of concerns about mismanagement, malfeasance, and/or poor performance.[18] As early as 1868, it was noted that conservancy was carried out by contract in Lahore, with a "contractor [who] maintains an establishment of sweepers, carts, bullocks, donkeys, &c, for removal of filth, and undertakes to keep the streets, drains, &c clean." Prior to the instituting of a contract system, the municipality's "servants had nothing to do but to collect the night soil in heaps, its removal being left to the cultivators of the estates around Lahore, who had gradually acquired strong prescriptive rights in the valuable manure they obtained" (Government of

Punjab 2006 [1894], 316). Citing "uncertain and incomplete" timing and method of removal, the rights of cultivators were "broke[n] down" and "leas[ed] out to another contractor who paid for them." Then, the LMC would "revert to the former system, allowing the cultivators to carry off the sweeping subject to definite rules and times after the conservancy establishment has done their early morning work of collecting the stuff from houses and alleys and have deposited it at certain fixed places" (2006 [1894], 316). At that time the cultivators paid between 5–15 rupees a month in order to keep a cart at stations where waste, mostly manure, was deposited. By 1914, these landowners, paying different amounts, owned "contracts with the [Lahore Municipal] Committee through their agent [and] were allowed to take the filth from certain areas." These carts arrived at the seventy filth depots constructed by the LMC in the early morning from the villages surrounding Lahore. "Sweepers," who were given "a few annas a month to attend the latrines" of the households that had "privately" contracted them, brought materials to these filth depots.

Despite the additional presence of "donkey contractors," who receive "Rs. 4 per head" and "promenade the streets and alleys and collect whatever filth they can find there," materials such as urine and rubbish remained out in streets and drains for a variety of reasons, either irregularly being taken to the filth depots or simply flowing into the drainage and sewerage infrastructure. At the time, there were also failed attempts to utilize "small covered iron receptacles" to convey these materials to filth depots and even discussions of creating a conservancy tram to improve and mechanize transportation, rather than donkey carts, baskets, human labor, and other kinds of techno-infrastructural entities.

By the 1930s, the LMC had instituted a "strong departmental presence," while questions continue to be raised about the cadre of workers, supervisors, and contractors operating within and outside its boundaries. Waste materials were still being deposited in filth depots or open grounds to be carried away further by municipal carts, zamindari contractors, and/ or private cartmen (Government of Punjab 1931, 95). Once again, contractual relations as they existed at this point were deemed inadequate. A zamindari contractor or private cartman, due to "no proper check on deliveries from the dump," could be given waste "free of charge" or take away an amount greater than he was supposed to. Moreover, "tales of illicit supply to cultivators" questioned the accounting practices of the sale of waste materials. The sanitation staff that oversaw collection and disposal of waste material were complicit in such illicit practices, as they exerted control over the filth depot or dumping ground. Such mismanagement and disorganization necessitated, as expected, "that the contract system should disappear altogether," as "the merits of departmental management" being "unassailable," and "alleged leakages should be counteracted by stiffer control" (1931, 95–96).

At this time, the sanitation workforce employed by the LMC included 17 supervisors and 1,050 sweepers—all of whom were under the control of a city inspector from the Health Department. Sweepers, in particular, were described as a "motley throng" that knew "pretty well how to look after themselves" and posed "a difficult problem":

> Now these sweepers are a somewhat independent body. They have a Scavengers' Union: they are much in request and are to some extent able to dictate their own terms. All except 98, employed in the main bazaars, are part-time servants, engaged at Rs. 8 per mensem. A great part of the day is their own, and it is understood that they make as much as Rs. 25–30 per mensem. The result of this irregular mode of employment are thoroughly unsatisfactory. (Government of Punjab 1931, 96)

The desire to control sweepers was an effort to make their work, as well as disposal of waste materials, more regular and predictable. Proper management was very much about the bureaucratization of waste work, in which state institutions at the municipal level would exercise control over the labor of low- or noncaste groups by instituting waged relations. At this point, however, only a small minority of these sweepers were municipal employees who received a municipal wage. The vast majority would still be considered customary or hereditary sweepers who organized their labor in relation to those who would compensate them, in both monetary and nonmonetary forms, for materials and work.

Another important class of subordinates were supervisors, especially the *dāroghah* who was the supervisory figure at the level of the ward. Their responsibilities were "to supervise the sanitation of areas assigned to them and attend to complaints by the public: control the jemadars, muster menial staff of sweepers, bhishtis, cartmen, etc., maintain their attendance registers and prepare monthly acquittance rolls" (Government of Punjab 1931, 96).[19] In the next chapter I analyze how the figure of the *dārog̲h̲ah*, despite several decades of spatial and infrastructural development, plays a critical role in contemporary Lahore's waste infrastructures, allowing state institutions at the municipal level to occupy a managerial role over the labor of waste workers, the provisioning of waste disposal services to the public, networks of patronage, and processes of circulation.

Despite the unpredictability of sweepers' work, supervisors were complicit and, to a certain extent, enabled the irregularity being bemoaned to go on:

> If a sweeper wishes to change his beat, to absent himself for a short period, or to secure the employment of a relative, he does so for a small fee to the Jemadar or Sanitary Inspector. It is even asserted that they pay a proportion of their salaries to these officers, in order to retain their names on the muster rolls and that the rolls contain a great number of fictitious entries, the same names appearing on the muster rolls of other departments. I mention all this not with the object of stigmatizing the controlling staff on uncorroborated evidence, but in order to demonstrate the necessity for better control. (Government of Punjab 1931, 96)

And, in an inspection visit to the Inner City following a complaint related to "untended drains and general neglect of sanitary arrangements," the *dārog̲h̲ah* "had not been in evidence for several weeks, and it was obvious that the needs of their neighborhood, quite modest as they proved to be, had been totally ignored" (1931, 96). Much of these criticisms—access to work, worker absenteeism, lack of supervision—continues to be levied against the *dārog̲h̲ah* for the undue control they exercise over waste workers and the provisioning of waste disposal services to the public. Even if education[20] could ameliorate "bureaucratic disregard for duty," the real task at hand in making the labor of scavengers and sweepers more regular and controlled was changing their working conditions and stricter supervision. Such changes, it was thought, would "bring some measure of order into what is at present a very loose and disintegrate organization."

This portrayal ("very loose and disintegrate organization") resulted from an order of urban life organized around categories of the public—an outer one located in particular spaces and sites (drains) and relations of work and exchange (contract)—and the private—an inner one to be located elsewhere (households) and in other relations of work and exchange (custom). The constant speculation about sweepers, supervisors, and contractors was a legitimating practice for extending the powers of government, thereby extending bureaucratic control over waste materials and work situated outside the domain of the public (see Rutherford 2009). Throughout this period, however, sweepers or scavengers labored under distinct relations of work and exchange, at times being labelled hereditary or customary sweepers and at other times (quite often simultaneously) being under the control of contractors or municipal institutions, where monetized exchange (i.e., wages and contracts) were dominant. Their labor, which brought together relations of work and exchange, extended across the order of urban life, rendering vulnerable categorical divisions and their attendant spatial practices, while concurrently becoming a site for extending the techno-legal apparatus of the bureaucratic state. This techno-legal apparatus, though imbued with the power to govern in the name of the public, incorporated caste-based relations by synthesizing custom and contract. The transformations in contemporary Pakistan described going forward build upon this order of urban life, in which caste-based relations have come to be embedded.

An Order for Urban Life

The category of the public, especially as it undergirds spatial practices and relations of work and exchange, is a politically contested one throughout cities in South Asia and globally (Freitag 1991; Glover 2007; Anjaria 2016; see also Low and Smith 2006; Harvey 2012).[21] In the case of waste materials and work, the claim of generality and universality made through the category of the public is discernible in not only how the disposal of waste materials from *public spaces* continues to be a primary responsibility of municipal institutions but also how solid waste management is to be provisioned and managed as a *good to the public* through the techno-legal apparatus of the bureaucratic state. For instance, municipal institutions are repeatedly criticized for failing to provision these services to the public in a fair or equitable manner and are viewed as corrupt because actors (i.e., workers, supervisors, political coordinators) exploit their positions within state institutions to pursue private interests and profit through wider networks of patronage. This rendering of the public also aligns with approaches to waste materials that prioritize institutional and technicist approaches such as governance reform and engineering of disposability. The category of the public traverses and brings together spatial practices, relations of work and exchange, and techno-legal apparatus of the bureaucratic states—all of which remain critical to understanding the dynamics of waste infrastructures across urban Pakistan. Yet, this category performs other work as well: it disentangles these things—spatial practices, relations of work and exchange, the techno-legal apparatus of the bureaucratic state—from the interest of any particular community, and in doing so, it simultaneously obscures and embeds caste into the order of urban life.

Waste work constituted as an infrastructure of urban life in Pakistan has been built upon expansive forms of life that are organized around caste-based relations and stretch across the Punjab and many other parts of the country. Under colonial rule, the city of Lahore expanded toward the south of Inner City, where the Civil Lines, Cantonment, and other localities burgeoned, while in recent decades more settlements have grown toward the south but expanded much further outward. These spatial dynamics, undergirded as they are by a logic of separation and containment, continue to inform infrastructures of disposability that shape the trajectory of urbanization across contemporary Pakistan. However, rather than those differentiations occurring along the racialized lines of colonizers and colonized, the differentiation of urban space now occurs along the lines of caste, class, and religion, though race along with ethnicity and gender remain salient as well. Here, the category of the public is elementary, as it enables caste-based relations to be concealingly incorporated into the order of urban life through a range of constitutive techniques, from spatial practices and concepts to techno-infrastructural entities to contractual waged labor. Although the category of the public has figured prominently in the institutions and infrastructures assembled in Lahore, processes of urbanization—in spatial, institutional, and infrastructural terms—and the quality of urban life across much of Pakistan have been consistently shaped by caste-based dynamics.

The proceeding chapters will detail the processes by which waste workers, whether working for the municipality or laboring under informalized relations, have migrated to urban centers like Lahore from more agrarian areas of the Punjab over the past several decades and found work in the country's expanding waste infrastructures. Many of these workers continue to be drawn heavily from low- or noncaste backgrounds who have historically been landless agricultural labor, embedded in a variegated set of relations with those considered to be upper castes and who enjoyed control over land across the Punjab. These forms of life have undergone patent changes over the past several decades, unmooring individuals and groups from many of these caste-based relations as they have come to be settled on Lahore's urban peripheries. Thus, it is not just the bureaucratic state, in the form of municipal governments employing sweepers, that is implicated in reproducing particular forms of life; indeed, as will be highlighted in the coming pages, informalized relations of work and exchange economy that have emerged out of the disposal of waste materials and consumption of commodities taking place on a mass scale, as well as the uneven urbanization that now characterizes contemporary Lahore's landscape, are also implicated.

Nevertheless, the order of urban life that emerged in Lahore during colonial rule sought to stabilize forms of life organized around caste-based relations by reproducing it through the techno-legal apparatus of the bureaucratic state. This project of reproduction through management has continued in contemporary Pakistan, as these institutions and infrastructures have continued to draw upon the labor of low- or noncaste groups, dealt with the dynamics of an unevenly urbanizing landscape, and confronted unprecedented levels of commodity consumption and waste generation.

CHAPTER 2

THE APPEARANCE OF THINGS

AASHIQUE, A *DĀROGHAH* (supervisor) in the Faisal Town area of Lahore, and I spent much of our time together in the ticketing booth-turned-field office for the Solid Waste Management (SWM) Department that I mentioned in the opening of the book. Except for a signboard above the entrance and garbage compactors intermittently parked outside, nothing about this field office makes its connection to the Lahore's waste infrastructures apparent. Expectedly, residents, shopkeepers, and many others regularly end up here accidentally—at times, mistaking it for Union Council offices where deaths, births, and divorces are registered, or presuming it is a field office for the Water and Sanitation Agency (WASA). Nevertheless, throughout the days, all kinds of figures—workers, residents, shopkeepers, supervisors, and managers—circulated in and out of its courtyard, each in their own way making Lahore's waste infrastructures happen.

Late one morning, after the morning attendance was taken, Aashique, Arif, and I were reclining in the courtyard, when Aashique received a call from Ms. Mariam—an assistant manager assigned by the Lahore Waste Management Company (LWMC) to oversee solid waste management in this locality. Soon thereafter, Ms. Mariam arrived in her *carry ḍabbā* (passenger van), and after handing Aashique a piece of paper, the two of them left abruptly. Before departing, Aashique turned to tell me to go back inside the office and wait for him. A little while later, Aashique returned without Ms. Mariam, sat back down where he had left us, and handed me a report cut out from the Urdu daily *Na'ī Bāt*, detailing several problems regarding living conditions in the Union Council where Aashique was the *dāroghah*—this was the same piece of paper Ms. Mariam handed him earlier. "Residents from UC 210 Faisal Town in conversation with *Na'ī Bāt* speak about their problems," it read at the top, with accompanying photographs of those who were sharing complaints with the newspaper. The headline announced, "In Faisal Town, UC 210, piles of filth, open manholes, and nonfunctioning sewerage." The subheadline stated, "Residents falling sick from contaminated water, not one water filtration plant installed, sanitation department doesn't dispose of waste for several days, streets and alleys are falling apart, most plots have crops for livestock, despite administrative complaints, no resolution to these problems, say residents." The report goes on to provide further details about each of the complaints in this locality of the provincial capital: In addition to rusting water pipes contaminating water and causing children and the elderly to fall ill, the report continues, "Asghar Ali, Fayyaz Ahmad, Taib Ali tell us that piles of waste are all over the place, the sanitation [*'amlah safā'ī*] staff do not show up in the streets for days." Finally, numerous images were arranged at the bottom of the report chronicling failing municipal services.

When I asked him who these people are, Aashique dismissed them, "They are just some political people [*siyāsī log*]." But, later in the day, Aashique was sure to pay a visit to a shop owner in the area who owns an electrical appliance store and is the president (*sadr*) of the Peco Rd. Business Association. We walked up a few stairs and entered through glass doors into the display room, with stairs to the right leading up to the second floor. Aashique is familiar with the attendants, and we casually walked into the back office, where the shop owner was seated behind a desk with an assistant who waited attentively. Aashique showed him the report, asking who the people mentioned in it were. The shop owner told us that they are residents who also have smaller shops and industrial units in the Union Council. Aashique did not inquire much further,

FIGURE 2.1. *Waste materials being cleared under the supervision of dāroghah, baildār, and attendance checker. Source: Author.*

seemed satisfied, and we walked out. Before leaving, the shop owner told Aashique to not worry; he knew the journalist who wrote the piece and would speak with him.

In the meantime, Aashique, Arif, and Salamat (a *baildār*[1]) deputed a dozen or so sanitation workers to the area where some of the pictures had been taken. This area fell under the "beat" of two sanitation workers named Munawwar and Babar who are respectively father and son. As we drove to join the "gang" of sanitation workers (Figure 2.1), Aashique recounts, "Workers don't work hard if I'm not around. They clean weakly and lazily," softly grabbing my shoulder to demonstrate their lack of effort and vigor. Upon our arrival, Aashique got immediately to work, instructing one sanitation worker to clear out plastic shoppers in front of a doorstep, while encouraging others to go toward the empty plot of land to create piles of trash. As the work was being done, multiple men converge on Aashique, each of them sharing complaints about Babar, commenting on how filthy the *mohallā* (neighborhood) had become over the past week, and praising informal workers who, at the very least, were reliable enough to take away their household garbage on a regular basis. In response Aashique threw one insult after another at Babar, as well as his father, and lambasted both for being more concerned with household trash, for which they received an additional payment from residents, rather than their municipal responsibilities for which they were paid a salary. Aashique then turned to address residents who had gathered there, declaring he would be held responsible if the *mohallā* did not get cleared of filth.

As the events unfolding that morning suggest, quotidian forms of work and exchange and social and political relationships are constantly mobilized to take away waste materials across Lahore's urbanizing landscapes. This chapter thus foregrounds the variegated set of activities, relations, and practices that have been constitutive of waste infrastructures in contemporary Pakistan. From the changing materialities that now constitute waste as "solid waste" to growing access to waste materials and work across municipal institutions and informalized work arrangements, to the shifting urban and agrarian landscapes, waste infrastructures have been and continue to be reworked in light of several distinct though interlaced scalar processes. Rather than being an ethnography of bureaucracy, this chapter pursues a tangential problematic: how has the bureaucratic state, through figures like the *dāroghah* and an accompanying techno-legal apparatus, appropriated and organized (albeit partially) the labor of low- or noncaste groups and different kinds of waste work that cut across and suture together Lahore's urbanizing landscape?

Investments into infrastructures of disposability in Lahore have not only expanded the bureaucratic state and its techno-legal apparatus but also entrenched the figure of the *dāroghah*, which, as discussed in the previous chapter, was a prominent one in colonial Lahore. Precisely because waste work implicates a broad set of relations that destabilize many of the distinctions that uphold the bureaucratic state, the work of the *dāroghah* then comes to maintain a particular appearance of things and persons, as well as the distinctions—most prominently, that of the public—that make possible and uphold that appearance. This continues to concealingly embed caste into the very fabric of urban life in Pakistan, making clear that the reproduction of urban life through waste work is concurrently the reproduction of forms of life organized around caste-based relations.

The Bureaucratic State and "Political Coordinators"

In contemporary Lahore, the disposal of waste materials has increasingly become a site of governance, in which the bureaucratic state and its techno-legal apparatus has intersected with markets for waste materials and work, networks of patronage and circulation, and processes of urbanization. Waste work has entered the "*routine* and *repetitive* procedures of bureaucracies" and led to its institutionalization, though in limited ways, within municipal government (Gupta and Sharma 2009, 11, emphasis in original; see also Weber 1978; Feldman 2008). The *limited* institutionalization of waste work raises a much more fundamental question about the relationship that the bureaucratic state has not only to waste materials and work but also to those activities, relations, and practices through which life comes to be reproduced in Lahore and beyond.

Much of the critical work on the state has emphasized a broad set of practices and procedures through which the bureaucratic state makes itself present within everyday life, just as ideas and representation allow it to maintain itself as an autonomous entity that is separate from and/or stands above other entities (see Abrams 1988; Mitchell 1991, 1999). The bureaucratic state, through its own actors and techno-legal apparatus, operates as an aggregated unity within everyday life that is rendered susceptible to disaggregation and projections by its very own constitutive categories and practices (see Gupta and Ferguson 2002; Hansen and Stepputat 2001; Krupa and Nugent 2015; Fuller and Benei 2009; Raheja 2022). Similarly, as several diffused activities, relations, and practices go into reproducing life in Lahore, the bureaucratic state must contend with a contradiction internal to its own functioning: being an aggregated entity constituted through its dispersal. Waste work constituted into an infrastructure operates and connects multiple, entangled regimes, whether that be the bureaucratized practices of state institutions, informalized work arrangements, networks of patronage and circulation, or caste-based relations.[2] As such, actors and institutions must manage a broad set of processes that inhere within waste materials and the work surrounding them.

One of most prominent of those processes is that of patronage, in which the figure of the "political coordinator" was prominent. Since the 1980s, just as the bureaucratic state has grown to provision waste disposal services to the public and the urban landscape in Lahore has been re-worked along the lines of caste, class, and religion, networks of patronage have expanded throughout the country, while democratic politics have been reinvigorated.[3] Patronage involves an exchange of goods and ser-vices for political power: those actors who have access to these goods and services facilitate their distribution among those (i.e. citizens) at-tempting to access them. Alongside networks of patronage, which may be undergirded by ties of *birādarī* ("kinship"), claims of citizenship have been consistently invoked in relation to many state policies and infra-structure projects being implemented across the country in recent years, with such claims being attached to a range of entitlements, whether they be public goods and services or social protections and welfare (see Siddiqi 2019). While *dāroghein* and workers are *not necessarily* patrons or clients, their respective kinds of work—supervision and disposal—are embedded within networks of patronage and the claims made by citizens to a public good or service like solid waste management.

In all the localities I conducted fieldwork in, there was always at least one "political coordinator" that *dāroghein* were perpetually in con-tact with, though so were municipal and informal workers and other field staff. Most coordinators working in these localities were from what Aasim Sajjad Akhtar has described as the intermediary classes, which are "comprised of traders, merchants, transporters and various types of petty producers, most of whom are, or historically have been, linked to the sec-ondary and tertiary sectors of the agrarian economy," and were supported by the authoritarian rule of Zia ul-Haq in order to shore up its own polit-ical legitimacy outside of formal democratic institutions and procedures (2018, 65).[4] These classes utilized access to state institutions and resources, as well as networks of kin and patronage, to become dominant in small- and medium-scale industrial and commercial activities. Even after the restoration of formal democracy, these classes, especially in urban Punjab, have continued to increase and formalize their clout by forming associa-tions (based around kin and/or commercial and business interests) and becoming active and prominent within political parties such as the Pakistan Muslim League (Nawaz), though that has changed with the rising influence of Pakistan Tehreek-e Insaaf. It should thus come as no surprise that political coordinators in these localities owned similarly sized industrial units or commercial enterprises, while also being part of market, merchants, and/or traders' associations, having an affiliation with a major political party, and having at some point been elected to local government (when they have been formed).

Political coordinators—whether as individuals or through parties and associations—thus utilized access to state bureaucracies like the SWM Department, and their labor-force and techno-infrastructural resources, to provision goods and services like solid waste management to the public within any locality. Since these coordinators do not inhabit state institutions themselves, the *dāroghah*, as a municipal employee, becomes a figure that negotiates the engagements among workers, citizens, bureaucrats, managers, and political coordinators themselves when solid waste management is being delivered as a public good. The tension between waste work as a pervasive social and political relationship and solid waste management as a public good to be provisioned to citizens by state institutions and actors has facilitated the growth of patronage networks: these infrastructures allow patronage to appear as the provisioning of a public good or service to its citizens by the bureaucratic state. These tensions have only become more salient as waste work has been constituted into an infrastructure of urban life in Pakistan.

Transitions: Waste, Work, and the City

Over the past several decades, the city of Lahore has been undergoing rapid urbanization that has had transformative effects on waste materials, work, and infrastructures. Prior to the expansion of piped sewerage, human feces ("nightsoil" in colonial accounts), sullage from open drains running along streets, or rubbish from streets and other open spaces was carried away by predominantly Dalit groups in Lahore. Much of this material was placed into a basket (*taslāh*) balanced atop their head and thrown away in an outdoor *kudi* (latrine) or *gun gaḍā* (filth depot), before being taken away by *bail gaḍī* (bullock cart) to the *fasīl* (boundary wall) of the Inner City. Many of these structures and practices remained in place in older parts of Lahore throughout the 1980s and even until the early 1990s, according to supervisors and workers alike. In Lahore's more recently constructed settlements, waste materials were oftentimes gathered in semienclosed structures known as a *darmālā* or other open plots of land, and in those settlements without underground sewerage, usually inhabited by the urban poor and working-class communities, sullage needed to be removed from open drains, being set aside to dry until it could be disposed of (as I describe further below). Across different parts of the city, household waste materials have been and continue to be burned as a waste disposal practice. As the *kudī*, *gun̤ gaḍā*, and *darmālā* have slowly diminished and sewerage infrastructures spread out across the urban landscape, waste workers with whom I conducted fieldwork dealt almost entirely with "solid waste," being assisted by containers, compactors, and other vehicles and equipment.

These techno-infrastructural shifts in Lahore's waste infrastructure have occurred alongside intergenerational shifts in work, settlement, and life for waste workers and their kin. Employed as a municipal sanitation worker for nearly forty years, Razia Bibi had been officially hired a few years before her marriage and the hanging of Zulfiqar Ali Bhutto (1979) but had been unofficially working alongside her mother, who herself started during the time of Ayub Khan (1958–1969), while her father had passed away when Razia Bibi was only a couple of years old. After the mother took retirement, Razia Bibi inherited the position since her brother was too young at the time to take the position. Additionally, many in her extended kin network have been and continue to be employed as municipal workers. Importantly, although Razia Bibi was born in Lahore in Gulab Devi Hospital, her mother and father came from Pattoki and Gajju Mata, respectively, where their extended kin network were embedded in agrarian relations of work and exchange—her father specifically engaged in work and trade involving livestock before being settled in Lahore and working in a factory near the city's old airport.

I also want to note the ways in which female and male kin relations played a critical role in Razia Bibi's life trajectory. Not only had Razia Bibi's father passed away when she was young, her husband worked for a period in brick kilns but then started working for the municipal government as a sanitation worker. After her husband lost his job because of drug and alcohol abuse, Razia Bibi, akin to her mother, became the primary householder, being forced to raise the children on her own, though with the help of her own siblings. This narrative was common among female workers, especially those employed by the municipality, who were either conscious of being the primary householder due to the absence of male kin or worked alongside male kin to support their households. As will become clear in later chapters, intergenerational trajectories involved shifting relations in work, land, and settlement, while also being accompanied by reworked gendered relations that cut across the domains of living and working. Alongside these intergenerational shifts are also other changes in waste work itself that have occurred within the lifetime of workers.

Sitting with Rameez one afternoon, I gained a sense of the actual extent of such changes. Those putting on a wedding in Faisal Town had contacted Aashique and retained Rameez's services for a modest fee, which Aashique and Rameez split. At the end of function, Rameez would sweep the *Eidgah* (open-air enclosure for Eid prayers) and assist in other cleanup activities. As we waited on benches for the function to start, Rameez told me about how this area of Faisal Town was once a *daihātī 'alāqah* (rural area), being sparsely populated and underdeveloped, but had now been built up into a densely populated residential area, with plentiful small- to medium-sized industrial units. When he first started working in this area over twenty years ago, the locality, Rameez told me, "was very dirty, there was [*open*] drainage. The roads were unpaved. It was in a very poor state. We first did not sweep or swept less at least. Those open drains, we cleaned them." I asked, "How did you clean it?" Rameez continued, "We had a *korpā*, it was like this [describing a metal trap-like tool], there was big stick attached to it, and we used it like this. We used it to remove the sewage. When it dried and became dirt after a few days, then we removed and placed it in a depression. The roads were uneven: in some places there was a pothole, in other places it was elevated. Then as we deposited trash over and over, we made it even, and we leveled it." Razia Bibi, though having worked much longer than Rameez, described similar things, having to clean an open drain (*nālīā͟n*) of sullage (*kard*) that caused them much discomfort because the liquid waste would splash back in their faces.

Despite Rameez highlighting how waste work was tied to other urban infrastructures, I remained wedded to those of solid waste management, in which gathering and transporting waste materials now constitutes the bulk of their municipal work. I continued, "But when did you sweep?" Making a clicking sound and shaking his head slightly, Rameez clarified, "We *of course also* swept. But less, because what's the point of the *jhāṛu* [handheld broom] when the drain breaks? Some motorcycle or bicycle passed by. The street's *banī* [boundary drain] was tiny, and a tire would hit it so it would easily break and the [sewage] water would spread throughout the *galī*. We first made the street *pakkā* [paved] and only after making it *pakkā*, we made a much bigger *bandh* [boundary drain]. Then after that this *galī* became fine, clean." Confused, I asked, "Who did this all?" and then, Rameez responded, "Us." Rameez later clarified for me that municipal workers in this locality raised the *banī* by using several bricks and covering them with a mixture of dirt and cement. As urban landscapes, especially in localities such as the one I am describing, have developed, underground piping has replaced open sewage drains running alongside the streets.

Rameez also described how changes in infrastructure, the built environment, and work were bound up with institutional ones: "Previously, the system [*of waste disposal*] was not very good. The trash, you know, many piles used to sit in the *darmāle* (three-walled, uncovered structure used to store waste temporarily). The area was empty, just like how this area is empty, most of the area was empty. Many, many piles used to sit out. Then over time, as the department told us, 'Give us the trash.' Those private trucks, we sent them filled with trash. Slowly, slowly, the dirtiness ended. It didn't happen at one time." What emerges from Rameez's description, as well as that of others, is how the work they have performed has been historically intertwined with infrastructures of disposability that are embedded in built environments and the movement of materialities within them. Yet, his mention of "dirtiness" ending slowly and not all at once gestures to the investments made into institutions and

infrastructures of solid waste management across Pakistan, which have
expanded the bureaucratic state and its techno-legal apparatus, impacted
the conditions under which waste work has been accessed and performed
by workers like Rameez and many others, and assigned a managerial role
to the *dāroghah* within Lahore's waste infrastructures.

Solid Waste as an Object of Management

In municipal acts and ordinances passed in Pakistan from the 1960s onward, terms like "dirt," "dust," "rubbish," or "stagnant water" have become
steadily less common, with preference given to more contemporary ones
like "sewage" or "liquid" and "solid waste" and municipalities now being
responsible for acts like "removing," "conveyance," "transportation," "disposing," and "managing" these material things. Since the 1970s, institutions and infrastructures of solid waste management have expanded at
the municipal level in Pakistan and globally.[5] In tandem with the formation of the Lahore Development Authority in 1975 (replacing the Lahore
Improvement Trust) as the city's primary urban planning and development agency, the creation of WASA institutionally separated drainage
and sewerage from other departments within municipal government and
materially differentiated "sewage" from "solid waste." As there was no
dedicated SWM Department, waste collection and disposal fell directly
under the Municipal Corporation of Lahore (MCL), with the medical
officer of health overseeing the performance of field staff, especially sanitation workers and supervisors, and the acquisition and status of machinery and vehicles.[6]

In conjunction with these efforts, the World Bank-funded Lahore
Urban Development Project included components related to "Solid Waste
Collection and Disposal." At the time, it was estimated that a large portion of waste collected by the municipality (around 50 percent) was taken
away for use for cultivation purposes, while the remainder was transported
from "dust bins" to "filth depots" and eventually disposed of in dumping
grounds located "in depressions and low lying areas and wherever else
land is available" (Lahore Development Authority 1980, viii). The disposal
of waste materials was "taken care of by approximately 5,500 sweepers
operating about 90 lorries and trucks, 26 bullock carts and a number of

hand carts" (viii). Much of funding for this project would be directed at enhancing "collection, transport and disposal of solid waste on a city-wide basis through provision of bins and containers, vehicles, equipment for the municipal maintenance workshops, upgrading of transfer stations and selection of sanitary landfill sites" (World Bank 1994, 3).[7] These investments involved procuring "equipment and machinery, storage skips, containers and different types of refuse collection vehicles, establishment of a modern work-shop, provision of transfer stations, land-fill site, training and consultancy" (1994, 15). The project was described as "largely successful,"[8] noting that disposal capacity had increased "from 1300 metric tonnes (MT) to 2100 MT against total generation of 2600 MT/waste per day" and the procurement of land for a landfill site and gas extraction plant at Mehmood Booti (see Map 0.2). Much of what was described at this time as "solid waste collection and disposal" came to be transformed by and into "solid waste management" in the coming decades in tandem with wider processes of urbanization, informalization, and consumption-based economies. As a result of these institutional and technological investments, the SWM Department, with its own administrative and field staff and machinery with the MCL, was created in 1996.

Since then, the SWM Department has only expanded by growing its workforce of sanitation workers, supervisors, bureaucrats, and engineers and increasing investments in techno-infrastructural entities. By 1999, 360 million PKR had been spent on machinery (mechanical sweepers, containers, skips), and calls were made for more funding to procure other machinery (arm rollers, tractors, and suckers, or *galī* suckers).[9] Then, in 2005, the District Assembly noted how Lahore's growing population (at the time, 7.5 million) and expanding geography (1,770 sq. km) meant that "new settlements and localities" were generating approximately 4,000 metric tons of waste on a daily basis, and the 6,897 sanitary workers, conservancy staff, and supervisors could only dispose of 2,600 metric tons, meaning that 35–40 percent of daily waste generation "remain scattered and uncollected in the streets."[10] The District Assembly thus agreed to "increase the number of sanitation workers ... by 20 percent," and "expenses of salaries for these newly created jobs" would be covered if "*employees are hired through contract or work charge*" (emphasis added).[11]

Concurrently, increasing the size of labor force through precarious employment was attached to the introduction of "skilled staff," rather than "unskilled labor," as well as techno-infrastructural entities like dustbins, larger containers, "a mechanized system of cleanliness," and a computerized weigh bridge.[12] This was also the same time when a minimal sanitation fee, collected through WASA, would be imposed on households.

Over the past several decades, through the development of solid waste management, investments have made been into infrastructures of disposability such as machinery, containers, weigh bridges, and dumping grounds and a labor force of sanitation workers, drivers, supervisors, and engineers. These have been legitimated on developmental grounds: institutions and infrastructures of solid waste management were necessary to plan for, manage, and optimize Lahore's geographic and demographic expansion. The institutions and infrastructures put into place approach solid waste as a material and epistemological object produced on a mass scale by the city of Lahore and, thus, one in need of management (Butt 2020a). A quality of generality characterizes the act of management, in which techno-infrastructural entities and human labor are organized around aggregated, mass waste generation. This quality of generality aligns with the continuing endurance of the public as a category implicated in spatial practices and relations of work and exchange.

As the opening vignette suggests, however, in their management of solid waste, institutions such as the SWM Department, especially through the supervisory figure of the *dāroghah*, are implicated in myriad social, political, and technical relations through which waste materials are actually disposed of and/or circulated within and beyond the city of Lahore. The development of institutions and infrastructures sketched out above has thus accorded a managerial role to the bureaucratic state in relation to Lahore's waste infrastructures: it must ensure that solid waste produced by Lahore and its population is managed through techno-infrastructural entities and human labor, such that any harms or dangers posed to the public by these materials are mitigated. Waste infrastructures become one site among many for the bureaucratic state to exercise its managerial role, while, concurrently, contending with the fact that management itself depends upon wider processes through which waste materials are disposed of and circulated and urban life comes to be reproduced (see Butt 2020c). Such a role has had lasting implications for those whose labor constitutes infrastructures of urban life in the country.

Accessing Waste Work

Throughout Pakistan, markets for waste materials and labor have expanded in recent decades, which has facilitated how individuals from low- or noncaste backgrounds have entered this line of work either through municipal employment or informalized work arrangements (see Butt 2019). Distinct governmental and private institutions oversee waste disposal and management in different administrative parts of the city, which structure these markets in important ways. The Cantonment Board falls under the Pakistani Army and looks after waste disposal services for areas within its administrative boundaries, while housing societies have several kinds of entities that they engage with for these services—whether that be individuals or kin-based groups of workers. More recently, waste management companies have been created in urban centers in Pakistan and compete for contracts to provision these services in different localities. As the repeated discussion of increasing the workforce of workers, supervisors, engineers, and bureaucrats alludes to, the SWM Department, and now the LWMC, have been and remain formidable figures within this labor market. Since the SWM Department, as a state institution, had such a presence within these labor markets, it has shaped access to and the conditions of waste work for many.

Municipal Work

Across the three classifications of municipal workers—permanent (*pakkā*), work-charge (*kachchā*), and contractual (*ṭaikadārī*)—the intervention of a figure who either has a connection to the SWM Department or was involved with local or municipal government was necessary—the *dāroghah* being the most prominent of these figures. *Pakkā* workers needed to submit medical exams, fingerprints, and other necessary documents at the Town Hall building where the offices of the Health Department and Municipal Services were located—these being the branches of municipal government that oversaw waste disposal prior to the formation of the

SWM Department. These documents were consolidated into a service book, which consisted of biographical information, an order of employment, and a list of allowances. Municipal workers relied upon superiors such as the *dāroghah, nāzim,* or *nāi'b nāzim* (elected officials within Union Councils), or another political figure to help in organizing much of these documents. As municipal workers told me, having these documents prepared by a *dāroghah* required paying him a minimal amount as *sifārish*.[13] A municipal worker who was placed in Faisal Town, Sadiq used to accompany his father who was also employed by the MCL and placed in the area of Icchra, where many of Sadiq's kin continue to work. It was his father that spoke with his own *dāroghah,* paying him "some money," and had his son and others within his extended kin network employed within this department. As may be evident by now, kinship was and remains important within this department and line of work. The position of a permanent worker who passes away or takes retirement is inherited by their eldest child, if the latter desires it, while others employed on daily wages or through labor contractors still rely on kin and other intimate relations in finding employment.

As alluded to earlier, the size of the labor force within the SWM Department has expanded since the late 1990s through *kachchā* (work-charge) employment. In 1999 Mian Muhammad Nadeem, a councilor for the MCL, advised the members of the assembly that "a specific class has established their monopoly on the sanitation department. Metropolitan Corporation has no alternative management for them. This means they have remained successful in their monopoly."[14] Mian Muhammad Nadeem recommended first that municipal workers be employed as *kachchā* workers who would not be made permanent, and second, others should be employed on daily wages to demonstrate to Christians that non-Christians are willing to do this work as well. Only then would their "attitude" improve, and would they work with "care and effort." Despite protest by one or two of the other councilors present, it was decided that municipal workers from then on would be recruited as *kachchā* workers, though the municipal labor force remains predominantly Christian.

Prior to the formation of the public-private partnership, it was estimated that nearly half of the labor force in the SWM department were *kachchā* employees. These workers had ninety-day contracts with the SWM department that had to be regularly approved. Contracts rendered workers into a precarious component of the SWM Department's labor force, which could be easily fired and replenished through the wider labor supply. *Kachchā* workers do not enjoy any increases in wages, do not receive social and retirement benefits (something prized by *pakkā* workers), and frequently worked Sundays. Though they had to arrange fewer documents compared to *pakkā* workers, *kachchā* workers similarly relied upon the *dāroghah* with whom they had some connection to arrange the work order, which was the bureaucratic document (akin to the service book) that ensured their employment in the department and a source of income. *Kachchā* employees' conditions of work were purposely made more precarious than those of permanent employees, as evidenced in the municipal debate, and yet, many *kachchā* employees have been working under these conditions for at least the past decade, if not more. Also, as *pakkā* workers retire and no kin inherits the position, *kachchā* workers are at times "regularized" into being *pakkā* workers.

Finding other waste-related work, as Rameez did that afternoon, is common among municipal workers, and the *dāroghah* often brokers these transactions and arrangements. In a wholesale market located in the Inner City, municipal workers, with the help of a *dāroghah*, collected *hafta* (bribe payments) from shopkeepers for their services—the two parties would share the payments clandestinely. In another area, a market's management paid a monthly salary to municipal workers who, after clearing their "beats," would collect a small fee from those who needed to use the market's toilets. Others in this area collected fees at the few public latrines still existing in the city, which are themselves given out to contractors. This quasi-legal and potentially illicit paid work was common among municipal workers.

Lastly, and probably most importantly, municipal workers, Rameez included, after or while carrying out their responsibilities as public employees, frequently turn their attention to "private work" (private *kām*) and collect waste materials from households in exchange for a minimal service fee. Like workers from the informal sector but to a much lesser extent, they separate out valuable materials that can be sold to junkyards.

There was also varying degrees of collaboration between municipal and informal workers. An elderly municipal worker, who retired toward the end of my fieldwork, had set up an arrangement with an informal worker who was Pashtun to split the work and income generated by collecting household waste. This income included both the service fees and valuable materials that could be sold to junkyards. Even though household waste collection is viewed as separate from their role as public employees, that latter role has facilitated their access to potentially valuable materials and other waste-related work, ultimately providing additional sources of income to supplement municipal salaries. That additional work and income was also a point of tension with supervisors and officials, who blamed municipal workers for being overly concerned with their "private work," not fulfilling their "public" responsibilities, and profiting unfairly from municipal employment.

Informal Work

Waste workers laboring under informalized work relations described similar trajectories regarding their entry into waste work. Though I describe the larger shift of which this was a part later in the book, Allah Ditta and his father had started working as *phairī lagāne wāle* (hawkers) across the Punjab even before Allah Ditta shifted with his wife to Lahore's outskirts in the 1990s. After coming to Lahore, the settlements of *jhuggiān* (huts) in which Allah Ditta and many informal workers resided were often located next to, near, or within localities being developed into private housing schemas, commercial establishments, and even at times public institutions. Though a lack of municipal presence in these developing localities facilitated their access to waste materials and work, informal workers built up their own relations with households in such localities. These workers contacted households through domestic staff who were throwing away household garbage or trash into empty plots (or parcels of land not built upon).

Another trajectory for entering this line of work was arrangements with municipal workers. While also working as a *phairī lagānā wālā* like Allah Ditta, informal worker Ghulam Ali was contacted by a Christian municipal worker who collected trash from several households in a few blocks within a locality. In their initial agreement, Ghulam Ali removed waste from these households and could keep the materials to sell to junkyards, while the municipal worker retained the monthly service fees collected from households. After a complaint from the *dāroghah*, these households were given over completely to this informal worker, who now both collects the monthly service fees and sells valuable materials to junkyards. Even if many workers emphasized anyone with a bicycle and netted sack ("kit") can start collecting waste from empty plots, containers, or even the side of the street, entering this line of work required building up social and political relations with domestic staff, households, *nāzims* or *nāi'b nāzims*, trader or merchants' associations, municipal workers, and of course, *dāroghein* in these localities. It is clear that informalized work relations exhibit a degree of recognition and legitimacy.

One afternoon, Manzoor (mentioned in the Introduction) presented to me a letter dated from November 10, 2002, that was signed by the *nāi'b nāzim*. Despite being written more than a decade ago at that point and having multiple creases, the letter was kept safe in a plastic sheet. Its contents were deceptively simple:

> As you may know, sanitation [*safā'ī kā intizām*], with regards to solid waste, was twice given over to contractors in Tariq Colony but due to their poor performance, the said contracts were terminated.

> After the termination, the contractor's operatives [*kārinde*] continued to work independently. These people had unlawfully occupied and built their homes on Model Town Link Road. The City District Government, with the help of the local police, evicted them from this area and due to their unlawful activity, I have given permission to an experienced man Manzoor, son of Akram, to take care of sanitation. I request you cooperate fully with him on sanitation matters. Please contact me at the number listed below with any complaints or suggestions.

Getting to this point, in which a letter formalized and legitimized his access to waste, was not a straightforward process. Manzoor, along with his immediate and extended kin, had been collecting waste in this area for approximately a decade and started to do so when only a few homes had been built. Importantly, he had been able to build relations with lower-level staff within the SWM Department, most specifically *dāroghein*. In fact, Manzoor had given almost 10,000 rupees to the supervisor in this area to attain his access to these households and continues to give small monthly payments so that his access will not be disturbed. Since then, Manzoor's sons collect waste from another locality, to which he had also gained access by mobilizing sociopolitical relations, documents, and money.

In another locality in the Garden Town area of Lahore, a worker presented to me a paper dated from 2001 that had been printed out and filled in with his name (Babar Ali) and signed by a stamp and handwritten signature of the *nāzim* for the Union Council (Malik Anwar Saleem). This document, addressing the honorable residents of this Union Council, instructed them to "cooperate with Babar Ali on collecting garbage from your households and cleanliness of streets and alleyways." Allah Ditta, though he did not hold onto such letters, did formalize his access through agreements with the *sadr* of various blocks within a ward, and kept safe documents such as a list of all the establishments (heads of households, exact addresses, and phone numbers) in a special folder that formalized and legitimized his access in other ways. He even had made customized receipts that were titled "Allah Ditta, Motorcycle and Rickshaw wāle," with each receipt including the date, name, house number, and payment amount. At the top of the receipt, under his title, it states, "Cleanliness fulfills half of one's faith," and at the bottom, "Note: If you have any complaints because of garbage contact this number." As both municipal and informal workers had to mobilize social and political relationships in accessing waste materials and/or a predictable form of employment, the bureaucratic state through its intermediaries impacted the workings of a formalized and informalized labor-force.

The Work and Language of Supervision

Within the SWM Department, the term *dāroghah* referenced a collective group of persons within the state apparatus that oversaw waste collection and disposal. The primary responsibility of *dāroghein* is unsurprisingly to supervise (*nigrānī karnā*) municipal workers, and as should be evident by now, informal ones to a certain extent, while also coordinating machinery and techno-infrastructural entities related to solid waste management and addressing complaints coming from within localities falling under their jurisdiction. However, whenever I asked what the *dārog̲h̲ah* actually does, the usual response was, "The job of *dārog̲h̲ein̲* is speaking" (dāroghe kā kām hai bholnā), and then, the additional point, "The *dārog̲h̲ah* gets work done" (dāroghah kām karvātā hai). This use of the causative form[15] (i.e., *karvātā*) of the verb "to do" (*karnā*) to describe the work of the *dārog̲h̲ah* was meant to underscore the fact that their effort is directed at causing others—an array of subordinates—to perform certain tasks. When addressing subordinates, kin terms like *beta* (son), *putr* (son), *chachā* (father's younger brother), *chachī* (father's younger brother's wife), and *vīr* (brother) were regularly used, while *baojī*, *sahb* (sir), *sahb bahādur* (brave *sahb*), *sarkār*, and *janāb-e-ali* were reserved for addressing superiors. Moreover, almost all the *dārog̲h̲ahs* I came to know emphasized they could only request (using the English word), ask for a favor (*ihsān*), or beseech or implore (*minnat karnā*). *Minnat karnā* entails a certain amount of humility, self-abasement, and a lowering of the self in terms of status.

For instance, one day, in front of municipal workers, an officer for the LWMC, who previously was a high-ranking supervisor in the SWM department, lambasted supervisors for failing to fulfill their responsibilities. He castigated supervisors by telling them they ought to be ashamed (*sharam aunī chāhīdī ae tuhanū*), advising them to maintain their respect and status, and emphasizing that the *dārog̲h̲ah* is *pagh* (turban), to be protected. "You are," the zonal officer made clear, "workers' (*mai-baap*, guardians) (see Gupta 2012, 56). And, on a separate occasion, an elderly sanitation worker had a younger male relative reinstated by crying in front of the *dārog̲h̲ah* and kneeling down to massage his knee and thigh—a performative gesture of submission. As waste work has become increasingly bureaucratized over the past several decades, so have these social and political relationships that not only draw upon notions of hierarchy, status, and respect associated with caste-based relations but also straddle the lines between access and exploitation, care and control, and persuasion and coercion.

The *dārog̲h̲ah* plays a critical role in facilitating or preventing workers' access to waste materials, work, and all the attendant benefits and services. At times, it becomes a technique for exploitation and rent seeking. *Dārog̲h̲ein̲* collect money from informal workers in exchange for allowing the latter to deposit waste materials removed from households into municipal containers, while many municipal workers give a portion of their monthly salary to supervisors in exchange for time off from work. Though Aashique never admitted it, municipal and informal workers alike told me they paid him for these very reasons. Simultaneously, Aashique, who also has a successful career as a property dealer, gave out small amounts of money (500 to 2,000 PKR) on an almost daily basis to municipal workers who needed help for unexpected expenses, such as medicines or bill payments. At times they would be paid back; at times they were not. While there was certainly no formal accounting of debts, both parties—*dāroghein* who gave and workers who received—described this giving as acts of love and care. As I elaborate in chapter 4, such nonreciprocal forms of exchange are imbued with a range of effects and are premised on social and political relationships, in which care and control are exercised over those who are assumed to be unable to provide or fend for themselves.

Political coordinators—whether attached to political parties, residential associations, and/or traders or merchants' organizations—and the *dāroghah* within their respective locality would remain in constant contact with each other. During the sacrifices for Eid ul-Azha, as antiseptics were being distributed in many localities, Khwaja Sahb (a senior supervisor) explicitly told a junior one, "Get them [the bottle of antiseptic] to anyone. All I care about is that they get distributed and political figures don't bother us," and finished by emphasizing, "Get them [political coordinators] off our backs, they are like barking dogs (kuttiān de tarān baunkde ne)." And, then, when the municipality destroyed "illegally" constructed structures during antiencroachment drives and construction waste that was not a municipal responsibility needed to be picked up, Khwaja Sahb received a phone call from a shopkeeper in a prominent wholesale market in the city. After the conversation, Khwaja Sahb explained to me that one of this shopkeeper's relatives was the minister for excise and tax, so that shopkeeper had his relative exercise his clout through a series of intermediaries and had this sizable amount of construction waste removed. Yet, another shopkeeper who supposedly had a relative in the LWMC also claimed responsibility for having the construction waste disposed of. This was when the former shopkeeper called and had Khwaja Sahb announce, on his mobile phone's speaker to a group of shopkeepers that had gathered, that it was, in fact, the shopkeeper whose relative was the minister that had the construction waste disposed of, not the other shopkeeper whose relative was in the LWMC. The humor of the entire situation was not lost on any of us sitting with Khwaja Sahb that day—the small groups of supervisors and clerical staff laughing about its absurdity.

The majority of the *dārogḥah*'s work is directed at getting workers to remove and dispose of waste materials because of an order or directive coming from elsewhere—a resident, a political coordinator, manager, or bureaucrat. *Dārogḥein* utilized direct or veiled threats about loss of employment, undesirable transfers, or the intervention of a political figure to intimidate workers into passivity or docility. I do not want to minimize the reality or severity of these threats, especially in the case of "*kachchā*" or contractual laborers who lack job security. At the same time, since few are willing to perform this stigmatizing form of work in Pakistan, waste workers recognized that all these figures—the *dārogḥah*, political coordinators, households—depend upon them for their labor. And informal ones, though they rely on field staff for access to municipal containers, operate on the peripheries of formalized institutions. Waste workers were thus somewhat insulated from these threats, with many resisting, arguing back, and outright refusing to work. For these reasons, the *dārogḥah*, as well as others like political coordinators, have limited control over the labor process through waste materials are disposed of or circulated.

On a daily basis, *dārogḥein* like Aashique issue orders and commands, instructing workers, supervisors, and other field staff to perform certain tasks, which are limited by the amount of power and control they exercise over the labor process. Thus, linguistic techniques for persuasion and coercion must be mobilized to get any number of everyday acts of waste disposal done. When a donkey had died one night in an empty plot where a cluster of waste containers and an encampment of *khānah badoshl pakhiwas* (nomadic groups) was located, the animal's carcass had to be removed, which took up much time and effort and disturbed the regular routine. So, in the early afternoon, Aashique had to reallocate workers from different areas within the locality. After asking Salamat and Arif which workers were available at the time, Aashique told Salamat to go "grab" Petras and Rasheeda and have them jointly clear a few remaining areas. Salamat hesitated, saying Petras had worked the overnight shift, which caused Aashique to lash out, "If you tell him, he'll do it. If you say it in this way [*with hesitation*], then it won't happen. When you remain on top of someone, you can get them to work twice as much."

At this point, Aashique himself called Petras on his phone: "Wa alaikum as-salaam, may I ask, Sir, you worked last night? Are you going home to rest or do you not want to leave her (*ghena na chaddhna*), keep holding onto her *dupatta* [shawl]. No, no, if you want to come and stay there, I'll send you two together in an hour or so, what do you say? Fine, grab and come with your *jhāṛu* [handheld broom] and come to al-Badr plot (*jhāṛu paṛ ke al-Badr plot ā*), bringing her with you." In this exchange, Aashique first playfully (though respectfully) addressed Petras with the more formal *tussi*, even referring to him as *janāb* (sir), and then teased him about Rasheeda, with whom he was rumored to be in a romantic relationship though both were married. At the end, with Petras acquiescing to the request, Aashique switched to the informal and intimate *tūn̲* and utilized the imperative verb form (e.g., *paṛ ke ā*), issuing statements closer to a command or order.

The allusion that Aashique made to a romantic affair between the two should not be overlooked. It was a playful gesture, though one that was meant to shame both workers, especially Rasheeda, into work. That is to say, shaming was a technique of coercion and persuasion. Indeed, Aashique regularly made bawdy comments and jokes about the sexual promiscuity of female workers and possible affairs with others, while junkyard owners and intermediaries casually commented about women engaging in sex work among the extended kin network of informal workers. At other times, a male worker's physical strength and virility would be called into question. When Rameez once refused to clear a couple of areas surrounding containers, Aashique paused while issuing orders to others and, in front of a group of female workers, addressed Rameez, "I asked you because you had a mustache." As a mustache symbolized masculine strength and virility, the presumption was that Rameez may have had the sign of masculinity (i.e., a mustache) but lacked the actual qualities (i.e., the physical strength and willingness to labor). To further shame Rameez, Aashique then announced that the female workers standing there had carried out the extra work. The work had been done, so there was no reason to convince Rameez of anything; rather, shaming was a linguistic technique caught up in gendered and sexual norms surrounding status and respectability and was meant to induce others like Rameez to work.

On a separate occasion, Arif stopped Samuel, who along with his wife was employed through labor contractors and so lacked job security. In this instance, an argument could easily lead to a loss of employment for Samuel, and possibly his wife as well. Yet, when Arif stopped to ask why Samuel had not yet cleared the main service road, Samuel burst with anger: "I don't do my job? I shirk my work? I don't work? I'll tell you, tell me, I avoid work, so you insult me." Arif was at a loss for words, but Samuel did not relent, "You [*dāroghein*] talk a lot. I'm a working man, not a man who runs away and leaves work undone. And neither am I a man who listens." Arif, trying to interject, said, "You'll have to listen." But Samuel remained steadfast, "No I won't listen, I work, I don't listen to anything." And later in the exchange, he adopted a sarcastic tone when he called supervisors like Arif "*change lokon*," or good people. Being accused of shirking his work was an insult for Samuel, who subsequently accused Arif of acting illegitimately. Later Arif explained to me, "If we talk to workers with love or tenderness [*pyār se*], they do not take us seriously, seeing no difference between us and themselves and they no longer are afraid. If I talk to them angrily, then they will abide by my order." Workers themselves expressed similar views about speech's affective qualities. "There should be 'heat' in *dāroghah*'s speech," one worker told me, but then, also emphasized, "But, you see, Aashique's word has sweetness [*miṭhās*] to them." On some occasions, sweet words expressing love worked, and on other occasions, they did not—the same was the case for hot, angry words or disrespectful, shaming ones. Rather, the affective qualities of speech constituted a range of possibilities in *dāroghah*'s attempts of persuasion.

Linguistic techniques of persuasion—from angry words said to intimidate to playful ones said to cajole, to bawdy ones said to shame—were inseparable from nonlinguistic ones—loss of employment, disrupting access to waste materials, or reduced pay through tampered attendance registries. Whenever a tiff over work escalated into a heated argument, workers speculated the *dāroghah* would mete out punishment surreptitiously later by having salaries reduced, or when a project for door-to-door collection was being implemented, the *dāroghah* enforced directives by preventing informal workers from using municipal containers. Though directed at getting others (especially municipal workers) to perform waste work, the work of the *dāroghah* was often the result of an order, command, favor, or directive coming from elsewhere, whether within the bureaucratic state or through networks of patronage.

The Appearance of Things

Since the latter half of nineteenth century, institutions and infrastructures in Lahore have been perpetual sites of investments—affective, financial, and technological—that have sought to organize waste work within the parameters of the bureaucratic state. As such, these institutions and infrastructures have been built upon and transformed waste work as it has historically been performed by low- or noncaste groups. Its techno-legal apparatus, especially as it has expanded through the development of solid waste management, continues to impose an order upon urban life, in which categorical distinctions are brought to bear upon organizing spatial practices, relations of work and exchange, and techno-infrastructural entities surrounding waste materials. What infrastructures of disposability have done is built managerial layers out of and on top of waste work as a social and political relationship. They have created a division between those working with waste materials and those managing them as solid waste.

Such layers are elementary to everyday work of the *dāroghah*, in which they contend with the pervasive nature of waste work—something that stretches across and connects the techno-legal apparatus of the bureaucratic state, extensive networks of patronage, and the circulation of waste materials and money. The *dāroghah* can strategically exploit and profit from their managerial role, but it also imposes limits upon their own position, work, and power. Yet, in contending with a broad set of processes—spatial practices, relations of work and exchange, waste and labor markets, and patronage—the work of the *dārogẖah* reproduces the representation that the bureaucratic state is the manager of waste materials within everyday life. Thus, to be deemed successful, the work performed by waste workers must be taken by the *dārogẖah* and made to appear as the good of solid waste management being provisioned to the public by the bureaucratic state through its techno-legal apparatus.

These initial chapters have adopted a state-oriented approach to examining the work and social and political relationships that go into taking away waste materials across Lahore's urban landscape. The purpose in doing so was to demonstrate how waste work has or has not been enfolded into the bureaucratic state, as well as the effects that this has had on the actual work of taking away waste materials and the lives of those who have performed that work. Precisely to distill out these processes, the account thus far has obscured, though certainly gestured along the way to, the extensive nature of waste work, as well as the variegated processes of which it is a constitutive component. At this point, it should be stressed that the bureaucratic state and its techno-legal apparatus fundamentally seek to stabilize the relations and practices that go into disposing and circulating waste materials. Put simply, bureaucracies are prominent though constrained actors in the reproduction of life as a distributed process.

As waste work has been organized into an infrastructure of urban life, the bureaucratic state, through the everyday work of government, takes all the activity that goes into reproducing life and happens within and outside its purview and makes that activity appear *as if* it falls under its management. While the procedures and techniques of the bureaucratic state seek to render stable and propagate such an appearance of things, pervasive forms of life, in which caste-based relations have been prevalent, have been instrumental to how the city's waste infrastructures have come to be organized. We can now zoom out from the managerial role occupied by the bureaucratic state and its techno-legal apparatus and redirect our gaze to how life comes to be reproduced through an expansive set of entangled processes, from the remaking of waste materials into commodities to the suturing together of an unevenly urbanizing landscape to the intergenerational trajectory of waste workers and their kin on Lahore's urban peripheries.

CHAPTER 3

SURPLUS AND ITS EXCESS

UMAIR'S JUNKYARD IS in the Faisal Town area of Lahore. On a chilly January morning in 2015, a range of customers (*gāhak*) were steadily passing through. They mostly come from two of the nearby localities—one an upper-middle-class neighborhood and the other a working-class *bastī* (settlement). Younger children and older women carry household waste—plastic bottles, old newspapers and school notebooks, cardboard and tin boxes, and CDs—to sell for extra cash. Domestic staff from more affluent households haul similar items but ones that are of a higher quality and in larger amounts. Then, there are the municipal workers, informal workers, and janitorial staff from a nearby hospital whom Umair gives advances to. Though minimal in amount, being no more than a couple thousand rupees, these advances remain crucial to his junkyard's viability: they ensure those who are given advances sell the materials they collect only to Umair. Finally, then, there are those items such as appliances in need of repairs or furniture to be refurbished that attract the attention of passers-by who regularly stop to ask about their prices but rarely purchase anything. Exchanges happening within Umair's junkyard are inseparable from working with waste materials.

Umair and I spent most of that morning sitting on wobbly plastic chairs underneath the junkyard's tarp roof while we sorted and disassembled waste materials. It being only my second visit to a junkyard, my hands were still too delicate for the pummeling and thrashing required of disassembly, and I had not yet picked up the necessary knowledge for sorting. As we worked throughout the morning, my pace was slow and deliberate. I regularly stopped to ask Umair about the materials. At one point, Umair brought out an empty collapsed sack; as we packed it with plastic trash, it started to take on more and more of a rectangular shape. Umair then weighed it on the iron scale that sits out front—the sack placed on one end and weights of different measures placed on the other. After it came to a balance, Umair set it aside for the *biopārī* (intermediary) who would arrive shortly to purchase it. This was when, peeking inside this bag, I asked, "What kinds of plastics are in here?" This bag, Umair told me, contains mixed goods (*darā māl*) while another bag in the back, which is already sorted, contains only sorted waste, specifically PET (polyethylene terephthalate) bottles with the caps removed. The mixed goods will be split into the higher quality and more expensive items (*sāf māl*, lit. clean goods) and the lower quality and less expensive items (*kālā māl*, lit. black goods). Sensing doubt on my end, Umair pulled out multiple pieces to hand me. "Can't you see?" he asked emphatically. I responded affirmatively but also asked, "Still how do you recognize the difference between *sāf māl* and *kālā māl*?" Breaking off a piece of plastic, Umair placed it in a bucket of water. The first piece of plastic remained afloat—this was *sāf māl*. The next piece sank to the bottom—this was *kālā māl*. Each of these items will fetch different rates among *biopārīān̲*.

After a couple hours sorting, we turned to disassembling a VCR, extracting out whichever metals we could, and placed them into piles on the ground—a task that kept us busy for most the afternoon. Through flying shards of plastic and rising particles of dust, Umair emphasized that nothing will be thrown out. The electrical board, for which he has neither the necessary tools nor knowledge, will be sold through another *biopārī* from the city's main electronics market located at Hall Road. Then, grabbing a piece of wire that had a thick rubber-like covering, inside of which was foreign (*valā'itī*) copper—one of the most expensive metals that circulates— he said, "It takes too much time and effort to remove, so I'll sell the item at a lower rate." I nodded. I started to recognize foreign, higher quality copper as I removed belts, motors, and coils from the device. Hammering, unscrewing, and even tearing our way through it, very little was left of the VCR in an hour or two, and by the end, a chill in the air and the physical force required to break down the device had made my fingers red and tender. All that remained of the VCR were metals of various kinds organized into piles, its encasing, and the electrical board. As I got up to leave, a large truck arrived to load the plastic materials we had sorted earlier. They will be taken away to a warehouse across the River Ravi in Shahdara,[1] where they will be further sorted and transformed into something else.

In fact, just a few days earlier, I had visited a few warehouses and manufacturing units near Band Rd. (see Map 0.2) with Ali Bhai, who is a *biopārī* that rents warehouses for paper waste in the cities of Lahore and Gujrat. The first warehouse we visited was full of "shoppers" (plastic bags), and several workers were separating the all-white ones from those with color. The ones with color printing were being cut to separate the all-white portions. In the other warehouse, sorted plastics were being shredded into smaller pieces, washed in chemicals and water, and dried on the roof (Figure 3.1 and 3.2). We then ambled to a manufacturing unit close by to see how shredded plastic was made into pellets.

FIGURE 3.1. *Shredded and washed plastics. Source: Author.*

FIGURE 3.2. *Shredded plastic drying on roof. Source: Author.*

In a dimly lit basement permeated by the smell of melted plastics, two sinewy young men weaved through low-hanging wiring as they operated the pellet-making machinery. Shredded plastic coming from warehouses nearby was put in a spinning cauldron that further dried and softened the materials. Once ready, the shreds were fed into a pipe, underneath which ran a rod lit by gas that melted the pellets inside. A slow process, it takes approximately four hours for one cauldron of plastics to flow through the piping, one of the workers told us. The melted plastic extrudes out as several strings through the end of the pipe, falling into a pool of water. Cooling and solidifying, these materials were then collected, broken into sections, and passed through another machine that cut them into pellets. Last, we visited another nearby unit, where machinery and workers were making shoppers. Pellets, similar to the ones we just saw being made, were fed into machinery that moved the pellets, once again, through piping with the force of heated air. As we observed shoppers ballooning out one after another to be collected onto spinning reels, Ali Bhai and I stood surrounded by bags full of pellets to be used for production and reels full of shoppers to be used for consumption.

Surplus and Exclusion

Waste work, constituted as an infrastructure of urban life, cuts across and undoes many of the central distinctions upon which regimes of governance have come to be built—the public and private, inner and outer, and contract and custom. This continues to be the case when we examine waste work and infrastructures in relationship to what has come to be known and referred to as the *informal economy*. The notion of the informal economy historically emerged as a way of understanding the transition to capitalism that was presumed to be taking place in what was then considered the developing world. Populations, unable to be absorbed into the "formal" economy as waged laborers, were rendered into "surpluses" and compelled to secure livelihoods in the "informal" economy, which was presumed to exist outside capitalist social relations.[2] The informal economy was part of a state-centric discourse that sought to render visible and manageable a diversity of activities, thereby incorporating those activities and populations into the formal economy of newly independent nation-states.

As a state-centric discourse, the informal continues to have effects that stretch from heavily capitalized sites of commodity production to the worlds of waste workers, *kabāṛīāṇ* (junkyard owners), *bīopāṛīāṇ*, and all those whose livelihoods have been secured through working with and exchanging waste materials. Indeed, as should be clear from the previous chapter, infrastructures of disposability have expanded across Lahore's urbanizing landscape in the past several decades alongside and in tandem with those of circulation, in which relations of work and exchange have expanded such that contractual waged labor has been peripheral. Although I sporadically use the terms *informal, informality,* or *informalized*, they remain analytically unstable, where its constitutive divisions—formal and informal, not to mention capital and noncapital, public and private, and contractual and customary—tend to be blurry and overlain with one another.

Waste as a category conjures an impression that surplus is an ontological condition not only of material things but also of life under contemporary capitalism. This is the idea of surplus-as-waste—whether those surpluses are things or people that have been discarded by highly unequal, exploitative, and oppressive systems that stretch across the globe today (see e.g., Bauman 2005). However, surpluses are not ontological conditions but, taking our cue here from Marx, something premised on "the unpaid labour of others" (Marx 1977, 715). Conceived more broadly, unpaid labor took place as much in the domain of production, where the wage-form was elementary to the exploitative nature of the labor-capital relation—laborers sell their labor-power as a commodity to the capitalist who buys it by offering a wage and subsequently realizes surplus-value in the form of profit—as it did in the domain of reproduction—activities and energies going unremunerated but being appropriated by various techniques by the capitalist. Surpluses, especially in the form of surplus-value as profit that then contributes to accumulation, were realized in the domain of circulation, where the circuitous (and uneven) exchange of money and commodities happened. This notion of surplus, where waged labor and exploitation are entangled, sits orthogonally with my discussion of surpluses below, where surpluses, generated out of things (waste) and persons (workers) in production, involve forms of exploitation not premised on waged labor. How do we conceive of surpluses when the nature of exploitation has become more splintered and dispersed? And how are they entangled to the reproduction of life in Lahore along the lines of historical inequalities and interdependencies?

Numerous commentators have described shifting forms of exploitation such as contracting, subcontracting, and outsourcing that have emerged across Pakistan and South Asia.[3] On the other hand, among the waste workers, *kabāṛīān*, and *biopāṛīān* with whom I conducted fieldwork, such forms of exploitation were for the most part absent—and yet, surpluses continually get realized. The problem confronting us then is, in the absence of expected forms of exploitation, how a variety of surpluses are realized through relations of work and exchange that are organized around the consumption of disposable commodities and their circulation as waste for money, especially as these relations are ones that stretch across not only Lahore but much of Pakistan and beyond. A condition of exclusion, in which "the capitalist economy secures its resources minus the people who traditionally survived on it," is crucial to the realization of surpluses and an unevenly urbanizing landscape like Lahore (Sanyal and Bhattacharyya 2009, 36; see also Hall, Hirsch, and Li 2011). This condition of exclusion is similar to what Anna Tsing has described as "pericapitalist" sites, where "all kinds of goods and services are produced," by humans and nonhumans alike, to be "salvaged for capitalist accumulation" (2015, 66, 63). Though the term *salvage* dovetails conveniently with waste materials as a resource to be extracted, it is more expansive than its material referent. Salvage must be understood, as gestured to in the Introduction, as referring to how accumulation depends upon activities, energies, relations, knowledges, and yes, even materials over which it does not have control (see also Weeks 2011). In other words, accumulation depends on appropriating forms of life that are *not necessarily* organized for accumulation.

In understanding how this actually happens, we can turn to a distinction made between accumulation and need by Kalyan Sanyal (2007) in his rendering of informality. In that rendering, accumulation happens when surpluses are created in production, realized as profit through exchange of a produced commodity and money, and then directed to expand surpluses (i.e., accumulate). Profit, as one form that surplus value can take, results from a deducing the cost to the owner to manufacture a commodity and the amount acquired through its sale. Between the cost to manufacture the commodity and the income generated from its subsequent sale is where the exploitation of labor through a range of techniques (e.g., wage suppression, time and work disciplines, technological investments, or subcontracting and outsourcing) enables accumulation. The other circuit is that of need, where surplus is also generated in production and realized through circulation but is deployed toward the "satisfaction of need" and the replenishment of productive activity, not its expansion. Across these surpluses in circulation, arbitrage becomes a critical mechanism for realizing value out of the same waste materials by a differentiated set of actors—domestic staff, waste workers, junkyard owners, intermediaries, factory owners, and many others.

For instance, waste workers and *kabāṛīān*, especially smaller-scale ones like Umair, generate surpluses out of materials and persons to meet needs and, aside for a few exceptions, do not engage in accumulation by expanding circulation. Yet, they are doing "salvage" work for supply chains directed toward commodity production elsewhere, so as one gets closer

FIGURE 3.3. *Plastics being accumulated to be sold to manufacturing units.*
Source: Author.

to capitalized sites of production, a shift toward the circuit of accumulation occurs (Figure 3.3). Surpluses generated out of things and persons can be directed into circuits of accumulation, where waste work appears to be salvaging for accumulation, or they can be directed into those of need, where waste work appears as a means of securing one's livelihoods.

Additionally, waste work, as the next chapters demonstrate, is also a form of work that cleanses middle- and upper-class homes of potentially polluting materials and substances, while also making possible life for waste workers and their kin on Lahore's urbanizing peripheries. This is why the distinction between accumulation and need is important to keep in mind, since it foregrounds how waste infrastructures distribute forms of life unevenly across Lahore's urbanizing landscapes.

Before proceeding, let me briefly provide a general overview of how waste materials are supplied as a resource for commodity production and how that builds upon forms of life organized along the lines of caste, class, and religion. As already mentioned, in an initial act of separation, waste workers and others who sell these materials to *kabāṛīāṉ* separate garbage or trash (*kachrā* or *kūṛā*) from that which is considered profit, saving, remainder, surplus, gain, or excess (*bachat*). While the former materials will be disposed of in containers, dumped in empty plots of land, or burnt in small piles, the latter will be moved through numerous sites (*jhuggīāṉ*, junkyards, warehouses, shops, and manufacturing units) as they are accumulated, exchanged, and remade. Trash is disposed of, materials are sorted and sold, resources are purchased and reused, and a commodity is made and consumed.

Alongside such transformations are figures whose lives and livelihoods differentially depend upon the remaking of commodities: waste workers, domestic staff, children, or female kin dispose of these materials from a mix of public and private spaces, while intermediaries, specifically *kabāṛīāṉ* and *bīopārīāṉ*, purchase these same materials and then broker exchanges with suppliers working with manufacturing units. Along with the fact that waste workers come predominantly from Dalit groups and intermediaries are presumed to come from higher caste backgrounds, waste materials and work are gendered in many ways. Within Pakistani households across caste, class, and religious lines, women and/or domestic staff dispose of waste materials, while female kin within the homes of waste workers where these materials accumulate are the ones who do much of the work of sorting. All this underscores how historical inequalities and interdependencies, especially of caste, class, and gender, undergird infrastructures of circulation, thereby not only facilitating the realization of surpluses but also, shaping the quality of urban life across Lahore's urban landscape.

Remuneration and Need

Across the relations of work and exchange through which waste materials move as they are remade into commodities, remuneration, taking multiple forms, consists of the "deserved recompense" for *both* materials and work (Sargent and Duff 2019, 637). Remuneration is most apparent in salaries received by municipal workers from the SWM Department, service fees paid to informal workers by households, or monthly and daily wages given to those sorting and disassembling waste materials inside junkyards and warehouses. Concurrently, waste work, specifically collecting, transporting, disassembling, and sorting, allows waste workers to access the monetary worth of these materials. Most municipal workers sell the waste materials they collect to junkyard owners in the locality where they work on a daily basis, while others are given advances. Informal workers, on the other hand, bring back similar materials to the clusters of *jhuggīāṇ* comprising their homes and settlements. Within these households, a division of labor exists in the performance of waste work along gendered lines: while male kin are more commonly the ones who collect waste from localities, female kin are usually the ones who sort out valuables from the materials brought back to their households.

Along with these workers are *phaiṛī lagāne wale* (hawkers) who are itinerant buyers working across urban and rural parts of the country and have established different work and exchange relations with junkyards—some are given advances and even equipment (e.g., handcarts) to purchase materials while others work independently.[4] And many junkyard owners and intermediaries employ a mixture of kin and non-kin workers who are given monthly wages and provided housing, though daily wage (*Dihārī*) earners are also hired to cover extra work or specialized tasks.

There is, however, considerable variation in how remuneration actually happens. The organization of *when* to sell these materials depends upon the everyday workings and needs of households. Many workers sort and hold onto waste materials for periods of time, selling them on a fortnightly or monthly basis to generate income. However, depending upon one's financial means, materials will be held on to for greater periods of time to take advantage of price fluctuations that frequently occur in these markets. Those workers who have financial difficulties must sell most of their waste on a regular basis to cover daily domestic costs, such as rent (for the *jhuggiān*), food (both for humans and donkeys), fuel (for a refitted motorbike), and education and health-related expenses. These calculations are shaped by and dependent upon disassembly and sorting done by female kin within these households. On the other hand, workers who have achieved greater financial stability hold onto waste and sell it once prices shoot upward. In fact, multiple junkyards operate within *jhuggiān* by those who have been able to accumulate surpluses, which allows them to purchase from other workers and sell to larger junkyard owners and intermediaries. Despite moments of accumulation, much of the work and exchanges at this moment are directed at meeting needs. A major constraint to accumulation was the fact that indebtedness has become folded into the remuneration for materials and work.

As mentioned earlier, Manzoor gained access to household waste in a locality by building sociopolitical relations with lower-level staff and getting a letter signed by a *nāi'b nāzim* (an elected official of a Union Council) that formalized and legitimized that access. The previous *karinde* (operatives), as described in the letter, had incurred a debt of nearly 100,000 PKR (approximately US$1,000 at the time of fieldwork) to a junkyard. Because of this indebtedness, these *karinde* were no longer willing to collect waste from this locality. This is when Manzoor took on their debt to the junkyard and, in exchange, received control over the area. As the area was transferred to him, so was the debt. Over the years the debt has ebbed and flowed, but Manzoor has remained indebted to that junkyard. The junkyard gives Manzoor a lower rate for the materials he provides them—that reduced rate acting as interest. Another waste worker, Sadiq, took on debt worth 35,000 PKR from his *māmūn* (mother's brother), specifically for acquiring a donkey cart—something crucial to waste disposal and circulation at the time. In exchange for this, Sadiq explained, "My *māmūn* took 200 PKR as a weekly commission. This is why I stopped working with him." This is when Sadiq started giving his waste materials to another *kabāṛī*, Chaudhary Billah. The debt was transferred to Chaudhary Billah, who now receives these materials but takes a lower commission of 100 PKR, which is deducted from the total cost of the profit (*bachat*). None of the commission goes into reducing that debt, however—that must be paid off separately.

Moreover, an elaborate system of advances exists in which *kabāṛīān* provide money as credit to waste workers on a regular basis. That same credit being extended is also a debt to be repaid:[5] a *kabāṛī* will give advances of a certain amount to waste workers who will then sell waste materials collected from households (or other spaces like hospitals) back to whoever provided the advance. Once these materials are sold, the income generated by them can be kept or used to reduce the principal of the advance, which varies depending on the financial stability of the worker taking the advance. Waste workers strategically used these advances to cover the everyday costs of running and maintaining their households. Others, especially *phaiṛī lagāne wale*, are given advances that cover both the cost of buying waste materials from a variety of sources (e.g., households, shops, and smaller industrial units) and investing in vehicles and other machinery and tools.

Remuneration, here, takes multiple forms, from monthly and daily wages to cash payments for sorted waste materials to the adjustments of debts, credits, and advances over many years. Due to the limited prevalence of the salaried wage, these dynamics of remuneration become major techniques for exercising limited control over the labor process, especially the initial collection and sorting of waste materials as a resource by workers, which then allows others to generate and accumulate surpluses from the work of salvaging. Before examining how remuneration and need shift to payments and accumulation as one gets closer to sites of commodity production and consumption, we must first tread through how *kabāṛīān* and *bīopāṛīān* create and maintain relations of exchange and then examine how work and knowledge are organized within such relations. Then, we can return to how payments become a form in which surpluses are realized as accumulation.

Buyers and Brokers

The *kabāṛī* and *bīopārī* are well-known figures across Pakistan and South Asia.[6] Acquiring waste materials from one direction to sell in another other, these figures stand between these materials and their supplying as a resource in commodity production. The exchange of waste materials for money articulates multiple spatiotemporal scales: the collection of waste from particular localities; their movements across the city, country, and region (materials can be both imported and exported); and wider networks of circulation (be they legal, informal, or even criminal). Thus, one critical feature of the *kabāṛīān* and *bīopārīān* is their capacity to navigate diverse spatiotemporal scales of exchange through a "brokered" form of governance, in which they stand as intermediaries between "societal embeddedness of local actors and the expertise needed for network embeddedness in global transactions" (Crang et al. 2013, 22). Along with the work of sorting and disassembling waste materials and expertise about quality and prices of specific materials, securing waste materials as a resource for commodity production also involves infrastructures of circulation, especially related to transport, storage, remuneration, payment, and financing, and much of this infrastructure falls under the control of traders and brokers.[7] Their capacity to realize surpluses out of a labor process, especially as accumulation, arises partly from their access to and control over these infrastructures, not necessarily the labor process itself. As may be evident by now, a degree of autonomy characterizes the latter. In any case, the relations they create and maintain, in which kinship, trust, and mutual indebtedness figure prominently, intersect with infrastructures of circulation to realize surpluses out of exchanges that require navigating an array of spatiotemporal scales.

Many of the *kabāṛīān* and *bīopārīān* I came to know had a connection to Shakargarh Tehsil in Punjab. Although I was never entirely certain why or how those from this area became so prominent, it was undeniable they relied upon relations of kinship to establish themselves as *kabāṛīān* and *bīopārīān*, while kin-based labor was mobilized for performing waste work within junkyards and warehouses.[8] One such *kabāṛī* from Shakargarh was Chaudhary Billah, whose junkyard is placed on a rented piece of land located within a major settlement of *jhuggīān*. Chaudhary Billah started sorting and disassembling waste materials in a friend's junk-yard in the early 1990s. At one point, the two of them opened a factory (*kārkhānah*) that manufactured pellets out of recycled plastics, but this failed. After an infusion of money—the source of which remained un-clear to me—he was able to open his own junkyard. He was becoming a *kabāṛī*, no longer working waste materials himself but buying them from some (workers) to sell to others (*biopāṛīān*). Although I speak more about his entry into this line of work in the next chapter, what needs to be em-phasized, at this point, is how this transition depended upon a moment of accumulation, in which figures like Chaudhary Billah are able to pur-chase and sell waste materials in larger amounts and at an increased pace to generate further surpluses.

Indebtedness continues to be dispersed across relations of work and exchange that extend to and beyond sites of production. Chaudhary Bil-lah estimated that anywhere between twenty-five to thirty waste workers are indebted (including advances) to him in the ways described earlier, with the debt in the range of 700,000–800,000 PKR (approximately US$7,000–8,000 at the time of fieldwork). These loans vary in size and are often given for a range of purposes to waste workers, as junkyard owners are a major source of liquidity for those excluded from the for-malized financial sector. Those workers who sold their materials to him were described by Chaudhary Billah as customers (*gāhak*). Their status as customers highlights that workers come, under varying conditions of obligation and choice, to sell waste materials to junkyard owners, either for cash or an adjustment of debits and credits, as described earlier.

Junkyard owners are concurrently indebted to larger junkyards or warehouses to whom they sell their sorted materials. The warehouse (also run by a group of male kin from Shakargarh) from which Chaudhary Billah had taken a loan of 200,000 PKR (approximately US$2,000 at the time of fieldwork) had given advances in similarly large amounts to other junkyards as a technique for ensuring specific kinds of materials are procured for them. Junkyard owners repeatedly expressed suspicion about adulterated materials, casting doubt on their quality, or as Chaudhary Bil-lah described it, "People cheat a lot in Pakistan." The final section of this chapter will address how mutual indebtedness extends across *biopāṛīān*, suppliers, manufacturing units, and beyond to those who sell manufactured commodities for consumption. At this point, however, what should be underscored is the fact that mutual indebtedness is a technique for navigating the uncertainty about materials and distrust of persons, while simultaneously exercising control over both relations of work and exchange (i.e., specific materials are regularly supplied to junkyards and warehouses). As one moves toward *biopāriān*, trustworthiness takes on greater salience since the spatiotemporal scale of activity expands.

A *biopārī* also from Shakargarh, Ali Bhai, along with his brothers, rents two warehouses—one in Gujrat City[9] and the other in Lahore—where the family accumulates and further sorts waste materials. The work of purchasing, collecting, transporting, and sorting is done by several workers, some of whom are kin, employed through a mix of monthly and daily wages. Warehouses such as these are spaces located across Pakistan where waste materials of all kinds are purchased from junkyards like Chaudhary Billah's and Umair's and are collected and further sorted to be sold to other *biopāriān* supplying manufacturing units across the country and beyond. Despite drawing upon kin-based relations with others from Shakargarh, Ali Bhai also described challenges in building relations with junkyards in the early years of entering this line of business, saying, "We had more losses than gains." When the family first came to Gujrat, no one gave them goods. When I asked, "Well, how did you get them to sell only to you?" It was small things such as their style of speaking (*bolne ka lehjah*) and method of working (*kām karne ka tarīqah*) that demonstrate honesty (*imāndārī*) and allow trust (*ā'tabār*) to be built up, only then can one person believe another (*yaqīn ho gayā*), he told me. The concern with trustworthiness, instantiated in personal qualities, should come as no surprise since the suppliers with whom he has worked are not kin or other intimates.

In the case of one supplier with whom he has done exchanges worth several hundred thousand rupees over the years, neither of them has ever seen each other, only being in touch over the phone. In another conversations, Ali Bhai explained, "Just like now, you come to me, I speak with you with love (*pyār se*) and show you respect (*'izzat*). Business doesn't run on cheating." Yet, when cheating does happen, which certainly does, Ali Bhai emphasized, "you have to end up tolerating it." The cheating here refers mainly once again to the accuracy of and purposeful equivocation about materials being purchased. If a *bīopārī* is purchasing the high-quality "pure white," and some "boxboard" is placed, knowingly or unknowingly, in these goods, this will be useless for the supplier, who will remove its weight from the goods that are being purchased and a loss will be incurred by Ali Bhai. The more often this happens, the more the trust necessary for brokerage will be diminished.

Adeel, a *bīopārī* dealing in scrap and junk in the Misri Shah[10] area of Lahore (see Map 0.2), clarified that relations of brokerage are ones among acquaintances (*wāqif*), rather than strangers (*ajnabī*). As the two of us sat in his refitted passenger van on the way to Darogahwala (another industrial area of Lahore) to buy unsorted copper, Adeel elaborated these insights when he asked me what field my PhD was in. After I told him it was anthropology (*ilm-e-bashrīāt*), which is not a commonly used word in Urdu spoken in Lahore, Adeel looked confused, so I clarified that it was the study of culture (*shaqāfat*) or societal relations (*samājī t'luqāt*). Adeel grabbed on this point about societal relations. He stressed that *making a relation is not difficult; the difficulty lies in maintaining them.* As was the case with many others, trust was cited as a major component of maintaining relations, emphasizing relations are broken through cheating (*dhokā se toṛ jate heiṇ*), and then he described three methods by which that can happen.

The first is through the exchange of money or give and take (*lain-dain*). In exchanges, breaking one's promises (*v'dah khilafīāt*) reduces and diminishes trust and weakens the relation (*t'luqāt meṇ kamī tī hai*). The second method by which relations are broken is when more money than is necessary is taken for doing something. When someone has another person do something for them, especially the case with governmental departments (*safarish*), a *dhokā* occurs when more money than is required is taken for doing that task. The last technique by which relations are weakened is when one reacts poorly or wrongly to what another is saying (*kissī kī bāt se ghalat react karte haiṇ*). A few days later, Adeel demonstrated such a measured response when a *bīopārī*, with whom he had made a verbal agreement about a purchase, ended up selling materials to someone else since Adeel had not deposited the payment in his bank account in time. When I asked Adeel why he had done so, he shrugged, saying it was perfectly reasonable (*m'aqūl*) for this *bīopārī* to sell to someone else even if they had reached an agreement. In describing the means by which societal relations are disturbed or deteriorate (*samājī t'luqāt kharāb ho jāte hain*), Adeel was highlighting how trust, belief, forbearance, and other personal traits are crucial to sustaining relations of brokerage that articulate multiple scales of activity.

Across these figures, so much emphasis is placed on relations, indebtedness, and trustworthiness because of the fragmented and differentiated nature of these processes: lack of control over the labor process, equivocation about waste materials, delay in payments, dispersed infrastructures, and exchanges happening across multiple spatiotemporal scales. Standing as they do between the collection of waste materials and their remaking into commodities, *kabāṛīān* and *bīopārīān* are constantly negotiating the vicissitudes of these processes, and, unlike waste workers who are removed from commodity production, which affords them a limited amount of autonomy and control, they are closer to and more dependent upon production, which exacerbates their vulnerability to fluctuations in demand and prices for these materials. Now that the relations of work and exchange through which waste materials move have been clarified, we can now examine how the work of sorting and disassembly is embedded in unequal exchanges, where knowledge about materials and prices contributes to generating and realizing surpluses.

Unequal Exchange

A *bīopārī* in Gujranwala, Babar Anwar was busy attending to phone calls in his office at the back of a warehouse while other *bīopārīān* and suppliers visited for a variety of purposes. Eventually, he took a break and started our conversation with a statement I commonly heard throughout my fieldwork: "The first thing you need to be successful in this business is money." This statement stressed that figures like *kabāṛīān* and *bīopārīān* are acting like merchants, whose capital (money) is defined by an initial stock of money, procured through a variety of means, that is used to purchase goods and materials that will then be sold at a higher-than-initial price to make profit. The profit of the merchant does *not necessarily* come from excess labor being performed over and above necessary labor (i.e., "the unpaid labor of others"), as is the case with surplus value derived from the labor process penetrated by capital accumulation, but "arises from unequal exchange exclusive in the sphere of circulation" (Sanyal 2007, 116). Transforming profit into capital, the merchant is then able to *potentially, though not necessarily*, penetrate the labor process, something previously closed off as accumulation was happening in the domain of circulation, not production (where it was nevertheless generated) (see Banaji 2020, 122). *Kabāṛīāṉ* and *biopārīāṉ* rarely use their capital to penetrate the labor process around procuring waste materials as a resource. Waste workers are relatively autonomous from the control of these figures, though other techniques, especially indebtedness as described above, ensure the flow of waste materials into junkyards and can be utilized to exercise control. To put it simply, even at the risk of oversimplification, a condition of exclusion comes with limited autonomy for waste workers. Yet, if *kabāṛīāṉ* and *biopārīāṉ* have limited control over the labor process of waste work and the production process of commodities, then how are surpluses generated in production and realized in circulation?

The work of sorting and disassembly is organized within relations of unequal exchange, in which knowledge about materials and rates is crucial to generating and realizing surpluses. Larger scale *kabāṛīāṉ* and *biopārīāṉ* buy waste materials at a base rate that can be further sorted and disassembled into even more specific types. Each type of waste will then be sold to a particular *biopārī* at a specific rate. For instance, if the going rate for a particular kind of copper being offered by manufacturing units was in the range of 550 PKR per kilo, which it hovered around during my fieldwork, *biopārī* will either buy these materials at 530 PKR per kilo, selling them at 540 PKR to suppliers, or will buy mixed goods, sorting and disassembling materials and selling them at their respective rates. The supplier also makes profit because he will sell the materials he bought (at 540 PKR) to the manufacturing units at 550 PKR. This is why, when purchasing waste materials, *kabāṛīāṉ* and *biopārīāṉ* tend to look for mixed ones that *appear* to have high-quality materials in them. Uncertainty about materials results in constant bargaining and arguing about the quality of materials and the appropriate prices to be paid. The more effective one is at bargaining, the greater the potential for generating surpluses through sorting and disassembly becomes. Each moment of sorting and disassembly is preceded and followed by exchange, where waste materials are bought and sold. Surpluses in the form of profit are realized from the minimal difference in the rate at which materials are bought and then sold. Unequal exchanges allow marginal gains to be made across those figures, from workers and *kabāṛiān* to *biopāriān* and suppliers. Surpluses (as marginal profits) realized in circulation is previously generated in production through sorting and disassembly, where physical and mental labor are mobilized to identify materials for commodity production.

In his shop in Misri Shah, Adeel traded while Zubair sorted and disassembled. One of the most ubiquitous kinds of metals to pass through this shop was various types of copper because of its material ability to conduct electricity. Pipes, wiring, parts, and any number of other copper items arrived from a variety of sources, whether small-scale industrial units or large-scale public utilities (Figure 3.4). These metals would be cut to inspect the inside, scratched to reveal the actual coloring of the metal, cleaned to remove any dirt that had built up on the materials, or heated to detach one metal from another. These were all techniques for getting at the identity of a particular thing.

In our first meeting, Zubair explained to me that you can tell what kind of copper a material is by its break: he took wire cutters and snapped the copper wiring to reveal a brighter inner portion. If the copper on the inside is red, then this would be *valā'ītī* and purer—Zubair would call it 99.99%. If the copper on the inside was yellow, then it was *desī* (local) and was impure or mixed—no exact number was given. In another instance, Zubair put a piece of *desī māl* next to one of *valā'ītī māl* to show me a slight difference. This piece of *desī māl* had coloring (*rangat*) of brass mixed into it, which made it closer to the reddish-orange color of copper we usually imagine, but when set against a piece of *valā'ītī māl*, it was not nearly as sharp red (*surkh*). In addition to these categories of *valā'ītī* and *desī*, a third category of copper was *russa*. Used for telephone wiring and thick cables for factories because of its ability to bear a larger than normal electrical load that mitigated the risk of burnt wiring, *russa* is soft and heavy, and was also "99% pure" in Zubair's words. Along with color, relative lightness was another primary quality through which different

FIGURE 3.4. *Two different kinds of copper wiring. Note sheen of the cooper in the foreground. Source: Author.*

kinds of metals were recognized: lightness was often used to describe soft (*naram*) silver or aluminum that had a flexibility about it, and its rate during my fieldwork was 175 PKR per kilo while the rate of hard silver, which is heavier, was 140 PKR per kilo.

Extra effort and/or specialized knowledge was also at times necessary to identify and prepare waste materials. When Adeel acquired copper rods used in mobile phone towers one day, he and Zubair spent most of the day trying to figure out if it made sense for them to process them. Since there were two layers of copper—on the inside was a thin copper rod that was insulated with foam and surrounded by a thicker, ribbed rod—Adeel had Zubair weigh the rods, then burnt a few of them to remove the foam on the inside, and then weighed them again. This would give them sense of how much weight they had and whether it made sense for him to hire workers on *dihārī* (daily wages) to prepare the copper for being sold to the *biopārī*. They were willing to hire labor and reduce the weight because these rods were *valā'itī māl* and would fetch a good rate. They needed to be careful, however, since direct fire would burn the copper, removing the varnish, changing the color, or making it brittle and frayed. Even if copper was foreign and of high quality, mistreating the materials could move it from the category of *valā'itī* to *desī*, reducing the rate at which it could be sold. On other occasions, a more specialized worker, usually called a *kārīgar* (artisan), would be needed to identify waste materials. Quite often, this involved the use of acids to prepare and identify all kinds of materials. A group of workers who collect sludge that deposits in the drains running below gold shops in the Inner City bring this material to a group of kin who then wash and burn them in acid to ensure only dusty gold pellets remain. Separately, Zubair explained how acid is poured on to steel, a battery attached to the material, and then, the change in color identities its relative quality: if the material remains red for a while, it is 316 (a grade of steel considered to be of the highest quality), if it remains red for only a few seconds, it is 314 (a grade of steel considered to be slightly lower quality), and if it turns black, it is *desī*, *barthan* (dishes), or magnet—all lower qualities.

Sorting and disassembly are in fact knowledge about materials being organized and utilized in relation to knowledge about their rates on local and global markets. This knowledge is dispersed across figures involved in working and exchanging waste materials. The closer one gets to the site of production—whether that be a factory, mill, or plant—knowledge about rates becomes well established. For *kabāṛīān* and *biopārīān*, the ability to generate surplus through unequal exchange comes from their "role in the construction of market information because key to their social practices is that they broker these categories between other agents" (Beuving 2013, 3–4). The *kabāṛīān* are in contact with several *biopārīān* such as Adeel or Ali Bhai and so have partial knowledge about the standard rate being offered in local and global markets. Those below the *kabāṛīān*, specifically those who collect these materials (waste workers, *phaiṛī lagāne wale*, or domestic staff), do not have relations with *biopārīān* and thus have more limited knowledge about the rate being offered in these markets. At this moment, "not much is known," in the words of Adeel, because these materials are being sold *kabāṛīān* with limited sorting. They are simply gathered and then sold en masse—for instance, into plastic rather than all the specific kinds of plastics. Knowledge at this point does not take on significance with regard to realizing surpluses. As one moves closer to *biopārīān* and sites of commodity production, knowledge and information about materials and rates take on greater significance and become more standardize and unified; in fact, *kabāṛīān* and *biopārīān* exploit ambiguities about materials in their favor by manipulating information and knowledge about rates and materials to others, which then facilitates realization of surpluses through unequal exchanges.

Discarded things (i.e., plastics, paper, junk, and scrap) are not surpluses in any ontological sense but are rendered as such by virtue of being routed into "the pale of value" (Gidwani and Reddy 2011, 1625) *as commodities*.[11] Sorting and disassembly are ways of knowing and working with waste materials, in which mental and physical labor are mobilized to recognize, evaluate, and standardize specific qualities of these materials and effect concrete and abstract transformations necessary for commodity production.[12] These transformations are how surpluses are generated in production, which are subsequently realized in circulation through unequal exchange.

Yet, it should also be kept in mind that those transformations arise from the fact that waste work is an instance in which "physiological labor, concrete labor, and abstract labor are performed simultaneously in the act of producing a commodity" (Gidwani 2018, 170). Sorting and disassembly as concrete labor produce use-values by exercising effort upon a world in which waste materials have proliferated on a mass scale through the consumption of disposable goods and commodities. Much of that effort, at least for waste workers themselves, is directed at meeting needs and thus is dictated by the temporal rhythms of work and life, not by a wage based on an abstracted unit of time. As simultaneously abstract labor, however, sorting and disassembly discern and distill out the exchange value of waste materials through mental and bodily effort, technologies (transportation and weighing), and money.[13] Such transformations are what generates surpluses, which can be realized in either circuits of need or accumulation. While surplus as need is realized in the forms of remunerations described earlier, surplus as accumulation is given form through payments. Transformations—whether concrete or abstract—arise from the fact that waste materials and work are embedded in relations of work and exchange organized around commodity production and dispersed across an expanding urban landscape.

Payment and Accumulation

As one moves closer to sites of commodity production, waste materials are increasingly treated as goods (*māl*) in the possession of *kabāṛiān* and *biopāriān*. Unlike materials and work for which one is remunerated, goods are transferred through payments. Bill Maurer has described payment as *"the act and infrastructure of value transfer ...* Payment is orthogonal to exchange. To put it in other terms: there may be a pyramid of money, but there is scaffolding and infrastructure extending from each level of the pyramid outwards and inwards, holding it up" (2012, 19, emphasis in original). These payments straddle the lines between the accountable world of the formal banking sector, regulated as it is by state fiscal policy, and the covert contours of informal exchange, articulated through its notions of sociality and trust.[14] Among *kabāṛiān* and *biopāriān*, rarely are payments done with an immediate transfer of money, which is partly why so much concern about personal qualities related to trustworthiness described earlier arises. Done through some combination of cash, checks, and/or account transfers, payments, for *kabāṛiān* and *biopāriān*, are temporally protracted moments when surpluses generated in production are realized in the form of money, which can then be utilized to generate further surpluses and be crystallized as accumulation.

Waste materials are acquired by initially paying a portion of the total amount in cash, the rest being promised on *udhār* (referring to debt, credit, and/or advances), and eventually, finalized with a check, bank transfer, and/or cash. Waste materials are thus given with the expectation that payment will not be completed immediately but will be finalized at some point in the future. Much of the delay in payment arises from the fact that supplying waste materials depends upon their use in production and consumption. Manufacturing units extend lines of credit to suppliers in exchange for the goods (waste) they deliver to these units, and it is this line of credit, along with their own capital, that a supplier attached to a unit uses to purchase goods (waste materials) from a *biopāriān*. Yet, as book publishers, one of whom is a relative of mine, in Urdu Bazaar explained to me, paper wholesalers, for instance, give advances to mills when putting in orders for a certain amount of paper that they will then provide to those producing paper commodities—publishers (of books), printers (everything from cards to advertisements), copy-makers (school notebooks), and retailers. When consumption is expected to be high (e.g., just before schools are expected to open and commodities like notebooks and textbooks are being purchased), wholesalers will extend advances to manufacturers to produce paper, which increases demand for paper waste across the chain of suppliers, *biopāriān*, and *kabāṛiān*.

When goods are being bought and sold on an uninterrupted basis, payments are carried out with limited delay across these supply chains, with waste and money circulating without friction and surpluses being realized. During these times, *biopāriān* are comfortable purchasing more goods than they have money for, making up the rest through *udhār*, but when there is a fall in demand for goods and rate drops, they are hesitant about relying on credit or advances, which, if delayed for too long, become burdensome debt. Nevertheless, in times of stagnating demand and prices, *kabāṛiān* coax *biopāriān* into purchasing their materials because the materials *kabāṛiān* acquire (from waste workers or smaller junkyard owners) must be kept in motion to realize surpluses. According to Ali Bhai, these *kabāṛīāṇ* say, "If you don't have money, you can pay after a few days. No worries, pay whenever you get the money." *Bīopārīāṇ* at times accumulate waste even while demand stagnates because prices have dropped and an expectation that these goods will be purchased once demand rises, something that will also push prices back up and potentially lead to greater profit. Ali Bhai similarly found himself caught in an unexpected fall in demand and prices. A month or two before we had met, he had purchased 9,500 kgs of copy notebook (one of the most expensive categories of paper) from a *kabāṛī* on *udhār*. Expecting to sell the goods at 35 PKR per kilo and receive 335,500 PKR from the supplier who purchased these materials, a lower rate of 24.5 PKR per kilo was given to him, bringing the expected total down to 237,500 PKR. This lowered rate, along with longer than expected delay in payment from suppliers, resulted from a fall in demand for these goods on the production side. He waited several months before he decided to bear the loss in profits.

While the play of cash and *udhār* negotiates delays (both expected and unexpected) in payments, checks are utilized as a way to either complete payments or ensure that payments will happen at some point in the future. When Ali Bhai had given 500,000 PKR worth of goods to a *bīopārī*, the check he was given in return was not being deposited because the *bīopārī* had not been paid by the mill. Ali Bhai described the payment as having been made, even if the money had not been transferred. In the absence of legally binding contracts, possession of a check allays some of the fear about nonpayment.

Checks, in fact, were used in three distinct ways. First is "self-check," which has the name of the person for whom the payment was meant, and the second is an "open check," which has no name but simply an amount and signature of the payer. Adeel, for instance, would take open checks of a certain amount given to him, pass them to another *bīopārī* he was purchasing materials from, and then make up any balance in cash or another "self-check." Whichever account the money was coming from did not matter to *bīopārīāṇ*; most important was that payment is ensured. The third kind of payment was a "cross check," which has two parallel diagonal lines drawn on the upper left corner of the check. This check transfers money directly from one account to another but cannot be cashed themselves. At the time of my fieldwork, Pakistani tax law required that a 0.6% advance tax for those who do not file income taxes be deducted from cash withdrawals greater than 50,000 PKR from all accounts in a particular bank associated with one name. As all *biopāriān* I spoke with were non-tax-filers, doing a cross check avoids the payment of advance tax because transfers are made between the accounts of two different individuals within one bank. My conversations about cross checks were usually met with suspicion. However, it became clear that holding multiple accounts, like Adeel and many other *biopāriān* did, allowed one to transfer money and avoid paying taxes when making a payment. Rather than a percentage of a payment going into the state exchequer through an advance tax, the cross check was a technique for manipulating the techno-legal infrastructures of value transfer, ensuring that payments are made and maximizing the realization of surpluses within the circuit of accumulation.

The remunerations examined earlier and the payments described above are two connected though distinct moments in which surpluses, generated in production, come to be realized in the circulation of waste materials and money. The remunerations for waste materials and work realize surpluses to be directed at need, while payment for goods (also, waste materials) realize surpluses to be directed at accumulation. This circulation of waste and money occurs in different forms (cash, debts, credit, advances, checks, transfers) and has varying temporal rhythms (immediate exchange, delayed payments, and protracted debts). Many of the figures I mentioned throughout this chapter, from those who collect, sort, and disassemble waste materials to those who buy and sell those same materials, are simultaneously excluded from and dependent upon the production of commodities. The relations of work and exchange through which waste materials move are part of much larger processes, ones that exceed informality as a site for generating and realizing surpluses and manifest themselves across Lahore's urbanizing landscape.

Surplus and Its Excess

Let me conclude by returning to Umair's junkyard. After we finished breaking down the VCR, I inquired naively, "Tell me all the kinds of plastics you have." Umair indulged me. As he listed them off, with their respective rates, Umair described one plastic called celluloid that when snapped, releases, in his words, a rose-like fragrance (*gulāb kī khūshbū*). He did not have any that day, but a few weeks later, sitting on those same wobbly plastic chairs, I sensed rose-like fragrances spreading through my nasal passages after the celluloid was snapped. That smell, I later learned, comes from the camphor—originally extracted from the camphor tree but now synthetically produced—used to manufacture celluloid. My initial forays into waste materials and work were through such moments, where properties and qualities of waste materials were recognized through the elicitations they aroused within a body's sensorium at work. Yet, as Alexander and Sanchez (2018) have highlighted, waste materials have an indeterminacy about them, especially because they emerge at the peripheries of several overlain regimes of value. An attention to materiality is a partial view, one that, though revealing much about waste work, obscures, first, its nature as a social and political relationship undergirding uneven forms of life in Pakistan and elsewhere and, second, how it is embedded in multiple spatiotemporal scales of activity. In other words, there remains much in excess of waste materials themselves and the surpluses generated out of them.

For George Bataille, an overabundance (surplus) of energy characterized life on the planet, and not being dissipated through production, this excess energy comes to be expended in "a luxurious squandering of energy in every form," especially "useless consumption," nonprocreative sexuality, and modern warfare (1988, 33). The first excess to be kept in mind has to do with the expansive economic relations implicated in contemporary worlds of waste. How different forms of value are materialized out of waste materials through distinct kinds of work in Lahore's waste infrastructures depends as much upon highly interpersonal and localized interactions among households, waste workers, junkyard owners, intermediaries, and many others, as it does upon fluctuations in global markets for materials (e.g., oil or copper). This is why we cannot delimit ourselves to the materiality of waste, and to a lesser extent, the work and labor surrounding these materials, when examining contemporary waste infrastructures. Worlds of waste, and subsequently those forms of life attached to them, are forged through these distinct and variegated set of scalar processes.

The other excess is those forms of life, organized as they are around caste-based relations, that have taken shape in urban Pakistan and have been reinscribed through informality as a site for generating and realizing surpluses. Over the past several decades, consumption on unprecedented scales has shaped Lahore's demographic shifts, spatial expansion, and infrastructural growth, much of which has been oriented toward an economically and politically ascendant middle and upper class. What remains unclear in many accounts of waste and urbanizing landscapes is how and why two forms of life—ones that produce waste through consumption and those who make a life working with and exchanging those materials—operate alongside each other in intimately fraught ways (see Gidwani and Reddy 2011). Within Lahore's urbanizing landscape, waste infrastructures and economies have grown in such a way that offers opportunities for securing work and livelihoods among those from low- or noncaste backgrounds, allowing them to make a place for themselves in Lahore's unevenly urbanizing landscape, even if they continue to experience precarity, stigma, and exclusion. Precisely because of how livelihoods have become attached to waste materials and work within Lahore's urbanizing landscapes, we must unpack the relationship that informality as a site for generating surpluses has to the uneven forms of life that exceed those surpluses.

Informality has become a critical site for maintaining relationships between uneven forms of life, with infrastructures of disposability and circulation connecting them. Relations of work and exchange generate surpluses directed at circuits of need, upon which many workers depend for reproducing their own life and that of others (kin and non-kin) with whom they share a world in common, but other surpluses generated *simultaneously* out of those relations are directed at circuits of accumulation, which *kabāṛīān*, *biopārīān*, and many others depend upon for reproducing that same world. Viewed from circuits of accumulation, relations of work and exchange are salvaging surpluses for capital, thereby reproducing it. Viewed from those of need, those same relations are generating surpluses to reproduce life (one's own and that of one's kin). Outside those who work with or exchange waste materials, there are those for whom waste workers remove garbage, trash, and all other kinds of refuse; that labor, as I have suggested, is reproductive in nature, as it is directed at allowing the life of another to go on and flourish. Here, excess is caught up with the abjection[15] thought to inhere within things and persons: the stigmatizing and polluting qualities of waste materials come to be attached to certain bodies and persons, and not others. After surpluses have been generated and realized, the other excess that remains are those forms of life—one's own, one's kin, and that of innumerable others—that have been taking shape across Lahore's unevenly urbanizing landscape. The final two chapters turn their attention to those forms of life as they unfold at multiple, intersecting spatiotemporal scales across Pakistan—from the uneven intimacies shaping urban life in Lahore to the intergenerational life of workers and their wider social relations across Punjab.

CHAPTER 4

THE UNEVENNESS OF INTIMACY

IMRAN ALI COLLECTS WASTE materials from middle-class homes in Faisal Town area of Lahore. This is one locality among several that fall under the control of Allah Ditta, who is a relative of Imran Ali. Late one morning in April 2015, I accompanied Imran Ali and another waste worker into one such home in the Faisal Town area. The two had been asked to collect some extra trash on the roof. We climbed three flights of stairs through the home but never saw the family—who remained on the first floor behind screen doors. As they saw us pass by, they asked whether I am with them and who I am exactly. Imran Ali told them, "He's with us and writing a book." We walked up a set of steep stairs to the second floor, which was vacant and littered with empty and half-filled soft drink bottles. Its paint was peeling off, and mold was growing on the walls. We then went onto the second-floor terrace and climbed another set of spiral staircases onto the roof, where several bricks were arranged with burned-out candles (*chirāgh*) and bottles of oil scattered about. While the other worker filled a netted sack with construction waste (*malbah*), Imran Ali gathered empty bottles, crumpled paper, some leaves, and dirt strewn about the roof. We then went back downstairs, but before leaving the house, an older woman asked Imran Ali to wait, calling him son (*putr*) and handing him 200 Pakistani rupees (approximately US$2 at the time) for the extra work. Back outside, in front of the house, the two of them stood on the side of the street, where they deposited the materials onto their donkey cart (*gadhā raiṛhī*), being sure to put aside what could be sold.

Imran Ali's work separates a small fraction of the waste generated in Lahore on a daily basis from those who produce it while requiring others, especially waste workers, to grow quite close to those same discarded materials. Separation from and proximity to waste are not simply a matter of physical distance in urban Pakistan—they are fundamentally social in nature. For instance, Imran Ali claimed his caste was "nau-Muslim Rajput." Attaching "nau-Muslim" to Rajput, which is considered higher status, Imran Ali asserted descent from a Rajput Hindu lineage that had recently converted to Islam. Another worker, however, refuted his claim. "This is wrong," he said. "No such people [*qaum*] exist. They are just Musalī." "Musalī" similarly refers to those who converted to Islam but from the Dalit group known as Chūṛā, which I described at much length in chapter 2. Musalī are also assumed to be "sweepers" and do not claim Rajput lineage. By using the term *Musalī*, this worker unequivocally relegated Imran Ali to an ascribed low- or noncaste status, then went on to claim, for himself, the higher status of being *Khokhar*, which *is* presumed to be of Rajput lineage. Although this man and Imran Ali shared the same form of work, these exchanges reveal two distinct though related ways of distancing oneself from waste materials and work: one is about physical distance, or being far from, rather than close, to waste, and the other relates to social distance, or being close to waste simply by circumstance (i.e., working with it), rather than by birth. Discernible in both our movement through the house that day and the contested claims of these workers are tensions of closeness and distance—among persons, waste, and work. Such tensions, in fact, highlight how caste has been built into the kind of intimacy that has emerged and shaped the unevenness of life in urban Pakistan.

Waste materials and work are sites for mediating social relationships in urban Pakistan, relationships in which people constantly negotiated intimacy across caste, class, and religious lines. This chapter focuses on the work performed in removing and accumulating waste materials, especially before such materials are deposited or reclaimed at landfills (Millar 2018; Reno 2016), in order to situate waste work within distributive processes whereby waste materials are made absent for some, just as they are made present for others.[1] Previous chapters have examined how the bureaucratic state has come to occupy a managerial role in relation to waste infrastructures, just as relations of work and exchange have been organized to procure waste materials as a resource for commodity production. This chapter, along with the proceeding one, extends these insights by examining the imbrications between bureaucratization of waste work, the informalization of livelihoods, and the spatial reorganization of life in urban Pakistan. Put slightly differently, the expansion of the bureaucratic state and livelihoods of waste workers are enmeshed with the texture of urban life through a range of distributive processes, one of which is the uneven distribution of waste across the urban landscape.

Waste work is instrumental to how distributive processes engender different intimacies with waste materials, such that particular bodies and persons, according to historical inequalities and interdependencies, have varying degrees of proximity (bodily, social, or moral) to those same materials. Intimacies exist among waste workers, middle- and upper-class homes that depend on them for waste disposal services, and waste traders who purchase sorted waste from these workers to sell to others. These waste intimacies reflect and reproduce wider transformations in social orders and hierarchies, which are then discernible in the spatial, affective, and material relations across urban Pakistan.

The notion of "waste intimacies" foregrounds how forms of work, social relationships, and affects, in unevenly distributing substances, bodies, and persons, produce attachments to a world that is shared yet deeply unequal. In urban Pakistan waste intimacies reproduce separations and distances between persons according to social differences and hierarchies inflected by caste, class, and religion as historical categories. This chapter's discussion of the differential proximity of persons have to waste materials and their potential pollution gestures to Mary Douglas's (2002, 152–56) account of how the body's porosity makes persons susceptible to defilement—wherein substances enter and leave the body through acts of exchange. This body, for Douglas (2002, 4) as well, is importantly a social one. In older studies of caste (e.g., Marriott 1968; Marriott and Inden 1977), the exchange of food was shown to be one of the means by which polluting substances could be potentially transmitted, requiring that such exchanges be organized by strict regulations that could control the flow of substances across hierarchically arranged castes. Purity was thus maintained by ensuring that substances, which were either polluting themselves or coming from persons whose touch was deemed polluting, were not transmitted across bodies and persons belonging to those different castes. Whereas norms and codes of conduct upholding caste purity and hierarchy have diminished over the past several decades, waste infrastructures have expanded across urban Pakistan to take away waste materials (themselves composed of potentially polluting substances) from certain spaces (i.e., middle-class households) to elsewheres, real or imagined. Rather than resuscitating a theoretical framework of purity and pollution to analyze caste in urban Pakistan today, I emphasize three central features of waste intimacies in materials below: (1) the symbiosis between waste and intimacy in constituting social life, (2) the management of intimacy as unfolding across social groups and between self and other, and (3) intimacy as forged through historical inequalities and interdependencies.

Waste Intimacies

Waste intimacies are predicated as much on forms of distancing and antagonism as they are on forms of proximity and interdependence. In Pakistan, caste is, at times, formulated as something that can be inherited across generations, allowing those who claim to work with waste materials by happenstance to differentiate themselves from those who are presumed to do this work by birth. Such claims, at least partially, are premised on the notion of a freely consenting individual engaging in waste work, rather than the socially constrained person compelled to do so through genealogical inheritance (Povinelli 2006).[2] Relatedly, waste intimacies do not immediately bear on things like sexuality, love, or romance; rather, these intimacies shed light on how those practices, especially related to different kinds of risk and harm, are organized and interpreted by social and political actors. This is an important point to keep in mind when considering what waste intimacies tell us about intimacy more generally. Take, for instance, someone like Imran Ali, who collects and sorts the waste of middle-class homes: he occupies an intimate relationship with those households, one that is simultaneously socially distanced and oftentimes fraught with antagonism, hostility, and harm. How caste, waste, work, and person have been brought together is instrumental in reproducing historical inequalities and interdependencies upon on which these sorts of intimacies and urban life more generally have come to be built.

Intimacy is a projected and condensed social relation that expresses certain interdependencies and ambivalences.[3] For instance, Lauren Berlant (1998, 282) describes an intimacy that "builds worlds; it creates spaces and usurps places meant for other kinds of relation. Its potential failure to stabilize closeness always haunts its persistent activity, making the very attachments deemed to buttress 'a life' seem in a state of constant if latent vulnerability" (see also Berlant 2011). Similarly, Michael Herzfeld (2005, 3) calls attention to what he describes as cultural intimacy, in which certain facets of a "cultural identity" become at once "a source of external embarrassment" and an "assurance of common sociality."[4] These approaches have prioritized intimacy as a relation of familiarity and closeness rendered unstable because of something external. Yet it becomes evident that intimacies are consistently marked by ambivalences when one considers that intimate relations are suffused with a wide range of affects—from love, care, and sympathy to disgust, shame, and powerlessness (Herzfeld 2005; Kristeva 1982; Berlant 2011; see also Ali 2021; Rashid 2020). In fact, the ambivalences involved in intimacy are key modalities through which actors across the lines of caste, class, and religion relate to the unevenness of life in urban Pakistan. This vision of intimacy underscores such ambivalences because they provide insight into an unevenness internal to intimacy's constitution.

Waste work is a prominent social activity in which persons and bodies potentially come into close proximity, touching the same objects as they move in a sequential way, from the object (i.e., commodity) used up and discarded as a waste product to its collection and exchange, which will remake the object into something of use once again. The social nature of waste work draws our attention to those forms of relatedness that are reproduced as waste materials are disposed of and/or circulated. In her fascinating exploration of interspecies relatedness in Central Himalayas,

Radhika Govindrajan sketches out an approach to relatedness that is attuned to "the myriad ways in which the potential and outcome of a life always and already unfolds in relation to that of another" (2018, 3). She goes on to qualify that forms of relatedness are "decidedly uninnocent," in which "mutuality and connection do not imply an erasure of difference or hierarchy" (2018, 5). The forms of relatedness traced out in this chapter are multiple and distinct, intersecting at various points and times. Disposability, for instance, instantiates a particular kind of relation that persons have to those material things (i.e., commodities) that constitute the quotidian bulk of their worlds. That relation of disposability is itself embedded within other relations of work and exchange, in which persons—most prominently waste workers, but also many others—come into close contact with waste materials, allowing them to access monetary worth of these materials and exchange them for money.[5] As previous chapters unpacked, these relations of work and exchange cut across the techno-legal apparatus of the bureaucratic state and informal economies organized around commodity production. This chapter further elaborates these relations of work and exchange by examining how they have organized uneven processes of urbanization, giving rise to forms of relatedness requiring constant negotiations of intimacies across caste, class, and religious lines. These forms of relatedness gestured toward two distinct though intertwined aspects of waste intimacies: they are as much about relations of proximity and distance within and across social groups as they are about the relations individuals have to the self, waste, work, and a world of others.

After tracing how waste work is instrumental to the reorganization of urban life in contemporary Lahore, the chapter then examines the affective relations surrounding waste work to demonstrate how these intimacies shape relationships between persons, in which a broad range of affects sustains relationships between those differentiated based on social hierarchies. The next two sections, respectively, analyze the material relations between waste workers and the middle- and upper-class homes from which they collect waste and interactions between junkyard owners and waste workers. These sections distill how, despite enduring associations between waste and caste, these materials are a source of monetary worth that offers at least the prospect for upward mobility, which in turn shapes the relationships that individuals form to their own self, waste materials, work, and others with whom they share a world. The final section turns to how intercaste and interreligious relations in urban Pakistan are reworked in light of violence, conflict, and other forms of antagonism.

The Substantialization of Life

Urban life in Pakistan has been frequently described as being characterized by antagonisms, based on either religious, sectarian, or ethnic divisions, informing and emerging out of everyday life, especially within intimate arenas such as neighborhoods, apartment buildings, and domestic spaces (see Khan 2006; Ring 2006; see also Maqsood 2017). Such accounts of social antagonism, however, have left caste unaddressed, which is a noted absence when one considers "caste is about attenuated and graded forms of intimacy" (Thiranagama 2018, 372; see also Singh 2011). Moreover, what must be accounted for is how differences between social groups, whether on the basis of religion, sect, ethnicity, or caste, come to be substantialized within everyday life. Foregrounding substantialization, in fact, lets us connect the reproduction of caste and the organization of waste work into infrastructure through distributive processes (one of which is the movement of waste materials) shaping life across Lahore's unevenly urbanizing landscape. Urban life in Lahore has grown directly out of a form of life in the Punjab that has been built upon caste-based identities and relations. This form of life has also undergone profound transformations that result from agrarian development, processes of urbanization, the hegemony of Muslim nationalism, regimes of citizenship, and democratic and authoritarian politics. This transformation has not meant this form of life, not to mention the caste-based relations upon which it has been built, has disappeared; rather, the form this life has taken a changed form within Lahore's unevenly urbanizing landscape. How do we understand the reproduction of caste through its transformation?

In an early account of transformations in caste in South India, Stephen A. Barnett noted that caste as a religious and ideological system that provided structures for organizing relations between caste groups was dissolving in light of economic development, urbanization, forms of cultural nationalism, and state-led projects of modernization and social transformation. This required, Barnett maintained, a distinction be made between "persistence of named groups called 'castes' from the persistence of the caste system," describing this shift in terms of substantialization, or the ethnicization of specific caste groups (1975, 158). When this happens, rather than codes of conduct related to commensality or marriage maintaining purity within and across hierarchically arranged castes, birth (i.e., natural identity) becomes a primary marker of purity. As caste as a system of relations and their attendant codes of conduct diminishes, other codes of conduct emerge that are at times unitary (i.e., cultural nationalism) and at other times diverse (i.e., class-based ones). This discussion bears directly upon the current context when one considers the hegemony Muslim nationalism has had across classes, castes, and ethnicities in Pakistan, as well as the success that Christianity has had (or not had) in providing unitary codes for Pakistani Christians across class lines.

Lastly, Barnett made a prescient observation that, even if there was an ethnicization of caste and more egalitarian codes of conduct were emerging that cut across class lines, "urban untouchables [were] excluded from ethnicization; while consistent transactions among urban castes are breaking down, they are carefully maintained vis-à-vis untouchables [*sic*]," with an idea "of a separate 'untouchable race' ... emerging among upper-caste city dwellers" (1975, 159). Similarly, Christopher Fuller (1996, 12) described the substantialization of identities, in which there has been an "alteration in the normative basis of caste—from purity as an index of hierarchical rank to difference as a marker of separation," which was "*a matter of degree rather than kind*" (emphasis added). Moreover, along with this shifting emphasis upon class-based markers of difference, the rendering of caste-based relations, ones that were more hierarchical in nature, has given rise to intercaste and interreligious relations that are at least perceived as more egalitarian in nature. What must be clarified at this point, however, is how the reproduction of forms of life built upon caste-based relations, identities, and codes of conduct has come to be distributed across bodies, spaces, and persons in a city like Lahore.

The continued presence of low- or noncaste groups in waste work throughout Pakistan's urban centers must be situated in relationship to Lahore's changing class and spatial relations. As mentioned earlier, much of Lahore's middle and upper classes are drawn heavily from higher-status Muslim groups who have historically had control over land in the countryside and/or maintained access to sources of power and status. Thus, waste disposal services are organized around shared aspirations of these middle and upper classes, such that more affluent localities have more reliable services. Expanding waste disposal services, resulting partly from class-based consumption, has opened opportunities for work, wealth, and mobility among waste workers themselves. The uneven distribution of these services has had the subsequent effect of differentiating certain bodies, persons, and spaces as "unclean," "dirty," and "impure," which has a disproportionate impact on those who have limited access to such services or who work with waste materials themselves. Recalling Barnett's observation, although transactions maintaining purity across castes may be dissolving and being replaced by ones more egalitarian in nature, low- or noncaste groups, especially those who have found a source of livelihood in waste work, continue to be subject to codes of conduct involving interdictions on commensality and marriage.

The distributive processes organizing urban life in Lahore have been facilitated by the transmission of potentially stigmatizing and threatening substances across bodies, spaces, and persons—all of which is ensured by waste work as an infrastructure. Once again, for Mary Douglas (2002) as well as others (Daniel 1984; Marriott 1968; Marriott and Inden 1977), the image of the body as an imagined coherent whole was susceptible to the transmission of substances (or transubstantiation) from the bodies of other persons. The different substances (e.g., animal skins, excrement, and so forth) that bodies came into contact with varied according to what kind of work these bodies and persons performed, as well as the spatial location of those bodies and persons at work. This is why the transmission of substances shapes how qualities of bodies, persons, spaces, and lifestyles are "substantialized" and operate as asymmetrical markers of difference and separation between those differentiated along the lines of caste, class, and religion.

And, even though commensality has been delegitimized on the grounds of religion (Islam and Christianity) and liberal notions of equal citizenship, the attachment of these substances to certain bodies and persons—especially those who come into physical contact with waste materials or those who are presumed to be low- or noncaste by birth—prevents caste-based relations and codes of conduct from completely dissolving. Even if religious traditions, nationalism, and citizenship regimes provide codes of conduct that are unitary in nature, those same codes come up against the fact that waste as comprising potentially polluting substances shapes transactions surrounding waste, work, and persons. Indeed, the organization of waste work into an infrastructure of urban life is meant to take away waste materials, as comprising substances, from certain spaces and make them present elsewhere.

An attention to substantialization reformulates connections between the materiality of waste and the construction of social identities by highlighting the role that waste materials, once disaggregated into their constitutive substances, play in organizing urban life. Waste as a category that references material things is characterized by varying degrees of indeterminacy. Later, the "ideological, symbolic, and social" (Hird 2012, 465) forms through which waste comes to be determined (i.e., known, organized, and managed) remains a source of considerable debate (see, e.g., Alexander and Sanchez 2018). Just as material things come to be determined as waste, they remain somewhat disaggregable through their constitutive parts and substances, which continually shape the interaction between persons in relation to waste materials and the work surrounding them. Substantialization—of waste and identities—allows for tracing how waste materials, through transformation and transmission, link the workings of economies and infrastructures to the uneven forms of life that have emerged across urban Pakistan.

Affective Relations of Waste Work

Households in Pakistan and throughout South Asia are exceptionally rife with anxieties about interactions across the lines of caste, class, religion, and gender (Ring 2006; Zulfiqar 2018; see also Dickey 2000; Frøystad 2003). The removal of different kinds of matter (or waste materials) is an elementary act of cleansing and purification that not only produces the home as a material and conceptual entity but also enacts gendered and sexual norms of domesticity and purity that saturate life, both public and private. Indeed, purity and pollution, which were produced through the disposal of waste matter by low- or noncaste groups (and not others), were values that organized a whole series of relations between and within hierarchically arranged caste groups. For instance, the purity of the "upper-caste" body was to be maintained through relations of work and exchange that removed potentially polluting materials from their households, attaching them to the bodies and households of persons belonging to the "lower castes." The relations of work and exchange that organized the movement of defiling matter were inseparable from practices of endogamy, which ritualized the control of women's bodies and sexuality across caste groups, thereby organizing individual and social reproduction.[6] Presumed violations of these gendered and sexual relations across caste lines were regularly and continue to be met by punitive acts of violence against both men and women, especially those belonging to low- or noncaste backgrounds. By ensuring the integrity of the household, as well as the bodies and person who inhabit it, waste work produces a contradictory set of affects centered on but also exceeding the space of the home, coming to saturate forms of life along the lines of class, caste, religion, and gender across Lahore and urban Pakistan.

Not only is waste work in urban Pakistan sustained by a normative sociality, in which caste, converging with class, religion, and gender, has remained central, but this form of work, as described in earlier chapters, has also been organized through distinctions of public and private that are themselves elementary to liberal imaginations of intimacy. The boundary between the house as a private, inner space and its outside as a public one rests upon a naturalization of home as a site of affection, love, and care among biologically related kin (Povinelli 2006; see also Beall 2006; Chakrabarty 1991; Kaviraj 1997). As noted in previous chapters, these distinctions—public/private, inside/outside, inner/outer—continue to structure work in Lahore's waste infrastructures in specific ways, from the governmental work (*sarkārī kām*) of municipal sanitation workers to the "private work" (private *kām*) engaged in by both municipal and informal workers. While distinctions organize this form of work and relations of exchange, they also have a fuzziness about them, which makes vulnerable the boundary between the household and its outside. This boundary thus operates as a permeable threshold of intimacy, in which substances, bodies, and persons move in between and across as waste materials are taken away and disposed of. Because intimacy must be constantly managed, this movement of substances, bodies, and persons across boundaries—of spaces, caste, class, and religion—both threatens and affirms affective relations across them.

For instance, in the opening vignette above, our movement through the middle-class home that day was highly circumscribed, as was the intimacy afforded to us. The space through which we moved was carved out of the household as internally differentiated, in physical and affective terms. Along the way, we crossed a threshold of intimacy, walking through stairs, corridors, and common spaces, but there were other, more intimate areas closed off to us, ones that we could not access. Traversing the passage open to us, I felt there was a violation going on. But that feeling was a recognition less of a violation and more of a passage into a more intense order of intimacy, the result of which was waste work being performed and social relationships being enacted. Similarly, when I did not accompany him, Imran Ali, even though doors were left open for him and he went about unquestioned, worked within delimited passages, being kept within an intimate but separate space within the home.

When I asked Imran Ali that day whether he felt any discomfort, he stressed:

> I've been working in these households since I could walk. Then I'd come here with my older sister before she got married. We'd work this neighborhood together. These households have complete trust in us. They leave the door open for me, and I go in and out with no one asking any questions. They treat me like their son.

This is why, according to him, he could easily demand of other domestic workers or children, "Go ask for something to eat for me," and why he was given cooking items, old clothing, and bedsheets, and even leftover food from a few nights earlier. Imran Ali, like many other workers, is indeed given all kinds of items, and that giving was spoken of, by both him and the households that gave, as sympathetic acts of love and care (*pyār-maḥabbat*). Imran Ali's use of fictive kinship—being treated like a son—highlights the custodianship implicit in control over a child as one who cannot provide for one's self and thus must be cared for by others. These everyday acts of giving are thus not reciprocal exchanges among equals. As with food exchanges, these exchanges were organized such that low- or noncaste groups could receive food from upper-caste groups but not give to those same groups (Marriott 1968; Marriott and Inden 1977). Similarly, upper-caste groups gave and received only from the same or equivalent castes and only gave to but did not take from lower-caste groups. Reciprocal exchanges happened among those of the same or equivalent castes, while nonreciprocal exchanges occurred among those of different or unequal castes. Reciprocity (or lack thereof) was a means for organizing caste hierarchy.

Unidirectional giving demonstrates that acts of love and care enact affective relationships among intimates who are not considered equals. And while the municipality regularly deployed the phrase "Cleanliness fulfills half of one's faith," to emphasize that waste workers provide a religiously invaluable service to the city, workers themselves emphasized that they are not accorded the necessary value (*qadr*), importance (*ah-miyat*), or respect (*'izzat*). Christian sanitation workers also repeatedly emphasized that residents, especially Muslim ones, have nothing but hate (*nafrat*) for them. One resident, commenting about a waste worker in his neighborhood, spoke of the shame (*sharam*) he feels when arguing over uncollected waste with such "a poor [*maṛā*] person." It was the presumed "lowliness" of workers that caused this resident such shame about the relation they both found themselves in. That shame, not to mention unidirectional acts of love and care, affectively binds intimates, thereby maintaining uneven relations among them.

Material Relations of Waste Work

Soon after coming to Lahore in the early 1990s, Manzoor and his kin started collecting waste from two localities known as Township and Shadman (see Figure 4.1 and Map 0.2). These localities are closer to the

FIGURE 4.1. *A neighborhood in Lahore, Pakistan, where waste workers collect refuse. Source: Author.*

center of the city, consist of two- or three-story residential structures, are made up of mainly middle- and upper-middle-class households, and have regular municipal services and amenities. The valuables removed by Manzoor and his kin from households in these localities are brought back and stored in the cluster of five *jhuggīāṉ* (huts) that compose their household, which is in a settlement of *jhuggīāṉ* on the city's peripheries near an area known as Thokar Niaz Baig. While homes in this settlement are separated by mud paths littered with paper and plastic trash brought back from wealthier parts of the city, several piles of waste are also scattered about Manzoor's home (Figure 4.2). As described in the previous chapter, these piles are rigorously sorted before being sold to *kabāṛīāṉ* and *biopārīāṉ*, who are located nearby or regularly visit these settlements. Moreover, the next chapter unpacks, in detail, the shifting forms of settlement, work, and life that workers and their kin have experienced across generations, as they have migrated and settled on Lahore's urbanizing peripheries and found a source of livelihood in waste work. However, what needs to be emphasized, at this point at least, is how waste work is crucial in reproducing spatial and material relations that suture together Lahore's unevenly urbanizing landscape.

In July 2015, right before the onset of the monsoon, I visited Manzoor while he and his extended kin repaired the *jhuggīāṉ* that made up their household. The wooden frames of the *jhuggīāṉ* had worn away. In repairing them, the eroded pieces of wood were pushed farther down into a crater while fresher pieces were tied to the eroded ones—this combination of eroded and fresh pillars would stabilize the *jhuggī*. These fresh pillars were prepared from reused wood that had been salvaged or were purchased second-hand. Once the poles of the frame had been prepared, they reused broken bricks, which had been acquired from neighborhood's construction waste or brought from a dealer, to build a slight embankment. Because the *jhuggī* is on a downward slope, Manzoor explained to me, this embankment would prevent rainwater from entering their home. And later that afternoon, their effort would shift to the structure's roof. Pieces of bamboo, being relatively thinner and more flexible, were placed horizontally and vertically to create a skeleton on which the roofing was placed. As some female kin cut pieces of old cloth into strips,

FIGURE 4.2. *Piles of waste in a* jhuggī. *Source: Author.*

FIGURE 4.3. *Strips of old cloth fastened to pieces of wood form the structure of a residential* jhuggī. *Source: Author.*

which were used to fasten the bamboo pieces into place (see Figure 4.3), Manzoor's wife explained, "These are old sheets that households gave us." They used several of these bedsheets for the roof, in which layers of cloth were wrapped in clear, plastic lining to prevent water from trickling in. Similarly, in another settlement, waste workers who predominantly collect cardboard waste repurposed those materials by stapling them together and wrapping them in plastic to construct their roofs.

As they performed these repairs, all the items one expects of a household were on display—several beds (*mañjī*); bedsheets and blankets; pans, dishes, and other crockery; storage containers full of clothing; and any number of valuable items (e.g., family pictures). This display of wealth was unsurprising: Manzoor regularly described waste materials as his *bachat* (profit, remainder, excess) and waste work as his *rizq* (means of subsistence). It was through the worth of waste materials and the work surrounding them that this *jhuggī* was repaired, maintained, and reproduced in a particular way.

The *jhuggī* in which Manzoor resides and the middle-class homes from which he and his kin collect waste are differentiated by construction materials, household commodities, perceived cleanliness, occupation, and wealth, and any number of other asymmetrical markers of difference. Though appearing as separate, the quotidian construction and repair of these *jhuggīāṉ*, and all the items that make them up, demonstrate their actual dependence on one another. Not only does removing waste ensure the cleanliness or tidiness of one household, it also facilitates the building, maintenance, and reproduction of another as different in urban Pakistan. The social and spatial differentiation—through households, occupations, and lifestyles of the middle classes and those of waste workers—clarifies how both groups mutually, though unequally, depend on each other. If waste workers receive and take away waste, money, and any number of other things, households receive something else, an intimate space cleansed of dirt, filth, and all kinds of substances—something that then gets attached to the bodies and persons who compose these classes. The organization of public spaces in urban Pakistan along the lines of caste, class, and religion are reflected in more private spaces and forms of life. The affective and material relationships sketched out so far thus extend beyond the shared intimacies between or among groups; they come to permeate an intimate aspect of one's own life.

Surrounded by piles of waste, Manzoor, with an odd mix of disgust and humor, caught me off guard when he chuckled and said, "After living in germs for so long, we've become germs ourselves." During that same conversation, Manzoor drew my attention to the flies circling about the piles of waste and the dirt (*miṭṭī*) and dust (*khāk*) spread about, while describing how the paths between *jhuggīāṉ* turn into a sludge of trash and mud (*kīchaṛ*) during the monsoon. In light of Michael Herzfeld's (2005) suggestion that intimate components of one's life (e.g., home, behaviors, work) can become a source of embarrassment when addressed to an Other, I initially interpreted such statements as being addressed to me as a Pakistani American of a different class and caste background. Yet Manzoor's expression of disgust, tinged with humor, indicates a "psychophysical response of a subject whose virtual wholeness is threatened by holes" (Reno 2016, 40; see also Kristeva 1982; Millar 2018, 56). Since bodies are porous (Douglas 2002), things like germs and substances like mud take on biomoral valences because they can move between bodies and thus shape both one's insides and physical surroundings: Manzoor was prone to mention how his own disposition and that of his progeny (*nasl*) have changed since they migrated to the city, began as waste workers, and took up residence in this settlement of *jhuggīān*. One's own body, as well as that of one's kin, was susceptible to the transmission of substances attached to these materials, which could later have transformative effects on one's own and others' dispositions, behaviors, and status.

Manzoor's narrative reveals an important tension surrounding waste materials and work by bringing into relief how working with waste materials raises concerns around transformations—in materials, bodies, and persons. When mentioning germs as potentially stigmatizing things, Manzoor deployed a register of purity and pollution, making waste into something that attaches to and potentially transforms some bodies and persons, but not others. At the same time, Manzoor repeatedly mentioned those aspects of one's self and status, such as occupation, education, wealth, lifestyles, and behaviors, that would be considered class-based markers of distinction. The possibility of waste materials to transfer monetary worth through work and exchange is difficult to disentangle from their potential to transmit contaminating and polluting substances. Both transformations are possible when working with waste materials, which necessitates constant negotiations and management between one's self and others within a shared but uneven world.

Maintaining Separation and Distance

Being embedded in relations of work and exchange organized around commodity production, waste materials and work present contradictory possibilities for transforming one's self and others—one can be stigmatized through these materials, just as much as one can generate wealth through them (Nguyen 2016; see also Millar 2018, 53–59). These contradictory possibilities are most conspicuous for junkyard owners (*kabāṛīān*) who putatively trade in, rather than gather, waste materials. As described in the previous chapter, Chaudhary Billah transitioned from being a waste worker to being a *kabārī*, which was accompanied by a moment of accumulation that allowed him to buy and sell waste materials in larger amounts and at a quicker pace. I only became aware of this transition because of how he narrated his trajectory from waste worker to *kabārī*. He began by describing how higher-status groups from the area he was from (Shakargarh) became successful junkyard owners and intermediaries because they controlled transportation infrastructure, specifically horse-drawn carts (*tāngah*) used to transport goods such as lentils, rice, and sugar (jaggery). This group used its access to transportation to establish a foothold in the informal recycling of paper. When chronicling the success of higher-status groups, Chaudhary Billah mentioned that his own family were Gujjars, who are traditionally known as pastoralists who tend cattle across North India. In telling me this, he meant to highlight that he lacked access to those resources, which would have eased his trajectory of becoming a *kabārī*. Rather, he entered this line of work through working with the materials themselves.

Settling in an area of Lahore known as Icchra closer to the traditional center of the city with an estranged brother, Chaudhary Billah first found work transporting iron rods in Badami Bagh—an industrial hub of the city at the time (see Map 0.2). Near his brother's home was a junkyard owned by a neighbor who would eventually become a good friend. When this friend asked Chaudhary Billah to join him at the junkyard, he refused, telling me, "I had a lot of hate for this work" (Bahut nafrat thī iss kām se). Eventually overcoming his discomfort, Chaudhary Billah started sorting and disassembling waste in his friend's junkyard, and after a brief stint in a junkyard elsewhere, he returned to his friend's, where he remained for the next several years. At one point, the two friends opened a factory (*kārkhānah*) that manufactured pellets out of recycled plastics, but the venture failed. He would at times show me a book of carbon-copied receipts of the plastics they had purchased—the name of the plastic, date of purchase, weight, rate, and total value.

This moment was one in which Chaudhary Billah was transitioning from working with waste materials to trading in them. His closeness to these materials, for which he initially had only "a lot of hate," was starting to dissipate, and his own self-understanding was changing.

FIGURE 4.4. *A junkyard owner sits in his junkyard with mostly sorted paper waste in front of him. Source: Author.*

With an influx of money, the source of which he equivocated about, he said, "I was becoming a wealthy figure [*seṭh*], and all I do now is sit all day" (see Figure 4.4). Rather than disappear, the hate he previously had for this work has turned into ambivalence: during other conversations, Chaudhary Billah often lamented that he had to do "dirty work," even if it was more profitable than other kinds of business. Chaudhary Billah has not experienced the kind of upward mobility that would propel him into Lahore's middle or upper classes, but becoming a *kabāṛī* has afforded him the opportunity to generate income out of waste materials from a distance. This same distance then allows Chaudhary Billah to maintain a separation between himself and others who work with waste materials in closer proximity. Here, distancing within intimacy is also constituted through acts of self-distancing.

Though physical distance from working with these materials was growing for Chaudhary Billah, other kinds of proximity were emerging. Throughout this time, Chaudhary Billah shifted from his brother's home to an area in the southwestern edges of Lahore, where these settlements were also being shifted. Since then, for nearly the next two decades, the location of his junkyard would shift along with this settlement: as these settlements are forcibly and repeatedly removed by the municipal government and private housing settlements, they have slowly been pushed to their current location on the city's peripheries, which is a similar trajectory among junkyards that need regular access to waste materials. Not only is Chaudhary Billah's junkyard now situated at the end of a *pakkā* (paved) road that changes into a *kacchā* (unpaved) one that snakes throughout the settlement of *jhuggīān*, he has built a two-story, permanent house in this settlement, located only a few doors down from the space he rents for the junkyard. Though located nearby, Chaudhary Billah's permanent home (*pakkā ghar*) is, materially and socially, differentiated from Manzoor's *jhuggī*, which would usually be described as a "slum" or informal housing (*kacchī ābādī*). Since the early 1990s, Chaudhary Billah's livelihood, like that of others who supply these materials to industrial and manufacturing units across the country, has become increasingly entangled both with waste materials themselves and those who reside in settlements such as these. As such, junkyards, settlements, factories, and middle- and upper-middle-class homes have formed symbiotic relationships as urbanization has proceeded in Lahore, and it is waste materials and work that link these distinct actors across the urban landscape.

Because of these entanglements—of proximal settlement and shared work—Chaudhary Billah, like many others, regularly commented on the moral qualities and lifestyles of waste workers: sharing stories of women engaging in sex work or the prevalence of drug and alcohol abuse among young men. This commentary was also part of his own self-narration: Chaudhary Billah was emphasizing qualities of character and lifestyles—either one's own or that of others—to thematize a "gradual process of transformation" of the self in relation to waste, work, and a world of others (Millar 2018, 59). The story through which Chaudhary Billah narrated his trajectory into this line of work was not a straightforward one about how he became a *kabāṛī*. Rather, it was one that highlights the kinds of distancing at play within intimacies fraught by an unevenness from the onset. Specifically, Chaudhary Billah distinguished between those who either temporarily work or only trade in waste, being of higher status, and those who actually collect waste, being expectedly of lower status. That distinction needed to be maintained precisely because it could be cast into doubt: Manzoor repeatedly insinuated that Chaudhary Billah came from another lower-status group known as Telī, or oil pressers. Manzoor's allegations were meant to be revelatory—Chaudhary Billah, though he claims higher status and has accumulated wealth, is by birth no different from the waste workers from whom he distances himself. Regardless, Chaudhary Billah's narration of his own trajectory into this line of work is fraught by ambivalences characteristic of intimacies, in which neither autonomy nor dependence could be fully acknowledged in relation to waste work and others with whom he shares his world.

Shifting Limits

Sharika Thiranagama (2018, 358, 359) has recently described how interethnic and intracaste relations in postwar Jaffna, Sri Lanka, "are forged through recent histories of violence and struggle," which are discernible "through the concrete problems of co-existence (living together with some measure of engagement) and co-presence (living together separately)." The social relations analyzed so far have been intercaste and interclass ones, since these groups share an ethnic background (i.e., Punjabi). Though I have analyzed the kinds of engagements and separations at play across caste and class lines, I have not yet examined the associations between caste and religion and how they have reorganized social relations. Christians in Pakistan, whether engaging in waste work or not, are assumed to have a "lowly" caste background, while Christianity as a confessional community has not made caste irrelevant. Christians in India "identify themselves in terms of caste" (Caplan 1980, 215) in several different ways (see also Mosse 2012). And as Christians have experienced violence, social discrimination, and legal challenges, associations between religion and caste have only sedimented further among them. Such events now saturate collective life in the country, for Muslims and Christians alike, and raise the specter of how violence, conflict, and other kinds of antagonisms act recursively in relation to the waste intimacies described thus far. Next, I discuss associations between caste and religion to highlight two dynamics: first, how intercaste and interreligious relations are being reshaped in urban Pakistan, and second, how events in the country's recent history have delimited the parameters of individual and collective life in Lahore.

Early one morning in a prominent cloth market in the city, the tea seller (*chaiwālā*) arrived to take away empty mugs that sanitation workers, supervisors, a security guard (*chaukīdār*), and myself had used to drink chai. Before returning to his tea stall, however, the *chaiwālā* informed everyone seated there that Christians should bring their own mugs. Later, I returned to ask Arshad, who was the security guard, about this. "You see, they are non-Muslim [*ghair*-Muslim]," he said. "We don't get along. Before, the *chaiwālā* probably didn't know. Someone must have told him that the security guard who takes the chai away drinks it with Christians." When I replied that there is no prohibition against eating with Christians in Islam, Arshad recognized my point but added a qualification: "For people of the book [*ahl-e kitāb*], if our heart lets us, sure, but if we don't feel like it, it is acceptable [*wājib*] for us not to eat with them. We do not get along because they are nonbelievers [*ghair-mazhab*] and we are believers." Sensing my discomfort, he noted that nothing could be done to them by force (*zabardastī*) but remained steadfast that there was a real quarrel over religion—Islamic beliefs and practices need to be upheld and protected from perceived attacks, while love for the Prophet required Muslims to not tolerate any insult against his personality and honor.[7] Even here, distinctions between Muslims and Christians as religious communities are organized through practices of commensality, in which idioms of hierarchy and purity figure prominently.

Then, Arshad shifted suddenly:

> We don't do any of this. ... We curse at them when inviting them to sit with us to eat, and they do the same with us. There's no difference remaining between us. We are all mixed up with each other. Sitting together, cursing at each other. If we go toward Adam, then we are one. If we go toward the command of the Prophet [*hukm-e nabī*], we are separate.

This is a recognized difference between commonality of descent and differences of faith. Additionally, unlike the vast majority who hate (*nafrat*) sanitation workers because of their impurity and inability to become pure (*pāk*), Arshad emphasized that he and others who work closely with them have a different view. "We also see that they put their hands in filth, open drains, and all kinds of dirty things," he said. "So then we say, 'It's OK, *yaar*, at least they wash their hands.' They eat with these same hands, and we sit and eat with them. We eat from their dishes."

He used this point to tell me a story:

> I had a friend, William, and we worked in the same soap factory. I was the only one who ate lunch with him in the canteen. Then I would go to his home, and his mother would give me food in their dishes, and I never said anything. But there were others in their neighborhood who objected by saying, "Why does he come to their home? He's Muslim." You see, every neighborhood or people has its own mind-set about how to behave with one another.

Arshad added, "Their elders wouldn't joke with us, and our elders wouldn't joke with them either. Then, only 10 percent of Muslims wouldn't object to sitting with them, while the remaining 90 percent wouldn't sit with them, keeping a distance." Arshad's own account arose out of the shifting associations between caste and religion and subsequent changes in inter-caste and interreligious relations. He recognized that the form of related-ness between Muslims and Christians had shifted, and that earlier kinds of distances based on hierarchical caste relations had been rendered less clear. This, however, had not undone separations but given rise to kinds of engagement that reinscribed relations across caste and religious lines, re-lations that Arshad described as more egalitarian. These changing inter-caste and interreligious relations were caught "between hierarchical and egalitarian logics," producing "hierarchically segmented forms of civility" (Thiranagama 2018, 359). Indeed, before trailing off, Arshad commented, "We say, 'Forget about it, *yaar* Allah is the provider. He tells us to treat others such that others will not ridicule either you or your religion.'" This was a call to maintain engagement across caste and religious lines, even if separation was at times necessitated.

Walking away, I came upon Tariq, the sanitation worker who had drunk with us earlier. Seeing me, he said, "You see how they hate us? This is our value here [in Pakistan]. This is why other countries are better than ours." And then he asked me, "What did you learn?" I recounted Arshad's words, and Tariq assured me, "Yes, this is exactly how it is. ... This is a problem of religion, not work. Or this could be about the work too. If we weren't here, would they do this work, or no? *Yaar*, what are we going to do?" I asked, "Why did you remain silent when we were talking?" Tariq replied, "I don't even sit then, because there will be a disagreement. What's the point? It's better to remain silent. Their thinking won't change. They are small-minded folk. I told you this before. You must have written it down." In this moment, Tariq inverted the relationship: though these people think they are above us, they are in reality "small-minded." Tariq continued, though:

> We don't talk to anyone about religion. Otherwise, there will be a disagreement, and if I say any wrong words, something unexpected will come from those wrong words. You must've heard that sometimes a Christian is labeled a blasphemer [*gustākh-e rasūl*], then a case is registered against them, and they are sentenced to death by hanging. This is an Islamic country. They have power in it. We don't.

Throughout these exchanges, constant slippages are noticeable between religion and caste, person and work, commonality of descent and differences of faith, and Christian and sanitation worker. These slippages are premised on an association between religion and caste, and this allows for the stigma of waste to travel beyond the space of work itself and attach to "Christian" as a category of person who is non-Muslim.

These slippages were also discernible among waste workers from the informal sector who were predominantly Muslim. For instance, when asked about changing attitudes (*ravveyah*) of people since he started doing this work, Manzoor emphasized "Most households don't think we are impure [*palīd*]. They know we are all Muslims [*Muslimeen*]." When I pushed Manzoor on this issue, noting that Christians also worked hard and it has no bearing upon religion, Manzoor recognized my point but elaborated upon it with an anecdote of his own. A few years back, when a person, whose household had recently settled in the locality where Manzoor worked, was distributing rations during Ramzan, Manzoor was asked by them to recite the third *kalmah* (testament) as proof of his

Islamic faith, which would make him, in the eyes of the household, deserving of the charity. Making a related point, Allah Ditta emphasized households do not see them as impure since they do not work with human waste—that is, they did not perform work like unclogging gutters and drains—and most of their work is with garbage (*kūṛā kirkaṭ*). Although also differentiating himself from Christians, Allah Ditta made the additional point that Christian sanitation workers no longer work with human waste, as most of their work entails sweeping, while admitting that those who clean sewers and gutters remain exclusively Christian in Lahore.

Whereas such slippages between caste, religion, and work were discernible among many of those who I conducted fieldwork with, Tariq's use of the phrase "You must have heard" gestures to how caste informs a central and pressing political issue facing contemporary Pakistan: accusations of blasphemy and ensuing violent events that have repeatedly taken place all over country and how such collective events are imbricated with the denial of commensality among those having chai that morning.[8] His inability to object in that moment, because of what could possibly ensue, recognized that events in collective life were being recursively reproduced within everyday interactions, shifting the grounds on which intercaste and interreligious relations are formed. Intimacy undoubtedly "links the instability of individual lives to the trajectories of the collective" (Berlant 1998, 283), but in doing so, it places certain limits on the forms of relatedness in which many find themselves in urban Pakistan today. The complex set of affects described across this article—from shame, care, and embarrassment to hate, love, and powerlessness—illuminate the changing limits of intercaste and interreligious relations in urban Pakistan, where such relations have become sites of antagonism, conflict, and violence.

The Unevenness of Intimacy

Over the past several decades, waste work as a social and political relationship has been organized to constitute an infrastructure of urban life. The notion of infrastructures, as socio-technical assemblages, draws attention to how disparate actors, relations, and processes are brought together, however tenuously, in producing something distinct from and greater than their constitutive elements—that is, the reproduction of life itself. Unlike previous chapters, which have looked at these infrastructures in relation to the bureaucratic state and informal economies, this chapter has laid bare the work these infrastructures perform in shaping forms of relatedness—affective, material, spatial—that sutured together life in an unevenly urbanizing landscape in Pakistan. Along with the fact that they allow for collective life to go on in a city like Lahore, an attentiveness to their everyday workings reveals the symbiosis between waste and urban life. As Joshua Reno has amply made clear, waste work enacts a "constitutive absence" (2016, 7), taking away discarded or exhausted things from certain spaces (e.g., a middle-class household) that are then made present elsewhere (e.g., a *jhuggī* or dumping ground). These infrastructures, at the center of which is the work performed predominantly by low- or noncaste groups, distribute waste unevenly across the social body in urban Pakistan, differentiating particular bodies, persons, and spaces along the way. In other words, the social and spatial differentiation one sees in Pakistani cities is a historical product of how waste gets distributed and, importantly, by whom.

Caste-based identities direct multiple, intersecting distributive processes, only one of which is the movement of waste across Lahore's urban landscape. The next chapter traces out histories of settlement, work, and life that have shaped the intergenerational trajectories of waste workers and their kin, especially as they have come to reside on Lahore's urbanizing peripheries. And, as made clear earlier, higher-status Muslim groups, with control over land in the countryside and access to other forms of capital, have been able to situate themselves in Lahore's middle and upper classes. Lastly, it should also be kept in mind that Christian communities in Lahore and across Pakistan are internally differentiated along lines of caste and class. The waste intimacies traced out above were meant to highlight how distributive processes inform the forms of relatedness as they have emerged in urban Pakistan. The disparate degrees of proximity and distance between waste and persons produce the mutuality and interdependence required for social life, where actors—waste workers, households, junkyard owners, intermediaries—are all differentially situated. These intimacies importantly foreground the symbiotic constitution of waste and urban life, such that one can critically reexamine the historical inequalities and interdependencies undergirding both.

As a social relation, intimacy is a constant source of ambivalence. This ambivalence is usually chalked up to attachments to something else (e.g., unrequited love or a naive vision of the good life), attachments that are problematic yet formative for the self and other. What such renderings of intimacy misrecognize is how ambivalences ensuing from intimacy grow directly out of the very conditions that make intimacy possible. Intimacies across historical moments have been consistently organized around different forms of inequality. Waste intimacies draw our attention to the diverse forms of work, social relations, and affects through which life, both public and private, is made possible and reproduced in uneven ways, while emphasizing the antinomies of autonomy and dependence as they emerge through waste work as a social and political relationship. By being attentive to those ambivalences, we can begin to discern the unevenness on which intimacy is built and, eventually, the grounds on which we, like many others, come to stand. These grounds, however, are faulty, causing those who stand on them to be unhinged and in constant search of finding their footing in those social relations presumed to anchor them. We gain much by attuning ourselves to the unevenness of life built on such intimacies—life in which actors constantly come up against the antinomies of autonomy and dependence while navigating their own sense of self in an unequal world shared with others.

CHAPTER 5

THE POSSIBILITY OF REPRODUCTION

IN THE EARLY DAYS of my fieldwork, a municipal worker, who would retire in the coming months, emphasized to me that this job—sanitation work—is not like a field (*pailī*) that can be inherited and used for cultivation. Though municipal employment is inherited across generations, this worker was pointing out the fact that waste work is not a tangible asset that can be potentially passed down to future generations, in the way that a field used for cultivation can be. Using such an idiom—a field for cultivation—is unsurprising as many waste workers in Lahore have migrated to the city from more agrarian parts of Punjab. At this point, we can also return to the statement made by Rameez mentioned in the Introduction: "A home should be one's own, even if it's a straw hut" (ghar āpṇā hove, bhaven kakhāṉ dī kullī hove). And as should be clear by now, the *jhuggiāṉ* (huts) settlements that are the home of many informal workers are socially marked and stigmatized, something that has facilitated and legitimatized their dispossession and removal by public authorities and private entities. These statements and experiences foreground the centrality of the home as a primary site of social reproduction for waste workers and their kin across generations and, as such, is implicated in a wider set of transformations in work, settlement, and life.

The homes of municipal workers like Rameez, whether owned or rented, were permanent houses (*pakā makān*) constructed over many years, while the homes of informal workers like Allah Ditta were almost always *jhuggīān* that had been placed on either governmental or private land and remained ephemeral structures. The Urdu and Punjabi word for home (*ghar*) is differentiated from the word for house (*makān*) by virtue of the fact that the latter references specifically a constructed building while the former includes a broader "sense of physical as well as social and inter-personal space" (Mughal 2015, 220). The home is a material and conceptual entity, which, in its internal organization and external façade, expresses and materializes historical transformations in social orders and hierarchies.[1] This is why, most if not all the workers I came to know underscored relationships among the lands upon which they have been settled, the homes in which they have resided, and the work they have performed, and how those relationships have shifted and been transformed over time.

These shifting relationships among waste workers and their kin bring into relief how "the presence of the past" and the "presence of the future" are mutually, though uncertainly, imbricated in making and reproducing life across generations (see Koselleck 2004). The efforts of waste workers and their kin described below highlight two distinct but interconnected scales of reproduction: one being the reproduction of intergenerational life and the other being the reproduction of collective life. For these reasons, social reproduction, as the ways in which inequalities are differentially inherited across generations, is intertwined with the reproductive nature of waste work itself. Organized as it is around the production of waste materials that result from the consumption of disposable commodities taking place on a mass scale, waste work in urban Pakistan, as in many other parts of the world today, has become bureaucratized and coordinated through institutions, infrastructures, and work regimes that are aimed at sustaining the collective life of cities. Delineating linkages between social reproduction and the reproductive nature of waste work is meant to highlight how historical inequalities and interdependencies have been materialized, though in a transformed state on Pakistan's urbanizing peripheries.

Life on an Urbanizing Periphery

The homes and settlements in which waste workers reside could easily be subsumed within the "global array of cities of disposal" (Appadurai 2013, 125). The disposability[2] of things, spaces, bodies, and persons would guide my initial forays into the homes and settlements of waste workers as well. For instance, as highlighted in earlier chapters, *jhuggīān* settlements were spaces where waste materials are not only accumulated, sorted, and exchanged but are also used to construct the built environment itself. An attentiveness to disposability allowed me to trace how homes and settlements such as these are as constitutive of the city's waste infrastructures, as containers, garbage compactors, empty plots of land, and dumping grounds are. Inversely, that same approach deemed the homes and settlements of others like Rameez less relevant: though they also sort valuables out of waste materials to sell to junkyards, rarely are these materials brought back to their homes, usually being sold daily or deposited in junkyards, and the homes themselves are more permanent structures. Not only were these respective homes and settlements distinct in terms of physical properties and legal statuses, but divisions between work and life were also seemingly drawn differently for municipal and informal workers—the latter brought back waste to their homes, while the former did not. However, by foregrounding waste materials and the work surrounding them, a framework of disposability obscured, first, shifts in land, settlement, and work that have shaped the intergenerational trajectories of waste workers and their kin, and second, transformations in historical inequalities and interdependencies upon which collective life in Lahore has come to be reorganized.

Many waste workers reside in settlements that are or were once *kachchī abādīs*. In Pakistan and across South Asia, *kachchī abādī* is a term used in both planning and everyday discourses to refer to a broad range of settlements in which land tenure is uncertain, access to services and infrastructures is precarious, and inhabitants are quite often migrants employed in informal work (see Qadeer 1983; Hasan 2010, 2015; Hasan and Arif 2018). Though the term entered official discourse in the late 1960s, *kachchī abādīs* themselves started proliferating on a greater scale from the 1980s onward as the city's populations steadily increased—this being the same period when many workers I came to know started settling in Lahore. In the early 2000s, during the regime of General Pervez Musharraf, both military and civilian state institutions initiated a process of class-based development across urban Pakistan, or what has been usually referred to as "world-class city making," by promoting the construction of private housing settlements for middle and upper-middle classes, as well as the Pakistani diaspora. The development of housing, in particular, has been facilitated by changed legal mechanisms through which land can be acquired and sold, and has made real estate developers, property dealers, nongovernmental organizations, landowners, criminal gangs, political parties, and state officials into prominent actors in land and real estate markets across the country—all of which has brought unparalleled speculation in real estate, sharp spikes in the price of land, and varying degrees of exploitation (Javed and Riaz 2020, 137; Hasan 2010; Anwar 2012; Rahman 2022; Tassadiq 2022). As noted earlier, there has been minimal support by the Pakistani state for affordable housing directed toward the urban poor and working-class communities, which has meant they have been largely excluded from land ownership and compelled to access land and housing through other means and strategies.

Over the past several decades, the urban peripheries in Lahore have emerged out of "agrarian-urban transformations," where a range of coercive techniques (e.g., devalorization, dispossession, or violence) has reshaped agrarian uses of land and forms of work and life, while land itself has become a site for renewed value struggles—for instance, the extraction of surplus-value through rent has required land that was previously a means of subsistence be put to use as real estate.[3] As a result, a feature of the urban peripheries, in Lahore and elsewhere, has been how "discrepant land uses sit side by side in oscillating spirals of ascension and decline, where it is difficult to discern just where things are headed" (Simone 2019, 991). The urban peripheries form a patchy palimpsest, where agriculture, commerce, and industry are overlain with one another, housing societies and informal settlements vie for land, and the machinations of state institutions, real estate markets, and property dealers conceal the dynamic, if exploitative, processes wrought by agrarian-urban transformations. The world inhabited by waste workers is one that takes shape in the shadows of such transformations, where workers must navigate the uncertainties that come with living on an urbanizing periphery.

For waste workers, these uncertainties were fundamentally about the reproduction of a present life that could then make possible a future one.[4] Thus, this chapter unpacks three discrete kinds of efforts aimed at reproducing life on the urban peripheries: settling on land, building and maintaining a home, and exhausting one's self through work. These efforts exhibit a shared expectational quality,[5] which grounds them in the present but orients them toward a possible future. Waste workers constantly negotiate expectations for and threats to their futures in the present—as I show, dispossession, uncertainty, and precarity create "an eternal present-tense" because their worlds could "at any moment disappear, making everything familiar strange" (Harms 2013, 15). Yet it is not only an existing present or potential future that is at stake here. As Maura Finkelstein has suggested about urban landscapes saturated by dominant narratives of development and progress, especially ones in which class-based dynamics intersect with ethnicity and caste, "the nostalgia of perceived past stability" becomes a technique for negotiating expectations for the future when confronted by numerous kinds of uncertainties and displacements (2019, 87). Waste workers' relationship to the past was not a nostalgic one, though they did at times speak of the past as a time of abundance; rather, they experienced the past as transitory moments, from older forms of settlement, work, and life into more contemporary ones. They recognized the presence of the past, both for one's self and one's kin, but with the expectation of transcending it. Here, their experiences and expectations converge, though awkwardly, with not only dominant narratives seeking to legitimate Lahore's class-based development but also agrarian-urban transformations taking place on the city's peripheries. Nevertheless, because of specific kinds of inheritances, ambivalences came to mark waste workers' relationship to past, as well as their expectations for the future in the present.

Waste workers come from low- or noncaste groups that have historically been landless labor in the Punjabi countryside, working under variety of relations—from servitude to tenant farming to wage labor— with landowning groups from higher-caste backgrounds. Previous forms of settlement, work, and life operate as specific kinds of inheritances that shape the intergenerational trajectories of waste workers and their wider kin networks.[6] In that sense, waste work, though certainly stigmatizing and marginalizing, is just one inheritance among many for those who come from low- or noncaste groups in the Punjab. After examining how forms of settlement, work, and life have shifted and their consequences for waste workers, this chapter then moves away from these intergenerational shifts to focus on the exhaustion of working bodies. This form of work or labor—waste work—is reproductive and thus operates at the spatiotemporal scales mentioned earlier: reproducing intergenerational life across kin and collective life across the city. All this reproductive work, however, eviscerates, in specific ways, the bodies of workers themselves, not to mention potentially those of their kin (see Berlant 2007; see also Corwin and Gidwani 2021). Operating at the confluences of work and life, the exhaustion experienced by waste workers comes to be rendered "ordinary," understood as "the local spacing of eventfulness," shaping their expectations of possible futures in the present (Povinelli 2011, 133; see also Das 2006). This unfolding of events—some past or ongoing and others still yet to come or barely discernible—must be situated within how urban life has come to be differentiated across Pakistan. The reason for doing so is to register the extent to which reproduction—of Lahore, of communities, of individuals—has and continues to depend upon forms of life, and the caste-based relations upon which they have been built, being transformed through processes of urbanization.

Settlement, Work, Life

During a visit to Rameez's home, we were sitting in one of the two rooms that were being built on the second floor. Construction tools and materials lied strewn about, and two men—one elderly and the other young— were working on a flight of stairs outside that led from the terrace to the roof. The older man, who despite his age still moved swiftly, entered the room where Rameez and I were seated. He undid the tightly fitted cloth wrapped around his head, and then used it to wipe his face before draping it over his shoulder. Rameez introduced him, "This is my father [*vālid sāhib*]." Though Rameez had mentioned his father, whose name was Isaak

Barkat, over the years, we had never met before. I took this impromptu meeting as an opportunity to learn more about the family's past.

Their family was from a village in the district of Sheikhupura adjacent to Lahore. Prior to Partition, Christians and Muslims worked for prominent Sikh landowners in the village. "Christians and Muslims only became wealthy when the Sikhs left," Baba Isaak clarified, "They had nothing. They only received a portion [*hissah*] of what was cultivated and worked for the Sikhs." He estimated, "These landowners had over 60 *murabbe* (nearly 1500 acres) under their control and had 60 tenants on that land." This is unsurprising, as many low- or noncaste groups who had converted to Christianity were settled in Central Punjab and worked under Sikh and Muslim landowners, and after Partition, the landholdings of departing Sikhs (and Hindus at times) were often given over to Muslim migrants from eastern parts of Punjab that remained in India. Baba Isaak's kin, who were tenant farmers for Sikh landowners, found themselves in similar relations with Muslim ones after Partition. Their extended kin network engaged in agricultural work (*khetī bāṛī*) involving livestock: "At the time, we had almost 150 water buffalos and oxen," Rameez interjected, "They used the animals to plough the field. You know then, there weren't tractors." Baba Isaak went on, "The owners of the land would build a *kachchā makān* made of mud for workers on two or three acres [*killā*], telling them, 'Do my work.' We spent our days grazing animals [*dangar chārnā*] and ploughing the fields with ox-carts." They received portions (*hissah*) from whatever was produced during a particular season and, importantly, were settled on *shāmlāt zāmīn*.

In the Punjab *shāmlāt zāmīn* refers to "village common land" that was once "wasteland" that had been converted to "productive" usages. Historically, the owners of such lands were those individuals, as a collectivity, who were registered as settling a particular locality and who then designated a demarcated area *shāmlāt zāmīn*. This land could then either be allotted to others, who were not owners but had control over the land, or the original owners or those given rights of control could give out portions of this land to others for a range of uses and purposes. Though Baba Isaak's family kept animals on their land, *shāmlāt zāmīn* was also usually reserved for cremation grounds, masjids, *janāzāgāh* (sites for Muslim

funeral prayers), barbershops, and other services provided for those settled in the area. Many of those who were either settled on or utilized this
land were from nonlanded, service castes, who would be considered of
lower status. Much like Rameez's family, these groups were given rights
of access and use (i.e., working and living) but not those of ownership
and alienation.

In the 1960s Sheikhupura District, where their village was located, was
designated into an "industrially backward area" through the development
policy of Ayub Khan's government, and industrial units were built there,
as well in other areas "across the river Ravi adjacent to Lahore City" (Alvi
1997, 40). During this time, Baba Isaak, along with other male kin, started
working as a craftsman (*kārīgar*) making engines for different purposes
in the Ittefaq Factory in Shahdara, which is where Baba Isaak spent the
next twenty years of his life. When Baba Isaak described his entry into
industrial labor, he told me about his family's objections: "My father said
to me, 'You are the son of Chaudharys.[7] Your hands are in good shape.'
You see, my skin was fair, and we drank milk. He worried I'd stir things
up in the factory and get into a fight." His emphasis on hands, skin, diet,
and behavior (e.g., getting into a fight) was meant to highlight an agrarian form of settlement, work, and life, and how it was shifting, for Baba
Isaak and his kin, to industrial ones organized around the urban.

Then, in the late 1970s, the family moved to Lahore because their
kachchā makān in the village would be destroyed from flooding every few
years, especially since the piece of land they were settled was located near
the flood plain. They initially lived with Baba Isaak's in-laws in Lahore's
still rural peripheries, which were eventually developed into a part of the
Defence Housing Authority (see Map 0.2)—where his wife worked as
a domestic worker for many years. At this point, the role that gendered
relations have had in shaping these shifts in work and settlement should
also be underscored. Not only did Baba Isaak live with his wife's family (matrilocality), but she also contributed to the everyday workings of
their home as a domestic worker in the Defence Housing Authority as
a burgeoning locality. Indeed, resources such as access to land in Lahore's urbanizing landscape accompanied kin made or affirmed through
marriage, which would subsequently provide a degree of stability.

Nevertheless, though the wife's family did own the land upon which they resided, it was sold off unlawfully, resulting in the family not being compensated for the property. By using work allowances and benefits received after Baba Isaak retired from the factory, the family acquired a modest plot of land (5 *marle*, or 1,361.25 sq ft.) in the Green Town area of Lahore, which is a locality adjacent to Bāgṛiāṇ (where Rameez's family currently resides).

When the land was acquired in the late 1980s, Green Town was undeveloped, with the Pakistan Army owning much of the governmental land and other pieces of land being owned by prominent *birādarīs* in the area. The Catholic Church also had a substantial amount of land under their control in this area at the time, upon which a foreign priest started building homes for Christians. The Church allowed Christians to settle in the homes, who would then pay off the value of the land through small, minimal payments. Baba Isaak's family was settled in one such home. Importantly, this was a period when informal settlements were expanding rapidly across Lahore's landscapes, and despite a substantial lack of adequate housing, federal and provincial governments during this time started formulating and implementing policies and procedures aimed at regularizing such settlements (see Alvi 1997). Because of the formalization of their settlement, they attained property rights to this land before finishing their payments to the Church. The family resided in this home until they sold it in the early 2000s and the money was split among Rameez and his siblings, who then acquired their own plots of land upon which they built their own homes.

After retiring from the factory, Baba Isaak shifted to working as a *mistrī*,[8] mainly under a construction *ṭhekedār* (contractor), and became a daily wage (*dihāṛī*) earner. Over the years, he explained how he also had helped build homes for others, whether they were his own children, more distant kin (*rishtedār*), or other intimates (*'azīz*). Noting my eyes wandering toward the staircase under construction, Baba Isaak told me to go look at them. "Yes, I did," I responded, "They're great." Baba Isaak insisted, "But go look at least." We walked out onto the terrace. "Get out of the way," Baba Isaak instructed the young daily wage worker who was assisting him, and then turned to me, "Look at that. We've been working on this one since the morning. This is really difficult work. Get the materials [cement, sand, bricks], mix them, and build the stairs. And on top of that, I've also gotten old." Though we both chuckled, Rameez explained in a serious tone, "His lower back [*kamar*] is a big problem." Then, Baba Isaak emphasized, "Boys do not do this work nowadays. They run away." Baba Isaak had no experience with waste work like his son, Rameez. Instead, he spoke of transitioning from being settled as tenants on village common lands and performing agrarian work with animals outside Sheikhupura to finding employment in Punjab's industrializing centers, to coming to own land on Lahore's periphery while eventually engaging in daily wage work in the construction sector.

The intergenerational trajectory narrated by Allah Ditta reveals similar, though distinct shifts. Upon partition, the *birādarī* migrated to Okara from the Firozpur District in Punjab that would become part of India. "We came here, like Muhajirs. Here, we had no place to stay [*basīrā*]. No property or land," Allah Ditta explained, "We had everything there [in Firozpur]—property [*jā'īdād*], livestock [*māl dangar*], land [*zāmīn*]." Upon their arrival in Okara, the *birādarī* was settled on landholdings (*raqbā*) and worked as tenant farmers for landowners. They resided in a *kachchā makān* that offered them, in Allah Ditta's words, at least some protection (*āsrā*) from the elements. The agricultural work they performed involved the cultivation and harvesting of crops, rather than tending to and working with livestock (as was the case for Baba Isaak), and they also received portions (*hissah*) of whatever was being cultivated along with minimal wages. Just before Allah Ditta's birth, the extended family received a separate contract (*thekah*) to grow watermelons (*matīrā*) on a landholding of several acres. Harvesting watermelon at the end of a six-month season, they travelled and sold their goods to *arhtiyas* (commission agents) in various markets across the Punjab. Having seen his paternal side do this work, Allah Ditta described how the uncertainties that come with this kind of work—from dependence on credit for cultivation and everyday goods to unpredictable harvests caused by weather or lack of proper care—caused a shifted away from agrarian forms of settlement, work, and life.

It was his father's generation that shifted to waste work, which would also impact their settlement and life: "Leaving early in the mornings, he [Allah Ditta's father] would go from village to village, hawk junk throughout the day, and then, come home in the evening. And everyone since then, my paternal family established themselves in working with junk." Coming of age in the mid-1980s, Allah Ditta also started hawking junk along with others from his *birādarī* across Punjab. A person could only bike 20 to 30 kilometers away from their settlements, he told me, because, on the way back, they had the added weight of the junk they collected. Eventually after a few months, there would be nothing left to collect in that radius, so the entire family moved on to the next area, bringing the *jhuggī* and their belongings along with them. Before Allah Ditta migrated to Lahore, part of his extended family had settled in Faisalabad, where his father remained and opened his own scrap business.

When I asked Allah Ditta why he came to Lahore, he emphasized the family's inability to achieve prosperity (*khushālī*). "We came to Lahore trying to find any kind of work, or resources, so we can feed our children. This is what my elders said, 'Go to Lahore, Allah's generosity and mercy is there. It is the city of Data Hazur.'" So, recently married, Allah Ditta came to Lahore with his wife, and they settled with an uncle of his wife (who was also a distant kin of Allah Ditta) in an area known as Mustafa Town near the western edge of the city at the time (see Map 0.2). Similar to the intergenerational trajectory of Baba Isaak and Rameez, there was a degree of matrilocality being practiced by Allah Ditta following his marriage. This however only offered minimal stability in light of shifting forms of settlement within Lahore's unevenly urbanizing landscape. Or, as Allah Ditta described it, "We were there for about four or five years, and then, in 1999, they bulldozed us." Over the course of the next two decades, their extended kin network, like many in these informal settlements, has experienced a cyclic pattern of dispossession and resettlement, which became familiar through conversations and interviews.

They would be settled in an area that had not yet been developed—usually paying rent to the landowners through intermediaries—and as more *jhuggīān* would be placed and permanent homes, often middle-class ones, started construction, "property dealers" notified those residing in informal settlements that their *jhuggīāṉ* needed to be removed. Their removal was justified on the grounds that these *jhuggīāṉ* posed a public nuisance[9]—household items strewn out in the open, children and animals blocking thoroughfares, and noxious smoke from stoves lit by a mixture of wood and plastics. Then, property dealers would threaten them with forced removal, and when it did happen, that removal was usually described through acts of being "bulldozed," destroyed (*toṛ-poṛ*), beaten and thrashed (*mār-pīt*), and *jhuggīāṉ* being set ablaze (*jhuggīoṉ ko lagāte the*) in "operations" carried out by the Lahore Development Authority, the police, and/or other public authorities.

As mentioned earlier, speculative land and real estate markets have facilitated the exploitation of informal settlements and those who reside in them. For instance, in the early 2000s, an informal settlement started growing on land in the area of Multan Chungi that was previously being used to cultivate a variety of crops, especially corn and fodder. Upon seeing that the fields were unpopulated and not very profitable, a group of waste workers—some of whom were kin and others of whom were not—contacted the landowners after being dispossessed elsewhere. These landowners stopped cultivation, letting the group settle on the land, and started collecting enough rent to cover the financial cost of lost cultivation. It would be those settled in the area who removed crops and prepared the land by raising it to connect to nearby settlements and their infrastructures: "This land was very low, and we raised the land a lot," Manzoor explained, "You know, where our *jhuggī* is placed? I would say that we dumped twenty to thirty trolleys worth of *malbah* (construction waste) in that area." Levelling the land with the surrounding areas, they performed a service for landowners who would not have to take on the financial costs of preparing the land for its later sale and development. Moreover, landowners collect anywhere from 500 to 3,500 PKR per *jhuggī*, and with several thousand *jhuggīāṉ* in this settlement, the rent generated for landowners must be, as Manzoor and others regularly commented, in the hundreds of thousands, if not millions.

Caught in speculative and exploitative markets for land and real estate, Allah Ditta and his kin have been settled, dispossessed, and resettled in at least five different localities across Lahore's southwestern periphery. When we first met in 2014, they were located on a disputed piece of land, where one of the parties to the dispute had let them settle there as a way of preventing the other party from forcibly laying claim to the land (*qabẓah karnā*). They rented a piece of land that was enclosed by a brick wall and metal gate, inside of which were two *jhuggiāṉ* and a one-room structure with a ceiling fan, lighting, and basic furniture. When I returned in 2017, they still resided on that same disputed property but had shifted to a nearby *maidān* (open field) where a sea of *jhuggiāṉ* had been placed. Then, during another visit in 2019, the family had just been shifted once again after a complaint was made by the nearby housing society to the Lahore Development Authority, which carried out an "operation" to forcibly remove them. Describing their removal, Allah Ditta told me, "We piled our things in carts and rickshaws. It took us nearly four days to shift here." It would take them another month to fully rebuild the *jhuggī* itself. They purchased bricks, wood, and other materials for reconstruction, and though they did some of the work themselves, they had to hire a *mistrī* to strengthen the structure. They are now settled in an area just slightly further southeast of Bāgṛiāṉ where Rameez resides.

These intergenerational trajectories described by Baba Isaak, Rameez, and Allah Ditta reveal how previous forms of work and settlement shared among them have facilitated their disparate trajectories of settlement and work in the city. Specifically, they were engaged in agrarian forms of work and labor and settled on land that was not their own (i.e., common land or others' landholdings)—in both instances (work and settlement), they were dependent upon landowners. A striking feature of their narratives is the limited emphasis placed upon stigmatizing forms of work or labor such as "scavenging" or collecting "nightsoil." This of course is not to deny the significance of waste work to intergenerational life: kinship has been and continues to be instrumental to how waste work is accessed, while, across municipal and informal workers, one consistently finds individuals who are kin or entire kinship groups engaging in waste work. Moreover, though my own materials are limited due to less access to women, it is clear even in their narratives that gendered and sexual relations governing marriage, land, and work have been critical the reproduction of life, one's own and that of others. Though waste work has undeniable significance, shifts in forms of settlement, work, and life are expansive in nature and should not be overlooked when considering the migration and settlements of waste workers on Lahore's urbanizing peripheries.

Over the course of the past few decades, kin across generations have had to navigate, on the one hand, previous forms of settlement and work and, on the other, an unevenly urbanizing landscape. It is within such historical transformations that life, and the caste-based relations upon which it has been built, have been made possible and reproduced across these generations. As is probably evident by now, the home has become a primary locus for shifts in intergenerational life; what is less clear, however, is how indebtedness has been enfolded into those same lives.

Indebted Homes

Indebtedness has been an instrument for reproducing historical inequalities and interdependencies across Pakistan.[10] Similarly, waste workers described forms of indebtedness that have taken shape as intergenerational shifts in settlement, work, and life have occurred. Allah Ditta, for instance, described how, when cultivating watermelons on contractual land, his kin remained dependent upon credit (*udhār*) both for cultivation purposes and fulfilling everyday domestic needs, which tied them to landowners and shopkeepers (*kareānah kī dukān*) and motivated a generational shift to waste work. Others like Manzoor gained access to waste materials and work by taking on the debt of others who had themselves become indebted to junkyards. Other events, such as the death or illness of kin, caused entire families to descend into indebtedness that impacted one's own life and that of future generations. Conditions of indebtedness among waste workers and their kin participate in a condition of "fixity," in which the relations individuals and communities have to settlement and work become congealed in the making and maintenance of a home within and across generations (see Besky 2017). These conditions highlight how work and life have converged in ways that call into question any clear division between possibility and constraint, freedom and bondage, and care and exploitation.[11]

Waste workers used the English word "circuit" to describe the management of the home as a material and conceptual unit. Running the home's circuit requires the constant flow of money, goods, and other material things that ensure its everyday building and maintenance. Indebtedness thus becomes one key technique for guaranteeing that the circuit of the home continues smoothly and without interruption. The use of the word "circuit" to describe the home also gestures to its internal workings, in which it is not only the body of the waged worker that makes this circuit go on. Quite often, female workers, especially those employed by the municipality, were the primary householders, either because of the inability of a male kin to work or the pleasure that comes with working outside the home. In the case of Rameez, whose wife was not engaged in employment outside the home, the workings of this circuit flowed through her everyday effort, whether that was directed at care for children and other kin, receiving income for activities such as sewing and embroidery, or a whole host of obligation to kin and other intimates. The work or labor, whether paid or unpaid, was often insufficient to ensure that the circuit of the home ran smoothly and without too much interruption. Precisely for this reason, indebtedness became folded into the building and maintenance of the home.

Like other forms of exchange in which an obligation to return flows from what has been given, indebtedness is defined by "its ability to link the present to the past and future" (Peebles 2010, 226). The debt is created through the extension of credit, and it is completed once the debt has been paid off, but the temporality of those exchanges varies based on the terms of the debt itself (see Mauss 2000; Gregory 2012; see also Peebles 2010). Similarly, as a primary site of social reproduction, the home links a present state or condition of life to a potential moment in the future—either in one's own life or that of one's kin. Thus, what waste workers were drawing attention to in their repeated use of "circuit" was how a plurality and diversity of debts, each with their own temporal terms, are configured, through constant negotiation and adjustment, with the everyday workings of the home, which has its own rhythms and vicissitudes.

Soon after the initial plot of land upon which the extended family resided was sold, Rameez acquired another piece of land and started constructing an initial home through two loans. The Solid Waste Management Department assisted him in acquiring the first loan of 1.25 lakh, which required a gazetted officer to prepare a guarantee (*amānat*). "I got a stamp paper," Rameez explained, "The department verified [*taṣdīq kiyā*] the documents and stamped the paper. Only then did the bank pass my loan. It was from the National Bank of Pakistan because my salary comes through there. They would take their portion [approximately 2,000 PKR] before giving me the rest of my salary." Since this loan only covered a portion of the cost of the land, Rameez then took out another loan of 50,000 PKR out of compulsion (*majbūrī*) from a "dealer" who only gave out sizeable interest-based loans. In the first year, Rameez clarified, he only paid the interest (2,000 PKR), because he had been part of a "committee," which is a system of rotating credit where participants contribute a fixed amount of money and one participant each month receives the total amount being contributed. Upon receiving 60,000 PKR from the committee, Rameez put it toward the loan from the "dealer," paying off the heavily interested loan, though, in the end, he still ended up paying nearly 24,000 PKR in interest. The fragmented nature of indebtedness experienced by Rameez is quite common among the urban poor and working-class communities across South Asia, where individuals draw upon multiple sources of debt and credit in light of existing inequalities and interdependencies along caste, class, and gendered lines.[12]

These loans would be used to acquire the land, lay the foundation for the home, make it *chār-dīwārī*,[13] and create connections for access to water and electricity. In other words, this debt was transformed into credit that enabled Rameez to construct, in his words, a "*kachchā makān* with a wood roof"—akin to the straw hut he mentioned in our earlier conversation. Since public institutions such as WASA, LESCO, and Sui Gas only had constructed the main lines for utilities such as electricity, water, and gas, households extended water piping and electrical wiring of their own accord, so they could establish connections to these infrastructures. As described by Nikhil Anand (2017), connections are made with the cooperation and recognition on the part of public authorities, while also requiring employing plumbers, electricians, and other kinds of infrastructural workers. Even after making these, Rameez took out a loan for a few thousand rupees from a co-worker, for which the two prepared an agreement through the *kachehrī* (court house), setting out the terms of repayment and the amount of interest. As this loan was used to install a water meter in the home, which would recognize and make predictable their access to water, Rameez was willing to pay interest on the loan because the co-worker, in his words, "was providing me a service."

The building of the home, as is often the case in both formal and informal settlements,[14] was done slowly and incrementally over the next decade and was still underway when I visited in 2017:

> Every one or two months, a little bit at time. Sometimes, I'd get 1,000 rupees worth of bricks, or at other times 1,000 rupees worth of cement. A little bit of cement and apply that. In this way, we did a little bit at a time. Now, look, it has taken 6 or 7 months to prepare this second floor. And even then, it's still not complete. We still need to put on a door and paint the rooms.

The day I was visiting Rameez, the upper portion being built by Baba Isaak was meant for his eldest son who was to be married in the next few months. This upper portion also required Rameez to take part in another committee—this one required a monthly payment of 5,000 PKR, and he received 1.8 lakh PKR—and his father had also given him 1 lakh PKR, while Rameez also had some money of his own saved. Indeed, the work that was happening before us had been ongoing for several months—it had taken quite some time and still required more. As we got up to go back downstairs, Rameez quietly said to me, "Making a home is very difficult" (Ghar banānā bahot mushkil hai). The difficulty that Rameez was pointing to was not the physical effort of building and maintaining the home; rather, he was gesturing to challenges posed by the dual nature of indebtedness. Indebtedness can be treated, from one perspective, as the exploitative obligations of debt and, from another, as the necessary extension of credit—this is what invests indebtedness, as a source of wealth generation and distribution, with contradictory material and moral force (see Gregory 2012; Roitman 2003). What someone like Rameez is compelled to do is make the dual nature of indebtedness work for him, or at least, temporarily *and* temporally in their favor.

While indebtedness allowed Rameez and his kin to build and maintain a permanent home, for informal workers like Allah Ditta, indebtedness was embedded in waste work and the everyday workings of the home. This partly results from how divisions between work and life are not easily distinguishable for informal workers. Not only are valuable materials accumulated, sorted, and exchanged inside their houses, waste work and the income generated out of it are also distributed among kin, especially male ones, residing (however temporarily) within a household. For the most part, Allah Ditta and his brother-in-law evenly distributed the service fees collect from households, while the brother-in-law kept the valuable materials to be sold forward, and Allah Ditta's eldest son collected waste from households in another locality, though the son only received income generated from the valuables sorted out of waste. Similarly, other male kin, who regularly came to Lahore, resided in their home, and helped in collecting waste, receiving a *dihārī* (daily wage), either in the form of money or recyclables, or simply a place to stay. Female kin also collected waste from localities at times but did not receive monetary renumeration in the way that male kin did. Nevertheless, their effort was primarily focused on sorting waste materials inside the *jhuggīān*, not to mention any number of other domestic tasks, such as collecting water from public taps located nearby. The work of female kin that goes unremunerated is essential to reproduction of the households itself, as is the labor of male kin that is at times remunerated and at other times, not. Drawing upon kin-based labor allowed Allah Ditta to engage in other kinds of daily wage work, such as using his refitted rickshaw to become a delivery person for an appliance store in a nearby market. Even if other informal work arrangements present themselves, waste materials and work organize the running of these homes' circuits, in which gendered relations of kin are instrumental. Here, forms of indebtedness work alongside gendered relations of work and kinship.

Informal workers do not have access to the formal banking sector, as was the case for Rameez, so they relied upon junkyard owners and intermediaries as the most liquid actors circulating in these settlements. As mentioned in an earlier chapter, the most prevalent form of indebtedness was a system of advances: in exchange for a monthly advance of a certain amount, workers had to sell their goods (*māl*) collected from households to whoever was giving the advance. We should also recall how workers like Manzoor took on the debt that others had accumulated to junkyard owners to then gain access to household waste within a locality. This debt then was embedded into the system of exchanges, in which Manzoor sold specific items to the junkyard owner at a slightly reduced rate that operated as interest. In the case of advances, the payment received for goods can be kept by them or used to pay back the principal of the advance. For instance, if one takes an advance of 20,000 PKR and the worth of one's goods is 10,000 PKR, 8,000 PKR can be kept for one's self and the remainder can be applied to the principal of the advance. The amount applied to the principal depends upon a workers' "ability" (*gunjā'īsh*) at any particular moment. It should be noted that junkyard owners and intermediaries giving these advances also stand to benefit: they purchase the materials at a slightly reduced rate, which functions as an interest on the advance. Here, a system of advances transforms income into something else, which could switch between a debt to be returned and credit being extended.

Allah Ditta relied upon a monthly advance of several thousand rupees from the intermediary who purchases glass to pay off the "ration" from the general store (*kareānah ki dukān*) that is purchased on credit (*udhār*), and, during my long-term fieldwork, the family had taken separate advances of 10,000 PKR from each of the intermediaries who purchase cardboard (*gatā*) and plastic, to pay off expenses related to marrying their eldest son. In fact, on the day we were discussing indebtedness, Allah Ditta received a phone call from the *qist wālā* who collected payments for the motorbike that had been refitted to transport goods. Not able to make the payment at the time, Allah Ditta called the intermediary who purchases his plastics and told him to pay the *qist wālā* on his part. That amount would be added to the amount that Allah Ditta already owed him. The mundane maneuverings of advances worked alongside more extraordinary accrual of debt. For instance, along with the debt taken to gain access to waste materials and work, Manzoor's indebtedness to that same junkyard increased for a period through a combination of events: his mother's deteriorating health (the initial reason why they migrated to Lahore), the marriage of a sister, and an attempt at buying land that resulted in "fraud." These debts eventually reached nearly 6 lakh PKR, requiring Manzoor to go around and plead for help (*minnat tarla karna*) from kin and non-kin alike—this debt had been reduced to around 2 lakh PKR during my fieldwork.

When we met in 2019, despite being recently dispossessed from their settlement, Allah Ditta was more preoccupied with the marriage of his two eldest daughters in the coming weeks. To cover wedding costs such as preparation of dowries (*jahez*), the family had taken advances from a junkyard and borrowed money from relatives, while they were also accumulating as much waste materials as possible, which could be sold off to bring in extra cash to cover last minute expenses. These marriages had not only increased indebtedness but had also reorganized waste work within the home. A few months prior, his eldest son started living separately with his own family, so these two daughters started accompanying Allah Ditta. However, they also stopped after their engagements, requiring his wife, who usually sorts waste materials and performs domestic tasks, to start joining him in collecting waste materials from localities. This reorganization prevented Allah Ditta from engaging in other kinds of informal work that typically augment income generated from waste work. Events such as the departure of a son or the engagement of two daughters disturbed the circuit of the home, and adjustments aimed at restoring that circuit required increased indebtedness, if only for a short period. Here, indebtedness, enfolded as it is into the everyday workings and maintenance of the home, participates in ongoing processes of social reproduction.

Exhaustion

One afternoon, a foreman at one of the plazas in an affluent area of Lahore where Ghulam Ali collects waste ordered him to take away an unexpectedly large amount of waste that had accumulated in the basement. Ghulam Ali laid out on the ground a soiled piece of cloth (*palli*). After piling all the waste onto the cloth, he tied it from its corners, making it into a package that could be carried away on top of one's head. Because of its weight, Ghulam Ali needed help, and after the foreman refused, he asked me. Though uncomfortable, I acquiesced without showing any outward hesitation. After a failed attempted, where I thought he wanted me to simply carry the cloth with him, Ghulam Ali clarified he wanted help lifting it onto his head. I became even more uncomfortable. These cloths are reused for several weeks; they become damp from liquid secretions, are caked with dust and dirt, and are stained with dried filth. The cloth was unexpectedly heavy, so when the two of us lifted it, I lost my balance and the package fell back directly on my face. Unidentifiable particles billowed out. The cloth's damp coarseness pushed against my cheek. Shocked, I coughed profusely and turned away my face in disgust. The cloth fell to the ground. We tried again. This time, I bent my knees slightly, so I could get underneath the cloth, using my body as leverage, resting the materials on my chest, and pushing upward with my hands— all the while, my face turned to the side. Eventually, the cloth full of waste was resting balanced on Ghulam Ali's head.

For the rest of the day, I remained absorbed about the state of my body. Despite only lifting one of these clothes, my jacket was covered with dirt, dust, and other particles, and my hands were soiled and blackened, sheathed in a greasy film. As we walked away from the plaza, Ghulam Ali caught me preoccupied with my hands and laughed at my attempts to rub them clean, while explaining how he has become accustomed to have blackened hands. A little while later, when sitting down to eat at a nearby *ḍhābā* (roadside food stall), I washed my hands vociferously, rubbing the soap in between fingers and underneath nails, and right before breaking off a piece of roti, I used hand sanitizer just to be safe. Then, showering at home later in the evening, I took extra caution and time in shampooing my hair and lathering my body with soap, with fears about lice, germs, bacteria, viruses, and any other number unknown things and substances swarming through my head. Though this moment undeniably raised fears about polluting substances, something else was also at stake in this form of work.

At some point in their lives, most waste workers had suffered from dengue, typhoid, and hepatitis (*kālā yarqān*), while in the winter months, colds and flus became pervasive, and many vividly described the physical effects of hypertension, diabetes, cardiac disease, and gastrointestinal problems. Additionally, work-related accidents—being hit by a car while collecting waste on the side of a thoroughfare, a heavy sack (*borī*) falling on someone sweeping a basement, or loss of one's eyesight—were repeatedly marked as life-changing events that reverberated across generations, requiring a child to leave school and assist a parent at work or creating a debt that would take years to pay off. Such events, whether mundane or extraordinary, highlight how the effects wrought by waste work come to be embedded in the bodies and lives of those who perform it. To put it simply, even at the risk of oversimplification, scenes of working bodies, like the one just described where I struggled in assisting Ghulam Ali to lift a soiled cloth full of waste onto his head, are also ones of reproduction. Such scenes—whether of work or reproduction—should be viewed, in the words of Lauren Berlant, as ones of "slow death," which is characterized by "a condition of being worn out by the activity of reproducing life" (2007, 759). This notion of being worn out through the work of reproducing life raises the specter of how waste work comes to exhaust the bodies of workers, even as it reproduces intergenerational and collective life (see also Corwin and Gidwani 2021). The different responses to waste work—my anxious preoccupation and Ghulam Ali's habituated attitude—demonstrate how exhaustion is potentially registered (or not) in the bodies and lives of those who *actually* perform that work.

Sighs of exasperation when standing or sitting, kneading muscles throughout the day, or wrapping joints with ragged pieces of cloth with the hope of temporarily easing pain, were constants that always left strong impressions on me. On the other hand, waste workers stressed they had become habituated (*'aādī*) to waste work, not registering its pains, smells, or exhaustion, and yet, one of their most frequent responses to my health-related questions was, in a slightly sarcastic tone, "It's right in front of you" (*āp ke sāmne hī hai*). How exhaustion came to be diffused in their bodies and lives became clear to me after a conversation with a relative of Allah Ditta, who described things in the following way: "Our lives are passing uselessly. We don't know about its beginning or its passing. We don't understand how our lives start, and we don't know how our lives will end." This statement aligns with what Elizabeth Povinelli has described for the durative quality of endurance, or a "temporality of continuance, a denotation of continuous action without any references to its beginning or end" (2011, 32). Here, too, the work that sustains life is continuously being enacted but is marked by a certain temporal incoherence—a life's beginnings and endings are not easily comprehended. Feelings of exhaustion may be more punctuated (and thus, more noticeable) in one moment rather than another, which gives exhaustion the appearance of being anchored in a discrete moment in time, but exhaustion is fundamentally durative in nature, arising out of and unfolding through the continuous effort required of reproducing life.

On an everyday basis, waste workers must navigate the material conditions and qualities of their work and its potential to eviscerate their bodies. Most prominently, municipal workers still engage in public sweeping. With every swipe, dirt, dust, and any number of other particles that have accumulated in public spaces get kicked up and shifted about, permeating work environments and encasing workers in a translucent and granular fog. Workers regularly expressed concern about the impact that these particles had on their respiratory health and connection to other illnesses regularly afflicting them. Though sweeping was done standing, it required that workers bend slightly to exert enough force to move about waste materials, so they can be organized into piles that could be deposited into municipal containers. As bristles wear down and harden, they lose their flexibility, making it more difficult to gather waste, and workers must subsequently bend further to exercise enough force to sweep materials into piles.

Along with public sweeping, municipal workers use shovels (*bailchah*) to pick up dirt, cement, and leaves; picks (*kayeh*) to break up hardened materials; and a cutting tool (*khurpā*) to remove any filth clogging gutters. After filling handcarts with waste materials, portions are deposited on old sheets laid on the ground (similar to what Ghulam Ali did that afternoon), and the contents are flung into containers or the back of trucks. At the same time, informal workers deposit waste in between sheets layered on the back of a donkey cart or refitted motorbike, with each layer's contents also being hurled into containers and trucks one after the other.

These containers must also be hooked into garbage compactors, which lift and deposit waste materials into their backs. However, to do so, workers must first align containers full of waste with the hooks on the side of compactors. This requires they shove, jerk, and yank containers into place, until they are aligned and can lock into the hooks. Because of the strain placed on their upper bodies from this daily effort, workers, especially males, would stretch their shoulders and backs in the morning before starting work, lest they aggravate something while collecting and lifting waste, tossing sheets full of refuse, or shifting about containers.

All this strain on one's body also resulted in consuming medicines of all kinds. Though many visited homeopathic practitioners or utilized traditional healing (*desi ilāj*), many relied on pain killers such as paracetamol (acetaminophen) and narocin (naproxen) and analgesic creams, while corticosteroid injections, mixed with other vitamins, were regularly administered by local medical clinics. These injections would make workers feel "fresh" during bouts of exhaustion or illness. Almost every worker I came to know relied on this combination of drugs, creams, and injections to manage the constant pained state of their bodies. However, exhaustion is not only discernible in the pained body.

While on a break one morning, Petras explained the mental exhaustion that comes with waste work: "Because of these worries, a man becomes weak mentally. His bodily vitality also lessens. Then what will he do? His fitness is reduced." I followed up: "How is your health [*tabiya't*] nowadays?" Petras chuckled slightly and said:

> What can I say about my health? I've never had a problem with blood pressure in my life before. I never *even* thought of it. The other day I went to the doctor, and he said, 'Your blood pressure has become low.' I said to him [chuckling again], '*Yaar*, I don't even know about these things.' Illnesses are created from thinking too much. One's vision weakens from thinking too much. It affects your vision. It affects your heart.

In an earlier conversation, Petras had told me about how his father's vision had deteriorated from doing this work over many years as well. In fact, this was why, according to Petras, he and his mother started accompanying and assisting him, explaining that "three people were working on one salary." So, his own deteriorating vision was lamentable, though unsurprising. The day he visited the doctor, Petras had gone to get medicine because, as he described, "my body was aching, my legs were aching, and my shoulder muscles were aching." After I asked how the doctor had diagnosed him, Petras clarified, "Reasons? Well the reasons he told me are either from working too much, from fatigue [*thakāvaṭ*], or then from thinking too much. I told him both are our jobs—thinking too much and working too much."

Petras's statement elicited a laugh in both of us. Our laughter was surprising as the matter was quite serious: weakness (*kamzorī*) and fatigue (*thakāvaṭ*) caused by this form of work have reduced his immunity, which could potentially make him even more vulnerable to other afflictions and illnesses and further destabilize his already precarious condition of life. A litany of similar stories—in which work, illness, and debt were intertwined among individuals and social relations across generations—were shared with me by others. The trajectory of events in these stories almost always mirrored each other—a tailspin of uncertainty in the present that rendered one's own future and that of one's kin unclear. At times, events were narrated as barely significant occurrences; at other times, they were described as life-altering shifts. The ways in which such events are registered across the lives of workers gestures to the durative quality of bodies and lives across generations, which have become exhausted from reproducing life at multiple scales.

Without disavowing narratives of exhaustion just presented, the moment of laughter shared between Petras and me also suggests other orientations to toiling with waste that do not subsume bodies, work, or lives to exhaustion. For instance, Mariam, a municipal worker, while describing years of domestic strife she has endured, emphasized how leaving the home and coming to work brought her certain pleasures—gossiping and joking with other workers or meeting and chatting with residents and shopkeepers in the neighborhood where she labors. In fact, laboring outside the home, according to Mariam, took her, physically and mentally, away from domestic discord—something also described by other female workers who nevertheless emphasized the challenges they experience laboring in public spaces as women from low- or noncaste backgrounds.

Such pleasures distracted Mariam and others from the almost endless number of worries and concerns (*parishānīān*) attached to domestic life. These pleasures were everyday ones elicited through work and organized through gendered relations linking private and public life. It was not just exhaustion but also certain pleasures that emerged out of working, if not from the specific form of work or labor (i.e., waste work). Such unexpected pleasures reinforce the fact that entanglements between forms of life and worlds of waste do not determine the shape any particular form a life will take—for instance, as pure and utter exhaustion. Indeed, the lives of waste workers and their kin have been actualized in ways that are always in potential excess of these entanglements.

The Possibility of Reproduction

There is a historicity to the lives of waste workers, or the sense that life, as lived, entails historical consciousness about one's self and others—whether those others be kin from previous generations or future ones. In his discussion of similar questions, Reinhart Koselleck made a distinction between what he called the "space of experience" and "horizon of expectation." For Koselleck, experience is registered in the present but results from the passing of a moment in time—that moment having necessarily been "assembled into a totality" (2004, 260). On the other hand, expectation is oriented around a horizon, as a field of possibility, out of which "a new space of experience will open, but which cannot yet be seen" (2004, 261). "The presence of the past," sedimented in experiences, bears upon but is distinct from "the presence of the future," materialized through expectations. Similarly, previous forms of work, settlement, and life constituted the spaces of experiences, out of which the present came to be known and organized, while also unfolding within a horizon of expectation oriented toward future possibilities. Such nuanced though fraught temporal movements are also discernible within the home as a site of social reproduction, negotiations of indebtedness, the exhaustion of bodies, and unexpected pleasures—all of which connect pasts and futures in the present. What does this discussion of pasts and futures have to do with waste work in urban Pakistan, or elsewhere, for that matter?

Recent lines of inquiry have taken as their point of departure configurations of waste and labor across a range of contexts as a way of intervening into more generalized and presumably shared conditions of work, life, and value under contemporary capitalism, especially in urbanizing centers and their ecologies across the Global South.[15] In many of these accounts, the laboring subject—whether humanity rendered into "surplus populations" in the informal economy or animal life constituted as a biotechnology and waste infrastructure—is presumed to give us a privileged vantage point, from which we can critically evaluate the generation, distribution, and appropriation of value across urbanizing landscapes, which are increasingly fraught by unevenness and inequalities.[16] What seemingly has fallen out of view, however, are the historical identities upon which contemporary capitalism and cities continue to depend and reproduce themselves.[17] Similarly, despite the uptake in scholarship on waste work and infrastructures across South Asian cities, the fundamental role that caste, along with class, gender, or religion, have had in shaping the dynamics of waste and urban transformations has been largely unaddressed. Nevertheless, these historical identities, significantly, are inherited—they connect individuals and kin to an experienced past, even if it is an imagined one, and orient their expectations for the future. To subsume particular configurations of waste and labor into more generalizable and shared conditions would be an act of gross misrecognition—of the intergenerational trajectories of waste workers, the urban transformations reshaping the collective life of cities, and the actual conditions of working and living under contemporary capitalism.

Waste materials, the undeniable result of production and consumption achieved under capitalist social relations organized on a mass scale, are disposed of, not to mention circulated and contained, such that life can go on and endure at multiple, interlaced scales—from the individual to the intergenerational to the collective. There is a simultaneity to the reproduction of life and its exhaustion because of how reproduction itself is materialized through "infrastructural distribution of life chances, pasts, and futures," which can be seen in the experiences and expectations of Rameez, Allah Ditta, and many others (Murphy 2017, 141). An unevenness is made possible by waste work and infrastructures, in which the life of individuals, communities, and collectives have been differentially reproduced and sutured together across generations. While the intergenerational trajectories of waste workers are undeniably historically specific, those same trajectories concurrently reveal how multifarious processes of contemporary capitalism—from spatial and infrastructural development to consumptive economies to informalization and precarity of work—materialize and transform historical inequalities and interdependencies across urban Pakistan, as they most certainly do elsewhere.

MOST OF MY PRELIMINARY fieldwork in the summer of 2011 was spent trying to understand how the status of Pakistani Christians as a political minority had impacted their social and religious lives within the city of Lahore. As such, I regularly attended Bible studies, healing sessions, Sunday services, and any other number of quotidian events held at a Pentecostal megachurch located in a predominantly Christian *bastī* (settlement) known as 7up colony (named after a nearby factory producing the eponymous soft drink).

A few days before the end of preliminary fieldwork, one of the elders I had gotten to know Solomon Shaukat invited me to his home. Elder Solomon's home was not in 7up colony but rather, in an area known as Sehajpal that is sandwiched between Lahore's main airport and, at the time, a largely undeveloped phase of the Defence Housing Authority (see Map 0.2). Turning off the major thoroughfare that led me there, I found myself in an agrarian landscape, which was not entirely unsurprising since Elder Solomon referred to Sehajpal as a village (*piṇḍ*). I then carefully drove down a smaller road on a slight decline that sloped through agricultural fields and empty pieces of land. That is when I saw Elder Solomon, who had been directing me on the phone for the last leg of the journey, waving in the distance.

Over the usual mix of biscuits, soft drinks, and chai, Elder Solomon told me about how he was born again and baptized on December 17, 1972. At the time, the family resided in an area of Lahore known as Sherakot that was then on the city's outskirts and fell in the River Ravi's flood plain. That flooding regularly damaged their *kachchā makān*, requiring constant repair, while also consistently disturbing cultivation, which was their main source of livelihood. Similar to others like Rameez, Allah Ditta, and Manzoor, the family decided to make a shift to Sehajpal. For much of his adult life, Elder Solomon worked as a railway fitter but had to take early retirement after false corruption accusations were made against him. After a neighbor named Ibaad joined us, our conversation shifted to theological and religious matters, the Christian community in Pakistan, and everyday interactions between Muslims and Christians across the country.

Before I left Sehajpal that night, Elder Solomon had me meet the *numberdār* (village head) Haji Mirajuddin. By that point, the village had descended into darkness, and Haji Mirajuddin, with a waterpipe by his side, was seated on a *mañjī* (bed) in the central square illuminated by the surrounding storefronts. Elder Solomon introduced me as a PhD student researching the Christian community in Pakistan. Only a couple years had passed since blasphemy allegations against Aasia Bibi had erupted into national consciousness. These allegations were known to have resulted from an argument over the refusal to share water between Aasia Bibi, who was Christian, and another female agricultural worker who was Muslim. During my preliminary fieldwork, however, everyone I spoke with, Christian and Muslim alike, showed much tact and even at times avoided discussing both the Aasia Bibi case and interdictions on commensality. On the other hand, Haji Mirajuddin, who struck me as much older than Elder Solomon (himself well into his sixties), stated immediately and unequivocally that one could recognize Christians by the unpleasant smell (*badbū*) emanating from their bodies, further claiming one's bodily odor changes and becomes unnoticeable when one recites the Islamic testament of faith (the *shahada*). When I inquired about this smell, it was described as an odor that elicits disgust, the word *ghin* was used, which includes a visceral reaction of repulsion and mental discomfort. The statement made everyone seated there, other than Haji Mirajuddin, noticeably uncomfortable.

I want to remain with the specific word, *ghin*, Haji Mirajuddin used to describe the odor and the visceral response elicited in one's sensorium. One way of critical examining caste has been to make clear how the affect of disgust embeds caste as a system of social stratification within the viscera of the body, both individual and collective. Recently, Joel Lee has foregrounded *ghṛṇā* and *ghin* to examine "the centrality of disgust in the maintenance of caste order" (2021, 312). Lee traces the affect of disgust in literature circulating among the Hindu reformist organization Arya Samaj, specifically how they sought to undo disgust toward Dalits as potential Hindu brethren, thereby integrating them into the fold of Hinduism, while redirecting that affect in a majoritarian tendency toward Muslims as a minority of irredeemable outsiders. Alongside this reformulation, there were also contemporaneous oral traditions that "critique[d] disgust as antithetical to moral action and as opposed to life" (Lee 2021, 312). Much of what Lee highlights about disgust resonates in contemporary Pakistan: the ways in which a social structure known as caste hierarchy reverberates in the viscera when the self recoils from the odor presumed to emanate from the substance of the other. Recoiling away in disgust instantiates and affirms relations of separation and distance between the body of the (upper caste) self and that of the (lower caste) other. This is how we must approach Haji Mirajuddin's disgust, infused as it was with contempt and repulsion; it is an expression of forms of life in the Punjab built upon caste-based relations.

Such expressions of disgust, however, do not go uncontested in contemporary Pakistan. Many of us who were seated around the aging *numberdār*—Christians and Muslims of different caste and class backgrounds—were noticeably discomforted. Moreover, Elder Solomon and Ibaad provided explanations as we walked away that were critical of Haji Mirajuddin: the smell he presumed to come from the substance of a person, in reality, came from those of materials, work, homes, and neighborhoods, not those of the person. They, like many others in Pakistan today, deemed this kind of disgust, along with the form of life and caste-based relations of which it is a part, illegitimate. If reformulating disgust was, in this instance, a technique for critiquing caste, what happens to such critiques when we consider all the affects through which forms of life have reproduced themselves across many parts of contemporary Pakistan?

At times, those affects took the form of hate (*nafrat*) that one has for working with waste materials (as was the case with Chaudhary Billah), or how hate is channeled at those doing this kind of work, as well as Christians as non-Muslims in the country, something discernible during moments of violence following blasphemy allegations. Then, there were feelings of powerlessness and anger, as expressed by Tariq, that may arise because of the belief shared by some Pakistanis that the touch of those working with waste materials or those coming from Christian and/or low- or noncaste backgrounds can be polluting (*palīd karnā*), making the touched person impure (*nā-pāk*). It should be underscored that contempt and repulsion (often associated with disgust) entail feelings of anger and hatred toward an act, object, or person eliciting that response. As discussed in the previous chapter, these affects, in enacting and affirming relations of separation and distance, are as much about antagonism between social groups as they are about intimacy, with its own set of affects. Thus, the fictive kinship and love and care (*pyār-maḥabbat*) cultivated between households and waste workers over many years, or the pity taken (*taras khānā*) by households on such "poor persons" who eke out an existence for themselves and others by putting their hands in "filth." These complex, seemingly contradictory sets of affects reveal not only how pervasive particular forms of life have become throughout much of urban Pakistan but also what the critique of caste in Pakistan demands of us today.

One reason why I conclude with the story of Haji Mirajuddin's disgust is to foreground the central problem undergirding the pages of this book: How do forms of life, based upon caste-based relations, come to be transformed such that they are reproduced across many parts of contemporary Pakistan? The elicitation of disgust within a (casted) body's sensorium, as well as critical responses to that disgust, make clear how affective relations, both to one's self and others with whom one shares a world in common, have been reorganized as forms of life have congealed in Lahore over the past several decades. However, affects, whether of disgust or of love, are just one site among many upon which processes of reproduction have unfolded. An expansive bureaucratic state and its techno-legal apparatus; the consumption of disposable commodities organized at a mass scale; an urbanizing landscape shifting along the uneven lines of class, caste, and religion; changing configurations of work, settlement, and life on the urban peripheries—all these are sites upon which reproduction as a distributed process materializes itself. By discerning such sites, we also locate those moments when caste is unsettled and becomes a site of contestation. To critically unpack reproduction—of caste, of Lahore, of life—requires we work across any number of interlaced though distinct processes that unfold at a variety of spatiotemporal scales.

My other reason for concluding with this story may be less obvious. My interests during preliminary fieldwork were in globalizing forms of Christianity and Christians as a political minority in Pakistan. Although caste-based stigma was something I had been attentive to, I later formulated what happened that evening within analytic frameworks— e.g., ethics, publics, and secularity—that narrativized the worlds of Haji Mirajuddin, Elder Solomon, Ibaad, myself, and many others in specific ways. More than a decade later, I return to that encounter in Sehajpal to reflect on how the central analytic framework of this book—that of reproduction—can now allow me to tell a story about Haji Mirajuddin's disgust, as well as our discomfort with it, that looks very different.

It is a story of how caste across Pakistan not only has been and remains in a state of flux and transformation but also has continually become a site of contestation and struggle. Such a story moves us away from static and reductive notions of caste, which have for too long weighed down critical thinking about caste in Pakistan. It shifts our attention to those forms of life that have been taking shape across several decades now, and what possibilities for life have become available for those from low- or noncaste backgrounds who have entered this line of work during that time. The stories I have told in this book would not have been possible if I had not shifted my analytic framework and deployed narrative strategies that center the reproduction of life; only when doing so was I able to discern the multifarious activities, relations, practices, and life-making projects that have crystalized particular forms of living and working in contemporary Pakistan. As is the case with critical studies of caste, the frameworks we deploy to tell stories about forms of life attached to the worlds of waste, whether in Pakistan or elsewhere, have consequences for what is deemed relevant in the contemporary moment.

Forms of Life, Worlds of Waste

In the contemporary moment, waste has emerged as a problem that is both global and planetary in scale (see Chakrabarty 2021). The processes that sustain an intensifying form of consumptive capitalism by producing disposable commodities and extracting resources on a global scale are the same ones distressing the geophysical process that sustain all kinds of life, human or otherwise, on our planet today. Within this world of waste, substances and matter continue to be a site for differentiating humanity along the lines of globalized forms of inequality, whether that be due to gendered, racialized, colonial, and/or casteist forms of power. Such differentiation is discernible as much within national boundaries, where marginalized communities are most vulnerable to the toxic infrastructures necessary for the production and consumption of disposable commodities, as it is across various regions of the world, where the effects of anthropogenic climate change are unevenly distributed across nation-states. The differentiation of humanity is facilitated by the increasing differentiation of waste itself: waste now takes the forms of microplastics, particulates, and toxins, as much it can be found as leachate, deteriorating foods, and valuable recyclables, scrap, and junk. Waste, both massive and minute, produced for and by human consumption, courses through and saturates bodies, communities, and environments in almost every corner of the globe, producing a differentiated humanity in its wake.

Taking shape as it has in such a world, the interdisciplinary field known as discard studies has drawn critical attention to those historical processes—globalizing capitalism, the expansion of nation-states, anthropogenic climate change, settler and nonsettler forms of colonialism, uneven urbanization—out of which the worlds of waste and forms of life have emerged entangled with one another (see Liboiron and Lepawsky 2021). Considering the fact that the problem of waste in the current moment is planetary and global in nature, greater attentiveness has been given to "scalar practices" of waste (see Carr and Lampert 2016). As such, Gabrielle Hecht, in describing "the Anthropocene as the apotheosis of waste," asks us to "grapple with ... complex interscalar connections" that demand "new narratives and analytic modes" (2018, 111–12). Hecht goes on to tell a story about the extraction of uranium-bearing rocks in Gabon by the Commissariat à l'énergie Atomique and a colonial mining corporation and the numerous kinds of violences—from mining collapses to difficult-to-detect radiation exposure—inflicted upon those working and residing around sites of extraction. Similarly, Elana Resnick, writing about Romani street sweepers in Bulgaria, has traced "environmental degradation both in terms of destruction and decay and as the foundation for creative possibilities of managing life amid difficult circumstance," emphasizing how "new racial formations and modes of living emerge in ways that ... enable particular strategies for dealing with the structural inequities that waste accumulation exacerbates" (2021, 3). Here, too, scalar practices related to waste situate the work of disposal (sweeping) and circulation (institutionalized recycling) within an urbanizing landscape and EU-era policies and racialization of Romani people. Across these accounts, the scale that opens up, in which things like uranium, geologies, racial formations, and violences come together and unfold, are situated within those processes sustaining an intensifying form of global capitalism and anthropogenic climate change that continue to differentiate humanity across the various regions of a globalized world and render the possibility of life uncertain on the planet.

These approaches have given us important insight into how anthropogenic climate change caused by a form of global capitalism, with consumption, disposability, and extraction at its core, can be critically examined through scalar practices of waste. Yet, despite the multiple scales that appear before us, they are simultaneously flattened, such that what happens in a place (like Pakistan or anywhere else) is a particular instantiation of a more general process unfolding at the global and planetary scales. This flattening arises from the fact that critical studies of waste in the contemporary world continue to rely on extractive and damage-based narratives, in which those damages and harms inflicted upon persons, communities, and environments through processes of capitalist exploitation, colonial subjugation, and racialized violence become sites for producing knowledge that contribute to wider critiques of capitalism and the Anthropocene, as well as spurring intervention to uplift communities and rejuvenate environments upon which such harms and violences have been historically inflicted (see Liboiron 2021; Murphy 2017; Tuck 2009; Tuck and Wang 2013). However, what happens to our accounts of waste in the world today when we do not rely upon extractive and damage-based narratives? How has a narrative that prioritizes the reproduction of life shifted the stories we tell about places like Pakistan in the contemporary moment?

The stories told across the pages of this book have not avoided the fact that the problem of waste is global and planetary in nature. They have not elided the enduring effects of colonialism, the organization of capitalist production and social relations on a massive scale, or the reproduction of historical inequalities and interdependencies. All these events and processes have been incorporated into the stories utilized to narrativize those forms of life that have been reproduced in urban Pakistan. However, the theoretical framework of this book—that of reproduction—has accounted for forms of life built around and through worlds of waste without constantly referring to those global and planetary forces. The reason for doing so was to ensure that forms of life that have emerged in urban Pakistan are not subsumed unreflectively into the unfolding of globalizing capitalism or anthropogenic climate change. Nor did this book simply recount the unending series of violences inflicted upon those who, for historical reasons, have come to engage in waste work across urban Pakistan. Rather, this book delineated the multiple scales of activity, relations, practices, and life-making projects that have converged in shaping those forms of life as they have emerged through the worlds of waste in the current historical moment.

Many of these stories have been oriented toward the lives of waste workers, many of whom would be considered low-caste Dalits. Writing stories of such life is beyond the scope of this book, as well as my own abilities, so I defer to accounts by those who have actually lived those lives, which provide a much more expansive of sense of what is required—politically, socially, economically, ethically—for the flourishing of that life (see e.g., Dutt 2019; Yengde 2019). While I have avoided relying too much upon the harms and damages inflicted upon those who perform this particular kind of work, the question remains of how to narrate those forms of life, especially ones based on caste-based relations, that have been reproduced through their connection, in both material and ideological ways, with those substances and materials that constitute the worlds of waste in the contemporary world.

This question has recently been taken up by Dipesh Chakrabarty, who has foregrounded how the marginalization of the "Dalit body," which results from "its forced contact with death and waste matter" that allows upper castes (Savarna Hindus) to create and maintain "relations of oppression," is premised upon an imagination of the human body "as intrinsically connected to the non-human and the non-living" (2021, 118). Although it has been well established that the casted body highlights the porous boundaries of the human in relation to other bodies, persons, and forms of (non-) life, Chakrabarty's purpose in narrating the "Dalit body" is to imagine the human "as a form of life connected to other forms of life that are all connected to the geobiology of the planet and are dependent on these connections for their own welfare" (2021, 126–27). Even if the linkages between human life and other forms of (non-)life, as well as the planet's geophysical forces, are important issues, this narrativization of the Dalit body skirts the fact that caste purity was not just a relation with the nonhuman and the nonliving, or even the compulsory touching of "death and waste matter." As this book has made clear, those relations, with the nonhuman, nonliving, and all the substances and matters attached to them, have been embedded in shifting forms of life that have been historically organized around caste-based relations of work, exchange, settlement, and marriage and codes of conduct. We might gain much from a more expansive rendering of life as they bear upon contemporary worlds of waste if we remain attentive to the multifarious set of relations that constitute life and nonlife.

Here, we can turn to what Suraj Yengde has described as "global castes," which are fundamentally premised upon "belief in purity of soul and blood" that are "then validated through the distribution of work" and a hereditary system involving a "descent-based order" (Yengde 2021, 17). Forms of life based on such relations can no longer be limited to the Indian subcontinent, because of either the global movement of caste groups from within South Asia or the construction of social hierarchies akin to caste across different locales and regions. Many of the features of global castes Yengde identifies—purity of soul and blood, distribution of work, and reconciling descent—overlap with the racialization described with regard to the changing valuations of waste materials, work, and technologies (see e.g., Millar 2020; Resnick 2021; Reno 2015; Zimring 2015). We must track between the forms of life and worlds of waste in the contemporary moment, precisely because both—life and waste—are constitutively entangled at multiple, intersecting scales. In doing so, we can furnish stories that are neither extractive in nature nor premised upon harms and damages inflicted upon bodies, communities, and persons. These are stories about forms of life and worlds of waste, about persons connected to the past within an unfolding present, and the work required for such lives and worlds to be reproduced at a future moment in time.

In contemporary Pakistan, particular forms of life, in becoming attached to the worlds of waste across historical moments, have been instrumental in organizing urban life throughout the country. Crucial to telling this story has been how waste work, referring to the differentiated kinds of effort exercised on a world saturated by waste, has been constituted into an infrastructure of urban life. This form of work disposes waste materials just as it circulates them, while it has also shaped the uneven trajectory of urbanization across many parts of Pakistan. This story is also one that implicates the bureaucratic state and its techno-legal apparatus, the relations of work and exchange transforming waste materials into commodities, and the kinds of intimacies suturing together an urbanizing landscape. As these processes unfold at various scales of activity, those from low- or noncaste backgrounds have found sources of livelihood for themselves and their wider social relations in Pakistan's waste infrastructures. The reproduction of life—of individuals, of communities, of Lahore—demonstrate how central those forms of life built upon caste-based relations have been to the organization of urban life across Pakistan over the past several decades. These are the stories I have decided to recount about forms of life and the worlds of waste in Pakistan today.

This entanglement of certain forms of life and particular worlds of waste is an undeniable result of casteist, gendered, racialized, and colonial forms of power. Instead of telling stories about the violence, exclusions, and exploitation saturating these lives and worlds in urban Pakistan, this book adopted an alternative narrative strategy that thematized the reproduction of life. In the current moment, where forms of life, human or otherwise, have been rendered uncertain, being attentive to processes of reproduction, ones that may converge with the Anthropocene at the planetary scale or an intensifying capitalism at the global one but also ensnare other scales of activities, relations, practices, and life-making projects, might tell us much about the actual forms of living and working in the contemporary moment. This book was offered up in such a storied gesture, where the forms of life growing up in and through the worlds of waste can be narrated such that we can discern the work—material, political, intellectual, and ethical—required for reproducing life in our shared world today.

NOTES

PREFACE

1. City of Lahore Corporation Office, Corporation Proceedings, From 11/25/1952 to 1/20/1953, Record No. 580.

2. My usage of these two terms—*low- or noncaste* and *Dalit*—alternates depending on context. When referring solely to those groups who have historically been considered outside the four *varnas* of Hinduism (i.e., "Untouchables"), I utilize the term *Dalit*. When referring to those groups who would be considered "lower" castes, I use the collective term *low- or noncaste*, which includes those considered to be "low" castes (e.g., Julāhā [weaver] or Telī [oil presser]), as well as Dalits. One reason for alternating between terms is because it thematizes a key fault line within caste-based relations in Punjab: between upper-caste groups whose status resulted from being landowners and perceived as "cultivators" and lower-caste groups whose status resulted from being landless laborers engaging in other kinds of work (e.g., leatherwork or "sweeping"). The term *low- or noncaste* draws attention to this crucial fault line and thus, the central argument of this book: how forms of life built around caste-based relations are reproduced in a transformed state across urban Pakistan.

3. In urban centers across the Punjab and throughout Pakistan and North India, one sees the prevalence of those from low- or noncaste backgrounds, across religious lines, engaging in waste work across the lines of municipal employment and informalized relations (see Beall 2006, 1997; Butt 2020a, 2020b; Prashad 2000; Streefland 1979). It should also be noted that Pashtuns from Khyber Pakhtunkhwa and Afghanistan are also dominant actors across Pakistan's waste infrastructures; however, my fieldwork with such communities was limited, as explained in the Introduction.

4. Estimation of Lahore's waste generation is fundamentally unclear, especially since a census had not been conducted between 1998 and 2017. Even by conservative estimates, 5,000 tons of waste are generated by its population on a daily basis. This number is taken from Batool and Nawaz (2009). However, this number, and many of the others that circulate in Pakistan regarding waste production, are based on a study done in the 1990s that was explicitly commissioned to examine prospects for privatizing solid waste management in Pakistan (Engineering Planning and Management Consultants 1996).

5. The elementary act of taking away has been identified as a defining feature of waste work by many (see Doherty 2019; Fredericks 2018; Millar 2018; Nguyen 2019; Reno 2016; Stamatopoulou-Robbins 2019).

INTRODUCTION

1. *Pakkā* translates literally to "cooked," and in many parts of South Asia, it refers to all kinds of structures (roads, houses, etc.) that are viewed as more stable. Their stability arises partly due to the materials themselves (e.g., bricks and concrete rather than wood and mud) as well as their legal status as being recognized by the state. For instance, *pakkā* houses are stable structures made of bricks (or cement and concrete) and located on land to which one enjoys legal claims of property. This is in contrast to *kacchā* homes that are less stable structures located on land to which one's legal claims are absent or uncertain. *Jhuggīāṉ* discussed shortly would be considered *kacchā* houses.

2. A critical feature of contemporary life is the generation of waste as "mass waste," which shapes practices of modern waste management, economies that have grown around them at a variety of scales, and uneven urbanization (see Reno 2015; see also Alexander and Reno 2012, Alexander and Reno 2014; Gregson et al. 2015; Gidwani 2015). Whereas this scholarship on contemporary transformations in waste materials and interventions surrounding them has been generative, this book remains attentive to the histories of labor, migration, and urbanization that shape waste work and infrastructures in a variety of settings, as well as the aggregation of urban infrastructures that has occurred over several decades.

3. This is what David Gilmartin (1998), in an important essay on historical narratives of Partition and the creation of Pakistan, has examined as the tensions between the unifying force of moral community, forged through Islam as a religious tradition that provided symbols around which Muslims mobilized in British India, and the diverse forms of belonging among Muslim groups, with their myriad loyalties and attachments formed along the lines of "tribe," *birādarī*, class, region, and/or language (see also Jalal 1994)

4. In a discussion about Islam, Muslim history, and national culture among progressive and liberal intellectuals in the early years of Pakistan's independence, Kamran Asdar Ali (2011) has drawn attention that these intellectuals were largely Urdu speaking from North India and shared an *ashrāf* background, which placed them in tension with the vast majority of Pakistan's population with its own cultural and linguistic diversity. In a slightly different register, Naveeda Khan has emphasized how Pakistani nationalism remains an aspirational project, in which religious argument and disputes, whether in everyday life or the formalized domain of law, become "expressive of ongoing striving" (2012, 11). More recently, Mubbashir Rizvi has described how the national imaginary of the Pakistani state "evades particular regional, and ethnic identities in favor of Muslim universalism, even though the everyday life of Pakistanis is circumscribed by local ethnic, religious, and linguistic identities," while qualifying that those tensions between the unity of Muslim nationalism and local identities is "least visible in Punjab, where the Pakistani state's nationalist project is most hegemonic" (2019, 7). It is undeniable that the Punjab has benefited disproportionately from the centralization of state power, authoritarian rule, and uneven development in Pakistan. In spaces, whether geographic or intellectual, where the project of the Pakistani state and Muslim nationalism has attained hegemony, however, tensions

remain unresolved, allowing for categories like nation, religion, and community to sustain social and political life in unexpected ways.

5. The most prominent of "agriculturalist" or "cultivators" in the Punjab have been Jatts, but there are also many others (Awaams, Arains, Bhattis, Cheema, Chaudhary, etc.) that have fallen within this designation. Sayyids (those who claim descent from the Prophet) and Khokars (of presumed Rajput lineage) also have been placed into the designation "agriculturalist" or "cultivator." Among low- or noncaste groups, those directly involved in agriculture, and at times worked as cultivators, were carpenters (*tarkhan*), blacksmiths (*lohar*), oil pressers (*teli*), leatherworkers (*chamar*), sweepers (*churha*), and then, there were those who were not directly involved in agriculture or cultivation, such as barbers (*nai*), cobblers (*mochi*), bards (*mirasi*), weavers (*julaha*), goldsmiths (*sunniara*), potters (*kumhiar*), tailors (*darzi*), washerman (*dhobi*), butchers (*qasai*), water-carriers (*bhisti, jhinwar*, or *mehra*), and religious ascetics (*faqir*) (Gill 2019; Ahmad 1970; Wakil 1972; Alavi 1972; Eglar 2010).

6. For a more general discussion of designations of "caste" and "tribe" in the Punjab and the bureaucratic apparatus of colonial regime across British India, see Gilmartin (1988); Ali (1988); Barrier (1967); Cohn (1987); Fox (1985). These dynamics would shape not only agricultural policy and interventions in the Punjabi countryside but also political parties and social movements across the region's rural and urban centers (Fox 1984; Grewal 2009; Kerr 1980; Malhotra 2002; Talbot 1988).

7. For instance, Muhammad Ali Jinnah, in a famous and oft-quoted speech given to the Constituent Assembly of Pakistan in 1947, charted out the following framework: "We are starting in the days where there is no discrimination, no distinction between one community and another, no discrimination between one caste or creed and another" (Jinnah 1947, 546).

8. It should be underscored that Christianity has historically and continues to provide a critique of caste-based norms and codes of conduct by drawing on local idioms and religious ideas, thereby furnishing a "counternarrative" around such norms and codes of conduct, especially those related to purity (*pāk*) and unclean (*na-pāk*) (Singha 2015; see also Mosse 2012).

9. See Hussain (2020); Falahi (2020); https://pasmandademocracy.com/caste-religion/masood/sir-syed-ahmad-khan-and-his-justification-for-ashraf-hegemony/. For an account of the distinctions of *ashrāf* and *ajlāf*, see Ahmad (1967). Gyanendra Pandey (1984) examines similar tensions between Muslim elites and poorer weavers in one particular locality, specifically how those tensions were embedded in larger visions of moral community.

10. Platts's *A Dictionary of Urdu, Classical Hindi, and English* defines *ashrāf* as "Nobles, noblemen, grandees, persons of high extraction, gentlemen, gentlefolk; honourable men; [. . .] a class of cultivators who claim certain privileges;—adj. Well-born, of good family, noble; gentle, meek, mild; refined, courteous, urbane." (1884, 57). *Ashrāf* is the plural of *sharīf*, which is defined as "Of high rank or dignity, exalted, eminent, honourable, noble, of good family, high-born; possessing glory or dignity; legitimate;—a title of honour of any descendant of the Prophet, as also of the rulers of Mecca; a prince, a chief or head (e.g. sharīf-ĕ-qaum, 'chief or head of a tribe or caste'). . ." (1884, 727).

11. The primary *ashrāf* groups were Sayyids (descendants of the Prophet Muhamad), Shaikhs (descendants from the companions of the Prophet and also of Arab origin), Mughals (descendants from Central Asians Turks), and Pathans.

12. Platts's *A Dictionary of Urdu, Classical Hindi, and English* defines *ajlāf* as "Base, vile, mean, or ignoble people; the rude, the vulgar; the lower orders" (1884, 24). *Ajlāf* is the plural of *jalaf,* which is defined as "Hard, severe; churlish; mean, base, despicable;—a churlish fellow; a miser" (1884, 387).

13. The ashraafiya itself designated a precolonial formation (see Lelyveld n.d.). Leadership among Indian Muslims, whether they supported the demand for Pakistan or positions of the Indian National Congress, were drawn heavily from the ashraafiya, while these same groups also gained prominence in diverse array of religious institutions and movements throughout the colonial period. The most prominent justification for retaining the power of the ashraafiya by the colonial British state came from Sir Sayyed Ahmed Khan (see Falahi 2020, 2007).

14. The hegemonic status of such elites would nevertheless be contested following independence through public arenas (most prominently, print media and literary forms), regional claims of autonomy, linguistic conflict, and social and economic mobility (see Gilmartin 1998).

15. For an intersection of ashraafiya hegemony and Sindhi nationalism, literature, and progressive politics, see the discussion by Hussain (2019, 2020).

16. One important point to highlight is that, unlike *ashrāf* and *ajlāf,* the distinction between agriculturalist and nonagriculturalist does not rely as much upon claiming ancestry and tracing descent through foreign lineages. There are, of course, other caste designations that connect being of "higher status" with descent from Rajput lineages, as well as other groups viewed as pastoralists such as Gujjars.

17. In the highly influential work of the sociologist Hamza Alavi (1988), for instance, the Muslim salariat, consisting of "the urban educated classes who qualify for employment in the colonial state," were dominant in the Muslim League and the "driving force" behind the Muslim nationalism and the demand for Pakistan, retained their status after independence because of their control over the civilian bureaucracy and access to education. Moreover, Alavi commences his fascinatingly detailed ethnographic account of Punjabi kinship by unequivocally claiming, "In the Muslim rural society of West Punjab ... it is kinship system rather than caste which embodies the primordial ties which structure its social organization" (1972: 1; see also Ahmad 1970). More recent scholarship on Pakistan that has been influenced by the work of Hamza Alavi and others has paid so much attention to class as a category of analysis and a formalistic understanding of the modern nation-state that it has largely ignored or sidelined caste-based dynamics (Ahmad 1970; Akhtar 2018; Alavi 1972; Javid 2015; Martin 2015). A note exception to this work was Shahnaz Rouse's (1988) account of agrarian transformations in the Punjab following the Green Revolution.

18. Though Frederick Barth (1960) applied theories of caste to his study of the Swat Pathan, more recent scholarship, however, has started to analyze the perverseness of caste

in social life, as well as its relationship to politics in Pakistan's history (Asif 2020; Gazdar 2007; Gazdar and Mallah 2012; Hussain 2019b; Javid and Martin 2020).

19. See Chalfin (2019); Chatterjee (2019); Corwin and Gidwani (2021); Doherty (2019); Fredericks (2018); Gandy (1994); Gidwani (2013); Gill (2009); Hecht (2018); Liboiron (2021); O'Hare (2019); Millar (2018); Resnick (2021); Solomon (2019); Stamatopoulou-Robbins (2019); Zhang (2020).

20. Agamben's concern, here and elsewhere, is that because bare (or naked) life has become "the ultimate and opaque bearer of sovereignty" and "the dominant form of life everywhere," we have found ourselves in a moment where our appreciation of life has become impoverished—the forms of life we see becoming hegemonic around us are unable to "coher[e] into a 'form-of-life'" (Agamben 2000, 6).

21. This is part of what Agamben has traced as "a genealogical inquiry into the term 'life.'" (Agamben 1999, 239). The purpose of this project is to foreground a philosophy of absolute immanence located within the writings of Western philosophers such as Spinoza, Nietzsche, Deleuze, and Foucault. Life—biological, contemplative, blessed—are to be pushed onto the same terrain for political philosophy, where epistemology has become indistinguishable from ontology. As a note, my own formulation is separate from discussions of emergent forms of life related to biomedicine, genetics, and other kinds of biopolitical intervention into our conceptions of life itself (see e.g., Fischer 2003; Petryna 2013; Rose 2009).

22. For instance, in a speech to district committees in 1875, the Sanitary Commissioner of the Punjab Annesley Castriot Charles de Renzy levied a harsh indictment against those forms of life that hindered "progress" in sanitation and public health in British India, in which he emphasized: "The cause may all be expressed in one word, namely, 'dirt'! Dirt in the air, dirt in the soil, dirt in the water, dirt in the dwelling, dirt on the person, dirt in the clothes; and the remedy for excessive sickness consists simply in the removal of dirt." "Proposed Address to District Committees Regarding Sanitary Matter." No. 909, Lahore, November 5, 1875. From A. C. C. De Renzy, Sanitary Commissioner, Punjab, to Secretary to Government, Punjab, 959.

23. This is akin to what Rosalind Fredericks (2018) has called "governing-through-disposability" that describes changes in governance and urbanisms in Senegal over the course of several decades. Similarly, in Zsuzsa Gille's (2007) work on transitioning regimes for waste in Hungary, such terms draw our attention to how changing notions of disposability and worth are not simply instantiated in material things like resources and commodities but are part of a shift in the grammar of government, the state, and capital (see also Doherty 2019; Zhang 2020; Resnick 2021). And, although disposability has been an alluring framework for understanding contemporary capitalism, infrastructures of disposability in fact build upon and participate in a longer biopolitical project of the modern state, ensuring and securing the health of the population, though in often deeply uneven ways (Foucault 1991, 2007; see also Hamlin 1998; Joyce 2003; Prakash 1999).

24. In a well-known review article, Brian Larkin has described infrastructures as "the architecture for circulation," emphasizing that they "are the matter that enable the

movement of other matter. [Infrastructures'] peculiar ontology lies in the fact that they are things and also the relation between things" (2013, 329; see also Star 1999). Historically, infrastructures of all kinds have been organized in ways that imbue them with distinct rationalities of rule, governance, and markets, making them into key sites for claims making by citizens, patron-client relations, economic exchanges, urbanisms, and shifts in socialist, liberal, and democratic politics (Ahmann 2019; Anand 2017; Barry 2013; Collier 2011; Coleman 2017; Larkin 2008; von Schnitzler 2016). Similarly, infrastructures in Pakistan have been suffused with expectations of modernity, in which large-scale technological systems were attached to forms of government and state power, notions of civilizational progress and national development, and the possibilities of urban life (Khan 2006; Akhter 2015; Anwar 2015; Imran 2010; Mustafa 2013; Akhter et al. 2022).

25. Waste infrastructures can be seen as a sociotechnical assemblages comprising material things, bodies, persons, spaces, and forms of work. This assemblage book is akin to that which is described in the work of Jane Bennett: "Assemblages are ad hoc of diverse elements, of vibrant materials of all sorts. Assemblages are living, throbbing confederations that are able to function despite the persistent presence of energies confound them from within. ... The effects generated by an assemblage are, rather, emergent properties, emergent in that their ability to make something happen ... is distinct from the sum of the vital force of each materiality considered alone." (2010, 23–24; see also Deleuze and Guattari 1987; Povinelli 2016, 51–54). Though sharing an interest in the materiality of things, the concept of assemblage thematizes the capacity of self-organizing processes, in which elements and relations that constitute such processes produce things (i.e., "events") that are greater than these constitutive elements and relations. What is key about assemblages is the "concatenation of mediators," whereby elements are connected by coming into relation to one another and subsequently, through which processes and events unfold across historical moments and within social life (Latour 2005, 59). The concept of assemblages allows me to trace waste infrastructures in Pakistan across a variety of spatiotemporal scales, in which distinct things, relations, bodies, persons, rationalities, technologies, and forms of work come into and out of view. Moments in which such elements come together are contingent in nature, though their convergence is not accidental and can be examined in relation to a wider set of processes.

26. The City District Government of Lahore (CDGL) consists of the nine Tehsil Municipal Administrations that fall within the Lahore Division. Prior to the CDGL, Lahore was administratively organized as the Municipal Corporation of Lahore, and prior to that, the Lahore Municipal Committee. Currently, the Lahore Waste Management Company (LWMC) is entrusted with the power and authority to oversee waste disposal and management for the CDGL, though it is an administrative entity that falls under the Government of Punjab. Prior to the formation of the LWMC, this power and authority was invested in the Solid Waste Management Department as a part of the CDGL. The Cantonment, which consists of the Lahore and Walton Cantonment Boards and under which the Defence Housing Authority falls, is administratively and infrastructurally separated from the CDGL (see Map 0.2). The Cantonment has its own staff of municipal workers, supervisors, and administrative staff that oversees waste disposal and management.

However, much of the actual waste materials collected from within the boundaries of the Cantonment ends up in dumping grounds and landfills located in the CDGL. Most if not all of my fieldwork was carried out in areas falling within the CDGL.

27. This aligns with Mary Douglas's well-known formulation of "dirt as matter out of place." For Douglas, dirt "implies two conditions: a set of ordered relations and contravention of that order" (2002, 44). Waste is a conceptual and material entity, but importantly one, as highlighted by Douglas, that creates and enacts a set of relations between materials things, bodies, persons, spaces, and ecologies, in which the work surrounding such an entity becomes crucial to maintaining and reproducing those relations (see also Liboiron 2014).

28. The work of Manu Goswami (2004) has been influential to my framing, as she has highlighted how sociotechnical entities, like land and revenue settlement or railways, were interlinked with producing diverse spatial scales and their attendant imaginaries, whether those be of imperial geographies and global capitalist economies or anticolonial nationalism and the national economy. Similarly, the act of reproducing Lahore as a spatial and imagined entity entails sociotechnical entities being brought together to stabilize such an entity across historical time.

29. The capital-labor relation refers to how accumulation was made possible through exploitation of waged labor in the domain of production. Not only are sanitation workers employed by the municipality as wage laborers, but also this work is intimately tied to the production and consumption of disposable commodities on a mass scale. Concurrently, in Pakistan's waste economies, as is the case the world over, informalized relations of work and exchange have arisen precisely because of an absence of formalized, waged labor.

30. The insights of this scholarship have sought to examine not only how reproductive forms of work, which tend to performed by gendered and racialized subjects of labor, remain essential to capitalist social relations through their appropriation outside the wage form (see Bear et al. 2015; Herzig and Subramaniam 2017; Mies 1998; Vora 2015), but also how to imagine social relations and forms of economic activity outside those same capitalist relations (Gibson-Graham 2006). This is where these discussions around reproductive work converge with those of the informal economy. Keith Hart reformulated informality in the economy as "an economic variant of the general theory of formal organizations," though it was formulated in relation to social and economic restructuring happening in Africa in the 1970s and as a technique for engaging with development economists (1985, 58). Importantly, Julia Elyachar has examined how a vacuum between state and society has emerged, in which nongovernmental organizations and other actors from civil society have entered to take on issues around informal housing and poverty alleviation (2005, 2012; see also Roitman 1990; Roy and AlSayyad 2004). Whereas the discussion of the informal economy is vast in its nature, two key aspects of informality are the fact that it is an effect of state-centric discourses and distinctions (e.g., public and private), while also exceeding them as it comes to be embedded in networks of circulation unfolding at a range of scales.

31. A critical aspect of Subramanian's approach has been to foreground both symbolic and materialist elements through which caste inequality has crystalized across historical moments, which goes against both culturalist approaches that prioritize values of purity

(see e.g., Dumont 1980; see also Appadurai 1988 for a critique of Dumont's approach) or Marxist approaches that subsume caste as a religious phenomenon into class as an encompassing social and political category. Other work (e.g., Béteille 1991; Fuller and Narasimhan 2014) has similarly sought to understand how caste groups have reproduced their power and position across generations through access to similar forms of capital discussed by Subramaniam.

32. This emphasis of how urbanization, waste infrastructures, and urbanization in South Asia are implicated in histories of caste and ethnicity has recently been taken up (see Gidwani and Kumar 2019; Sreenath 2020; Kornberg 2019).

33. Dana Kornberg (2019) makes an analogous point when examining processes of "casteification" among Muslim migrant workers from West Bengal who have entered Delhi's waste economy. According to Kornberg, "casteification" in this context refers to how caste has become organized through social practices brought together, something that allows it to remain stable while also changing across time.

34. Ambedkar (2014 [1979] had described "endogamy as a key to the mystery of the Caste system"], 5), just as the figure of surplus women (and men) was one to be brought under control though not just through endogamy but also "*sati*, enforced widowhood, and female infanticide" (Mitra 2021, 17). More generally, there is now a long-established body of work that has sought to center Dalit feminism within Indian feminism, and tracking the ways in which Brahmanical hegemony and patriarchy are constituted jointly, shaping the ritualized and everyday forms of violence exercised upon Dalit women and men (see Arya 2020; Arya and Rathore 2020; Chakravarti 2018; Guru 1995; Rao 2005; Rege 1998).

CHAPTER 1

1. This was established along with other Improvement Trust Committees in other cities throughout British India (see e.g., Kidambi 2007).

2. *Kuchas* refer to passages within alleys that do not open out back into a street and end in a cul-de-sac.

3. In 1832, the Royal Commission of Enquiry into the Poor Laws (headed by Edwin Chadwick) initiated a process of sanitary and public health reform across Great Britain. Much of the subsequent institutional and infrastructural interventions would be directed at being more attentive to changing conditions of life and work in Britain's industrializing centers that had been devastated by epidemics of fever, typhus, plague, and cholera. This would emerge concurrently with interventions across the imperial world, which would be directed at securing and legitimizing rule over subjugated populations. Moreover, sanitary and public health reform was also connected to the laws directed at the regulation of prostitution, especially the Contagious Disease Act of 1864–8 (Ballhatchet 1980; Whitehead 1995; Legg 2009; Howell 2000).

4. These laws would be most prominently codified in the first penal code of 1862 and dealt directly with "offences affecting the public health, safety, convenience, decency and morals" (Sharan 2006, 4906). One can be held accountable for such offenses "if s/he carried out 'any act or is guilty of an illegal omission which causes any common injury, danger or annoyance to the public or to the people in general who dwell or occupy property in

the vicinity, or which must necessarily cause injury, obstruction, danger or annoyance to persons who may have occasion to use any public right' (Sharan 2006, 4906).

5. In Sialkot for instance, *athri* Chūre had "to plough and irrigate the land, carry manure, attend to the cattle, and do the hardest part of the threshing and winnowing," rarely worked for more than one family, and were renumerated in food, different measures of "cereals at harvest," clothing, and other items such as blankets (Government of Punjab 1895, 98). On the other hand, *sepi* Chūre were engaged with multiple households, were "scavengers of the house and byre," made "most of the dung fuel," and tended to the cattle, all while being given a portion of the harvest (1895, 98). Similarly, Chūre in the Lahore district were described as having "hereditary duties of sweeping scavenging for certain families, to whom they also render occasional assistance in field work by working at the manure folding and feeding the cattle, or in busy seasons helping to drive the plough," and even at times, making winnowing pans (*chhaj*) or grass thatches (*sirki*) (1895, 111).

6. There were other aspects of those relations—most prominently that of settlement and marriage—that have worked to reproduce these forms of life. See, for example, Ahmad (1970), Gazdar and Mallah (2012), Javid and Martin (2020), and Jodhka (2002) on caste dynamics in relation to land, settlement, democratic politics, and marriage in rural Punjab.

7. Government of Punjab, "Letter from Secretary to the Government of India to the Board of Administration for the Affairs of the Punjab regarding Public Work and Irrigation in the Punjab," Nos. 60–2 (April 1850).

8. This characterization of Lahore's landscape as one of ruins was echoed later on: "The debris of ages has raised the site of the city to a considerable height above the river. The city is built on several mounds rising to a height of fifty feet and under, with incumber depressions" (Government of Punjab 2006[1894], 284–85).

9. As Nida Rehman has described, characterization of landscapes as ruins offered "powerful historical legitimacy to the act of physical transformation" in colonial Lahore, especially with regard to ideas of the Garden City and the construction of a canal system across the Punjab (2014, 179; see also Rehman 2009).

10. Government of Punjab, "Sanitary Improvement of Lahore," no. 3. (October 1869), 522–23; see also Government of Punjab, "Lahore Fresh Water Supply to Civil Station of Lahore," no. 10 (July 1869). As he was a proponent of contagionism, De Renzy recommended the provisioning of a "pure" water supply and the flushing of drains, as cholera was found in the 1880s to be a waterborne disease resulting from the contamination of water by human excrement.

11. Government of Punjab, "Sanitary Inspections of Villages," no. 6 (May 1876), 175.

12. By the 1890s "substantial improvements" would be made into the water supply, which would be partly due "new water-filters, such as the Pasteur-Chamberland, with much denser filter beds capable of preventing the passage of micro-organisms" (Harrison 1994, 68). More generally, David Arnold (1993) had observed that was an overall improvement in the health of the Indian Army, though higher among British troops than Indian ones, while the health of the wider population would suffer considerably from epidemics of malaria, cholera, plague, and influenza, which raised deaths rates among Indians.

13. Vinay Gidwani, writing about capitalist development in colonial Gujrat and other areas of British India, describes these transformations as a "processes of channeling and forming in desired ways the errant matter of native subjects and their physical environments," which sought to engender "an optimal balance between the internment and circulation of nonhuman flows as well as human bodies" (2008, 14).

14. Prior to these reforms, British and Indian members were appointed to serve on the Municipal Committee. Limited "indigenous representation" in these committees was unacceptable to liberal critics as it went against the notion of "self-government," which was necessary to change "indigenous cultural practices" that impacted health and hygiene (Harrison 1994, 166). Even if committee members were indigenous and elected, it was not close to universal enfranchisement as only European and Indian "ratepayers" within a municipality could serve not them.

15. As was the case for settlement, "customary" rights were especially protected in the Punjab, a province in which the colonial state organized itself around a rationalized, scientific order that was distinct from but dependent upon the domain of custom as affective relations and kinship that was thought to constitute the Punjabi social and political order (see Gilmartin 1994a, 1994b)

16. Much of the work on sweepers and scavengers in colonial India has distilled out the tension between custom and contract, as well as tradition and modernity, played out in relation to organizing the labor of low- or noncaste groups across urban settings like Dehli (Prashad 1995, 2001) and Bombay (Masselos 1982) and in prominent sites like those of pilgrimage in the United Provinces (Khalid 2012).

17. For one such contract see Prashad (2000, 13), where the offer is made of Rs. 110 per mensem to clean a ward and the details of the breakdown of that amount.

18. This was common in other urban centers across the Punjab and the Delhi Municipal Corporation (see Prashad 2000, 12–14)

19. Vijay Prashad has analyzed the role supervisors played in organizing the labor of sweepers or scavengers, where such supervisors "appeared to the workers as their overlord, just as at time he might be their protector" (1995, 20).

20. Education, in this passage, operated within the colonial rule of difference, where Indian subjects, who were denied freedom, were being prepared for eventual self-rule (Chatterjee 1994; Mehta 1999).

21. The urban poor, whose access to land and work has been historically precarious, have consistently utilized public spaces to secure a place to live and access to work and livelihoods. Though contemporary "slum clearance" has its antecedents in the colonial period (see e.g., Anjaria 2016; Kaviraj 1997), these spatial practices have become contemporary sites of conflict between those who are seen to flout civility and public order by encroaching upon public spaces and those who desire to restore that civility and order by cleansing these spaces of this encroaching presence. Such a scenario has also been complicated, since urban elites and housing developers also draw upon their own "informal" strategies to encroach and build upon land in ways that go against the visions of space shared by the bureaucratic state and its planners (Moatasim 2019; Ghertner 2015).

CHAPTER 2

1. The *baildār* refers to a municipal worker who has been placed into a supervisory role but still occasionally carries out waste work.

2. Das and Poole (2004) have made evident that the margins of the state need not be a geographical metaphor akin to center and periphery but instantiates a political relationship, while others have emphasized how waste materials and those who work with them also exist on the margins of capitalist relations and social life more generally (see Gidwani and Reddy 2011; Doherty 2019; Alexander and Reno 2012; Alexander and Sanchez 2018).

3. On the resurgence of patronage and democratic politics in contemporary Pakistan (see Akhtar 2011; Javid 2011; Martin 2016). Ward Berenschot (2011, 2010) has drawn attention to how brokers and political fixers have delivered public goods within party-based democratic politics, especially through transactional acts of brokering that mediate relations between citizens accessing state resources and services and bureaucrats and other officials distributing those same resources and services. For a more general overview of patronage as politics in South Asia, see Piliavsky (2014).

4. Akhtar contrasts these classes from landed, bureaucratic, and military elites who became patrons because they had access to state institutions and resources and profited from agricultural and industrial development in the immediate decades following independence and before the regime of Zia ul-Haq. For the role of intermediary classes, see Harriss-White (2003).

5. Some of these practices include systems of municipal collection, sanitary landfill sites and incinerators, private waste management companies, and experiments in recycling, recovery, and reuse, which have also had an uptake in Pakistan as I discuss shortly. For an assessment of these developments in North America and Europe, see Gandy (1994).

6. City of Lahore Corporation Office, Corporation Proceedings, 1952–1953, Record Nos. 593, 595; City of Lahore Corporation, Corporation Proceedings, 1982–1983, Record Nos. 88, 107, 187, 197.

7. Members of the Municipal Corporation debated issues around this loan from the World Bank, such as its dispersal by the various tiers of government and stipulation on its repayment. See City of Lahore Corporation, Corporation Proceedings, 1985–1986, Record No. 51.

8. There were, however, greater than expected costs and delays in implementation. This extension had multiple reasons, part of which were "frequent management staff changes in the solid waste sector at MCL" (World Bank 1994, 4). Additionally, an increased cost by 72 percent was attributed to "substantially higher costs for solid waste management equipment (Rs. 177 million compared with Rs. 60 million estimated at appraisal)" (World Bank 1994, 5).

9. City of Lahore Corporation, Corporation Proceedings, 1998–1999, Document No. Unavailable.

10. Special Session of the District Council of Lahore, Resolution No. 193, 01/10/2005.

11. Special Session of the District Council of Lahore, Resolution No. 193, 01/10/2005.

12. Special Session of the District Council of Lahore, Resolution No. 14, 04/17/2006.

13. *Sifārish*, or intercession, is generally used when speaking about a situation in which the intercession of someone is necessary to achieve a desired goal or end, especially ones involving governmental departments.

14. City of Lahore Corporation, Corporation Proceedings, 1998–1999, Document No. 26–27.

15. The causative form is often used to indicate when the intercession of someone is needed in getting work done, especially when that work involves governmental bureaucracies, but is also regularly used in everyday speech when the actions of another are required for the completion of an act. Matthew Hull, in his account of bureaucratic practices in urban Pakistan, describes this verb form in the following way: "The mediation of actions is enacted in the frequent use of causative verbs in Urdu, formed through the addition of the suffix -*a* or -*wa* to the verb stem, which yields the meaning of 'to cause to have done' the action designated by the verb. ... The form represents the subject as the agent of actions done by another" (2012, 76).

CHAPTER 3

1. Shahdara is an area of Lahore across the River Ravi that, during the regime of Ayub Khan in the 1960s, became a major area of industrial development in Lahore (see Alvi 1997). Industrial activities of varying sizes continue to be concentrated in this area, especially warehouses and manufacturing units for processing plastics.

2. The notion of surplus comes from Karl Marx's formulation of surplus population, or industrial reserve army, as a direct outgrowth from the dual nature of capital accumulation, in which a greater number of workers are attracted to and rendered disposably by being "made relatively superfluous." (1977, 783). Ideas of surplus population and the industrial reserve army have been developed by Kalyan Sanyal (2007), who describes these populations as inhabiting the "wastelands" of postcolonial capitalist development. Others like Michael Denning (2010) have put forward similar arguments that wageless life stands prior to any notion of waged life under capitalist social relations, and the former should be taken as a starting point for thinking about a politics of work within contemporary forms of life. Though invested in the problem of unwaged labor, the informal economy articulates larger debates, especially among feminist critiques of Marxism, about the role that noncapital— either as unwaged reproductive labor, the commodification of labor power, or precapitalist social relations and hierarchies—has in facilitating accumulation and reproducing capital (Fortunati 1995; Collier and Yanagisako 1987; Tsing 2015; Bear et al. 2015; Gibson-Graham 2006). More recently, these insights have also been extended to take into account how biological and animal life becomes a site for appropriating surpluses and capitalist accumulation (Rajan 2006; Zhang 2020; Besky and Blanchette 2019).

3. In a series of early articles, Jan Breman (1976a, 1976b) described the informal sector in India as being one that was "fragmented" in nature, something stretched across urban and rural areas, and included a fourfold system of differentiated social classes operating within urban informal labor. More recently, Barbara Harriss-White (2003) has further elaborated the changing nature of informality, in which "intermediary classes" (the self-employed, farmers, moneylenders, and so forth) have become prominent and active,

with social relations and hierarchies along the lines of caste, class, gender, and place organizing relations within and across these classes. In Pakistan Aasim Sajjad Akhtar (2018) has examined how subcontracting and labor flexibility draws upon personalized ties and "extra-economic coercion" typically associated with patron-client relationships. The rise of informal labor in Pakistan, according to many (see e.g., Munir, Naqvi, and Usmani 2015), is part of Pakistan's shifting political economy, where deregulation and privatization have been accompanied by weakening labor unions, lack of political mobilization, expansion of the contract economy, and depression of real wages. For a longer connection between capitalism and informality, see Jan (2019) who has detailed how merchant capital in colonial Punjab was built upon informally organized markets, especially around kinship, caste, and religion. Moreover, the informalization of work and labor in Pakistan cannot be understood outside the political and economic ascendance of commercial and trading classes, especially the "bazaar trader" (*tajir*) (see Javed 2019). Similarly, many *bīopārīāṇ* would be viewed as engaging in commerce and trade, either through their own activities or through their connections to commodity production and consumption.

4. For an overview of these work relations in another Pakistani city, see Majeed et al. (2017)

5. This nature of the debt—specifically, that it can be a burden to repay or the extension of credit that makes other actions possible—has been of long-standing interest for anthropologists (see Mauss 2000; Gregory 2012; see also Peebles 2010). One can approach debt as another form of exchange, in which repayment (as an obligation) temporally organizes past and current conditions of life to possible future ones, thereby shaping subjective experiences of indebtedness. These points are elaborated in the final chapter of this volume when analyzing how indebtedness is embedded in the intergenerational trajectories of waste workers.

6. In the novel *Khudā Kī Bastī* by Shaukat Siddiqui (2015), for instance, one of the main characters is a *kabāṛī* named Niazi. Over the course the course of the novel, Niazi is repeatedly shown to be a morally dubious character because of his greedy disposition and lecherous behavior. Niazi initially convinces another main character, Nosha, to steal a car part from the mechanic that he works with. Not only would Nosha lose his job for stealing and increasingly start to pursue a path of making money, but Niazi gains favor with Nosha's mother, shortly thereafter marrying her and then poisoning her until she passes away. The moral dubiousness of a someone like Niazi comes not only from his greed and licentiousness but also from his presence within a locality with connections to larger networks. I also want to thank Manan Ahmed for drawing my attention to Siddiqui's novel.

7. Recently, Jairus Banaji (2020) has unpacked the act of trading within the longue durée of commercial capitalism, in which profit, as one form that surplus-value can take, is realized through the exchange of goods and money at different spatial scales and temporal rhythms, all of which requires a considerable amount of infrastructures that sustain these trading networks (see also Sanyal 2007, 114–17). Though circulation has at times been overlooked by Marxist accounts, another strand of scholarship has drawn attention to how merchants, firms, companies, and other kinds of trading networks exercise control over

infrastructures of circulation to realize profits out of goods and commodities as they are exchanged on markets (see Bernstein 1976; Harriss-White 1999; Jan 2019; Roseberry 1989).

8. For a similar dynamic, see Kaveri Gill (2009), who traces how a Dalit community known as *khatiks* use caste networks and solidarity to consolidate their position within markets for recycled plastics.

9. Gujrat is the capital city of Gujrat District and lies about 150 km almost directly north of Lahore. On the way to the city from Lahore, one passes through the core of Punjab's agroindustrial landscape. This road cuts through cities such as Gujranwala (a city I return to later in this chapter) and Sialkot, both of which are major centers of industrial production in Pakistan, while a steady stream of fields makes evident the region's agricultural economy.

10. Originally meant for labor migrating to the city who were finding employment in industries such as the railways in the first half of the twentieth century, Misri Shah has become a major hub of the junk and scrap metal market in Pakistan. Materials arrive here from across the country and abroad and depart on their way to other areas of Lahore, Pakistan, and foreign countries.

11. Waste brought back into the pale of value is achieved by the workings of markets for waste materials. Çalışkan and Callon have described markets as "socio-technical arrangements or assemblages (*agencements*)" that enable the "conception, production, and circulation of goods" and bring together technical, infrastructural, scientific, and other epistemological systems (2010, 3; see also Muniesa, Millo, and Callon 2007). Importantly, such markets are not outside of politics, especially when viewed as sites of struggle over the relative worth of goods and persons (Boltanski and Thevenot 2006). Though the sociology of markets and finance has made important contributions to understanding markets as comprising scientific, infrastructural, and epistemological components, it has predominantly concerned itself with formally organized and regulated markets, which nevertheless rest upon considerable informality, contingency, and indeterminacy (see e.g., Zaloom 2003; Pinzur 2016). Markets for waste materials and labor, especially as they concern me, exhibit greater fragmentation and autonomy, something that both embeds and disaggregates them from larger processes of market formation and circulation.

12. These concrete and abstract transformations rely upon scales of nominalization indexing historical arrival, changes in the global economy, geographies of uneven development and social differentiation, and relative quality based on presumed origin (see Guyer 2004, 83–94). Abstraction is one key modality through which value is generated out of waste materials, even outside of informal economies (Butt 2020). For discussions of how material things become objectified and abstracted through semiotic forms, knowledge, and techno-scientific practices, see Maurer (2006); Keane (2003); and Scott (1998).

13. The exchange-value gestures to how money becomes the dominant form of value and the standard against which other forms of value come to be evaluated and made commensurate; however, as should be clear by now, money takes on distinct material forms (cash, debts, checks) and is invested with meaning for what other actions and activities it makes possible (see Turner 2008; Maurer 2006). Even if exchange-value is a dominant way

in which money as a form of value is utilized, it does not exhaust the possibilities for the exchange of waste and money.

14. Payments come with their own articulations of trust and the social. For instance, Nelms et al. (2018) describe how payment innovations such as Bitcoin and the sharing economy entail a formulation of trust and the social as "just us," without the intervention of state and corporate entities.

15. Along with Julia Kristeva (1982), Bataille, who has been a central figure in thinking through abjection as a generalized and central feature of social life, approached abjection as at once based in material itself (i.e., abject things) and the nature of the social (i.e., abjection produces and affirms separations between classes of persons). Agamben criticizes Bataille for this fact, as the latter cleaved "naked life" from "forms of life" in favor of a "superior principle—sovereignty or the sacred" (Agamben 2000, 7).

CHAPTER 4

1. Sophia Stamatopoulou-Robbins (2019) has made a similar point about the distribution of waste in Palestine, which has become saturated with waste as a result of its relative absence in Israel.

2. Similar tensions between individual choice and genealogical inheritance play themselves out in how marriages, friendships, and other affinities across caste and religious lines have challenged and reworked the normative basis of sociality in South Asia (Das 2010; de Munck 1996; Mody 2008; Orsini 2006; Osella and Osella 1998; Ring 2006).

3. Intimacy emerged as an object of analysis to examine how gendered and racialized relations undergirded colonial and imperial projects. Illustrative in this regard is Ann Stoler's (2002) work on how racial classifications in the Dutch East Indies were subtended by gendered and sexual practices (e.g., parenting, nursing, domestic labor, and illicit sex).

4. Scholars using other approaches have investigated how intimacy is being reworked under globalization by mass mediation and public culture (e.g., Mazzarella 2004; Shryock 2004).

5. Drawing on the work of Viviana Zelizer (2005), Juno Salazar Parreñas (2016) has demonstrated how transnational volunteers in wildlife rehabilitation facilities in Thailand engage in transactional, nonmonetized exchange, which enacts a form of intimate labor that involves vulnerability and proximity with nonhuman animals. More generally, there has been a proliferation of forms of work, both paid and unpaid, that many consider intimate. These include domestic work, medical care, and sex work, and each is increasingly being commodified and regulated across geographic scales (see Boris and Parreñas 2010; Constable 2009; Wilson 2004; see also Glenn 1992).

6. See note 34, pp. 188.

7. Such themes are prevalent in blasphemy allegations in Pakistan, where statements or actions perceived as attacks on the honor of the Prophet (and Islam and Muslims more generally) elicit shame and must be protected through violent acts of love (Ashraf 2018).

8. Since the late 1980s, "633 Muslims, 494 Ahmadis, 187 Christians and 21 Hindus have been accused under various provisions on offences related to religion" (Amnesty International 2016, 10). Most killings have not been carried out by the Pakistani state—for example, 70 people accused of blasphemy have been lynched— while, as of 2018, 40 people had been sentenced to death or were serving life sentences (Human Rights Commission of Pakistan 2019, 120).

CHAPTER 5

1. The home as a material and conceptual entity that expresses social orders and hierarchies has been a long-standing interest among anthropologists. See e.g., Carsten and Hugh-Jones (1995); Cieraad (1999); Bourdieu (1970); Miller (2001).

2. These are cities where those who build and maintain the city, while concurrently doing the same for their own homes and lives, are "regarded as somehow disposable, degradable, and recyclable" (Appadurai 2013, 125). The framework of disposability is a common one in accounts of waste, precarity, and abjection in contemporary cities and capitalism (see e.g., Anand 2012; Chalfin 2019; Reddy 2015). This framework is related to, though distinct from, what Rosalind Fredericks (2018) has recently examined as "governing through disposability," in which disposability enters into logics of governance and urban life.

3. For an account of similar processes in Karachi, see Anwar (2018).

4. The disjuncture between the present and future is familiar from accounts of precarity among the urban poor and working-class communities (see Han 2018; Das and Randeria 2015; Millar 2014).

5. These expectations are akin to what Arjun Appadurai has described for aspiration, "as a navigational capacity" that is inseparable "from language, social values, histories, and institutional norms, which tend to be highly specific" (2013, 189, 290). Recent scholarship has drawn greater attention to how housing—its political economy, aesthetic design, and material properties—becomes invested with aspirations of multiple actors, from state institutions, real estate and housing developers, nongovernmental organizations, and inhabitants (Anand and Rademacher 2011; Archambault 2018; Elinoff 2016; Fennell 2015).

6. My account of intergenerational life draws on recent insights by Sarah Besky (2017) and Mythri Jegathesan (2018) who, both writing in the context of plantation labor, demonstrate how histories of settlement, work, and life are organized through investments in and the upkeep of homes across generations, which reflect shifts in postcolonial labor markets and state-citizen interactions.

7. "Chaudhary" usually refers to a prominent landowner. Here, Baba Isaak used this term to refer to his own father because of his control over livestock, rather than land— these both being sources of wealth and prestige.

8. Here *mistrī* refers to "bricklayer," but *mistrī* more generally refers to anyone doing manual, physical labor. Thus, in Pakistan one could also use the term to speak about a car mechanic. Also, the construction sectors in Pakistan have expanded considerably during this period, which has made contractors into a key feature of urban labor markets (see Akhtar 2011).

9. This is akin to what Asher Ghertner has examined as "nuisance talk," which "operates as the key principle according to which discourses of the slum are both organized in everyday speech and translated from the neighborhood into a broader rationality for governing space" (2015, 79).

10. This is most discernible in unfree labor prevalent in a variety of industries, especially related to construction: for instance, in brick kilns, many workers are Christian and/or come from other low- or noncaste backgrounds and work as indentured labor because of intergenerational indebtedness (see e.g., Ercelawn and Nauman 2004). Relatedly, agrarian politics in Punjab depends upon intersections of tenant relations, debt bondage, and factionalism (see Martin 2009).

11. Sarah Besky (2017) elaborates on the blurriness of these divisions when she examines how plantation labor, as a particular configuration of settlement, work, and life, has been able to reproduce itself across historical moments. Others have made similar points about how the exchange of money, especially in ritual contexts, links the reproduction of individual lives with those of "social and ideological systems," thereby legitimating religio-political orders (Bloch and Parry 1989, 1; see also Lambek 2001)

12. This is quite discernible among women, for instance, who have been targeted by microfinance NGOS for loans and credit; these women also rely upon kinship, caste, and class relations in navigating the risks of these loans, as well as augmenting them with other sources of credit (see Kar 2017; Guérin, d'Espallier, and Venkatasubramanian 2013; Guérin 2014).

13. This refers to when a piece of land or house is enclosed by a boundary wall. This meaning is also entangled with the creation of a domestic space, in which women are enclosed and separated from non-kin, male outsiders.

14. See James Holston's (1991) account of "auto-construction" on Brazil's urbanizing peripheries.

15. This is discernible across a range of contexts. See, e.g., Doherty (2019); Fredericks (2018); Chalfin (2019); Chatterjee (2019); O'Hare (2019); and Millar (2018).

16. The work of Doherty (2019) and Zhang (2020) traces the intersections of urban development and the subject of labor in waste materials and infrastructures.

17. For recent exceptions to such tendencies in the study of waste, see Solomon (2019) and Resnick (2021).

REFERENCES

Abrams, Philip. 1988. "Notes on the Difficulty of Studying the State." *Journal of Historical Sociology* 1 (1): 58–89.

Agamben, Giorgio. 1999. *Potentialities: Collected Essays in Philosophy.* Palo Alto, CA: Stanford University Press.

———. 2000. *Means without Ends: Notes on Politics.* Minneapolis: University of Minnesota Press.

Ahmad, Imtiaz. 1967. "The Ashraf and Ajlaf Categories in Indo-Muslim Society." *Economic and Political Weekly* 2 (9): 887–91.

Ahmad, Saghir. 1970. "Social Stratification in a Punjabi Village." *Contributions to Indian Sociology* 4 (1): 105–25.

Ahmann, Chloe. 2019. "Waste to Energy: Garbage Prospects and Subjunctive Politics in Late-Industrial Baltimore." *American Ethnologist* 46 (3): 328–42.

Akhtar, Aasim Sajjad. 2011. "Patronage and Class in Urban Pakistan: Modes of Labor Control in the Contractor Economy." *Critical Asian Studies* 43 (2): 159–84.

———. 2018. *The Politics of Common Sense: State, Society and Culture in Pakistan.* Cambridge: Cambridge University Press.

Akhter, Majed. 2015. "Infrastructure Nation: State Space, Hegemony, and Hydraulic Regionalism in Pakistan." *Antipode* 47 (4): 849–70.

Akhter, Majed, Aasim Sajjad Akhtar, and Hassan H. Karrar. 2022. "The Spatial Politics of Infrastructure-Led Development: Notes from an Asian Postcolony." *Antipode* 54 (5): 1347–64.

Alavi, Hamza. 1972. "Kinship in West Punjab Villages." *Contributions to Indian Sociology* 6 (1): 1–27.

———. 1988. "Pakistan and Islam: Ethnicity and Ideology." In *State and Ideology in the Middle East and Pakistan,* edited by Fred Halliday and Hamza Alavi, 64–111. Basingstoke, UK: Macmillan Education.

Alexander, Catherine, and Joshua Reno, eds. 2012. *Economies of Recycling: The Global Transformations of Materials, Values and Social Relations.* London: Zed.

Alexander, Catherine, and Joshua Reno. 2014. "From Biopower to Energopolitics in England's Modern Waste Technology." *Anthropological Quarterly* 87 (2): 335–58.

Alexander, Catherine, and Andrew Sanchez. 2018. *Indeterminacy: Waste, Value, and the Imagination.* New York: Berghahn Books.

Ali, Imran. 1988. *The Punjab under Imperialism: 1885–1947.* Princeton, NJ: Princeton University Press.

Ali, Kamran Asdar. 2011. "Communists in a Muslim Land: Cultural Debates in Pakistan's Early Years." *Modern Asian Studies* 45 (3): 501–34.

Ali, Nosheen. 2019. *Delusional States: Feeling Rule and Development in Pakistan's Northern Frontier*. Cambridge, UK: Cambridge University Press.

Alvi, Imtiaz. 1997. *The Informal Sector in Urban Economy: Low Income Housing in Lahore*. Karachi: Oxford University Press.

Ambedkar, Bhimrao. 2014 [1979]. "Castes in India." In *Dr. Babasaheb Ambedkar: Writings and Speeches*, 13–22. New Delhi: Dr. Ambedkar Foundation.

Amnesty International. 2016. *"As Good as Dead": The Impact of the Blasphemy Laws in Pakistan*. London: Amnesty International.

Anand, Nikhil. 2012. "Municipal Disconnect: On Abject Water and Its Urban Infrastructures." *Ethnography* 13 (4): 487–509.

———. 2017. *Hydraulic City: Water and the Infrastructures of Citizenship in Mumbai*. Durham, NC: Duke University Press.

Anand, Nikhil, and Anne Rademacher. 2011. "Housing in the Urban Age: Inequality and Aspiration in Mumbai." *Antipode* 43 (5): 1748–72.

Anderson, Warwick. 1995. "Excremental Colonialism: Public Health and the Poetics of Pollution." *Critical Inquiry* 21 (3): 640–69.

———. 2006. *Colonial Pathologies: American Tropical Medicine, Race, and Hygiene in the Philippines*. Durham, NC: Duke University Press.

Anjaria, Jonathan Shapiro. 2016. *The Slow Boil: Street Food, Rights and Public Space in Mumbai*. Palo Alto, CA: Stanford University Press.

Anwar, Nausheen H. 2012. "State Power, Civic Participation and the Urban Frontier: The Politics of the Commons in Karachi." *Antipode* 44 (3): 601–20.

———. 2015. *Infrastructure Redux: Crisis, Progress in Industrial Pakistan & Beyond*. London: Palgrave Macmillan.

———. 2018. "Receding Rurality, Booming Periphery." *Economic & Political Weekly* 53 (12): 46–54.

Appadurai, Arjun. 1988. "Putting Hierarchy in Its Place." *Cultural Anthropology* 3 (1): 36–49.

———. 2013. *The Future as Cultural Fact: Essays on the Global Condition*. London: Verso.

Archambault, Julie Soleil. 2018. "'One Beer, One Block': Concrete Aspiration and the Stuff of Transformation in a Mozambican Suburb." *Journal of the Royal Anthropological Institute* 24 (4): 692–708.

Arnold, David. 1993. *Colonizing the Body: State Medicine and Epidemic Disease in Nineteenth Century India*. Berkeley: University of California Press.

Arya, Sunaina. 2020. "Dalit or Brahmanical Patriarchy? Rethinking Indian Feminism." *CASTE/A Global Journal on Social Exclusion* 1 (1): 217–28.

Arya, Sunaina, and Aakash Singh Rathore. 2020. *Dalit Feminist Theory: A Reader*. New York: Routledge.

Ashraf, Sana. 2018. "Honour, Purity and Transgression: Understanding Blasphemy Accusations and Consequent Violent Action in Punjab, Pakistan." *Contemporary South Asia* 26 (1): 51–68.

Asif, Ghazal. 2020. "Jogendranath Mandal and the Politics of Dalit Recognition in Pakistan." *South Asia: Journal of South Asian Studies* 43 (1): 119–35.

Ballhatchet, Kenneth. 1980. *Race, Sex, and Class under the Raj: Imperial Attitudes and Policies and Their Critics, 1793–1905*. London: Weidenfeld and Nicolson.

Banaji, Jairus. 2020. *A Brief History of Commercial Capitalism*. Chicago: Haymarket Books.

Barnett, Stephen A. 1975. "Approaches to Changes in Caste Ideology in South India." In *Essays on South India*, edited by Burton Stein, 149–80. Honolulu: University Press of Hawaii.

Barrier, Norman. 1967. "The Punjab Disturbances of 1907: The Response of the British Government in India to Agrarian Unrest." *Modern Asian Studies* 1 (4): 353–83.

Barry, Andrew. 2013. *Material Politics: Disputes along the Pipeline*. Chichester, UK: Wiley-Blackwell.

Barth, Fredrik. 1960. "The System of Social Stratification in Swat, North Pakistan." In *Aspects of Caste in South India, Ceylon, and North-West Pakistan*, edited by Edmund Leach, 113–46. New York: Cambridge University Press.

Bataille, Georges. 1988. *The Accursed Share: An Essay on General Economy*. New York: Zone Books.

Batool, Syeda Adila, and Chaudhary Muhammad Nawaz. 2009. "Municipal Solid Waste Management in Lahore City District, Pakistan." *Waste Management* 29 (6): 1971–81.

Bauman, Zygmunt. 2005. *Work, Consumerism, and the New Poor*. New York: Open University Press.

Beall, Jo. 1997. "Policy Arena: Social Capital in Waste—a Solid Investment?" *Journal of International Development* 9 (7): 951–61.

———. 2006. "Dealing with Dirt and the Disorder of Development: Managing Rubbish in Urban Pakistan." *Oxford Development Studies* 34 (1): 81–97.

Bear, Laura, Karen Ho, Anna Tsing, and Sylvia Yanagisako. 2015. "Gens: A Feminist Manifesto for the Study of Capitalism." *Theorizing the Contemporary, Fieldsights*, March 30. https://culanth.org/fieldsights/gens-a-feminist-manifesto-for-the-study-of-capitalism

Bennett, Jane. 2010. *Vibrant Matter: A Political Ecology of Things*. Durham, NC: Duke University Press.

Berenschot, Ward. 2010. "Everyday Mediation: The Politics of Public Service Delivery in Gujarat, India." *Development and Change* 41 (5): 883–905.

———. 2011. "The Spatial Distribution of Riots: Patronage and the Instigation of Communal Violence in Gujarat, India." *World Development* 39 (2): 221–30.

Berlant, Lauren. 1998. "Intimacy: A Special Issue." *Critical Inquiry* 24 (2): 281–88.

———. 2007. "Slow Death (Sovereignty, Obesity, Lateral Agency)." *Critical Inquiry* 33 (4): 754–80.

———. 2011. *Cruel Optimism*. Durham, NC: Duke University Press.

Bernstein, Henry. 1976. "Underdevelopment and the Law of Value: A Critique of Kay." *Review of African Political Economy* 3 (6): 51–64.

Besky, Sarah. 2017. "Fixity: On the Inheritance and Maintenance of Tea Plantation Houses in Darjeeling, India." *American Ethnologist* 44 (4): 617–31.

Besky, Sarah, and Alex Blanchette, eds. 2019. *How Nature Works: Rethinking Labor on a Troubled Planet*. Santa Fe: University of New Mexico Press.

Béteille, André. 1991. "The Reproduction of Inequality: Occupation, Caste and Family." *Contributions to Indian Sociology* 25 (1): 3–28.

Beuving, Joost. 2013. "Playing Information Games: Démarcheurs in the Second-Hand Car Markets of Cotonou, Bénin." *Social Anthropology* 21 (1): 2–22.

Bhattacharya, Tithi. 2017. *Social Reproduction Theory: Remapping Class, Recentring Oppression*. London: Pluto Press.

Birla, Ritu. 2008. *Stages of Capital: Law, Culture, and Market Governance in Late Colonial India*. Durham, NC: Duke University Press.

Boltanski, Luc, and Laurent Thévenot. 2006. *On Justification: Economies of Worth*. Princeton Studies in Cultural Sociology. Princeton, NJ: Princeton University Press.

Boris, Eileen, and Rhacel Salazar Parreñas. 2010. *Intimate Labors: Cultures, Technologies, and the Politics of Care*. Palo Alto, CA: Stanford University Press.

Bourdieu, Pierre. 1970. "The Berber House or the World Reversed." *Social Science Information* 9 (2): 151–70.

———. 1986. "The Forms of Capital." In *Handbook of Theory and Research for the Sociology of Education*, edited by John Richardson. Westport, CT: Greenwood.

Breman, Jan. 1976a. "A Dualistic Labour System? A Critique of the 'Informal Sector' Concept: I: The Informal Sector." *Economic and Political Weekly* 11 (48): 1870–76.

———. 1976b. "A Dualistic Labour System? A Critique of the 'Informal Sector' Concept: II: A Fragmented Labour Market." *Economic and Political Weekly* 11 (49): 1905–8.

Butt, Waqas H. 2019. "Beyond the Abject: Caste and the Organization of Work in Pakistan's Waste Economy." *International Labor and Working-Class History* 95: 18–33.

———. 2020a. "Accessing Value in Lahore's Waste Infrastructures." *Ethnos*: 1–21.

———. 2020b. "Waste Intimacies: Caste and the Unevenness of Life in Urban Pakistan." *American Ethnologist* 47 (3): 234–48.

———. 2020c. "Technics of Labor: Productivism, Expertise, and Solid Waste Management in a Public-Private Partnership." *Anthropology of Work Review*, 41 (2): 108–18.

Çalışkan, Koray, and Michel Callon. 2010. "Economization, Part 2: A Research Programme for the Study of Markets." *Economy and Society* 39 (1): 1–32.

Caplan, Lionel. 1980. "Caste and Castelessness among South Indian Christians." *Contributions to Indian Sociology* 14 (2): 213–38.

Carr, E. Summerson, and Michael Lempert. 2016. "Introduction: Pragmatics of Scale." In *Scale: Discourse and Dimensions of Social Life*, edited by E. Summerson Carr and Michael Lempert, 1–21. Berkeley: University of California Press.

Carsten, Janet, and Stephen Hugh-Jones, eds. 1995. *About the House: Lévi-Strauss and Beyond*. Cambridge: Cambridge University Press.

Chakrabarty, Dipesh. 1991. "Open Space/Public Place: Garbage, Modernity and India." *South Asia: Journal of South Asian Studies* 14 (1): 15–31.

———. 2021. *The Climate of History in a Planetary Age*. Chicago: University of Chicago Press.

Chakravarti, Uma. 2018. *Gendering Caste: Through a Feminist Lens*. New Delhi: Sage.

Chalfin, Brenda. 2014. "Public Things, Excremental Politics, and the Infrastructure of Bare Life in Ghana's City of Tema." *American Ethnologist* 41 (1): 92–109.

———. 2017. "'Wastelandia': Infrastructure and the Commonwealth of Waste in Urban Ghana." *Ethnos* 82 (4): 1–24.

———. 2019. "Waste Work and the Dialectics of Precarity in Urban Ghana: Durable Bodies and Disposable Things." *Africa: The Journal of the International African Institute* 89 (3): 499–520.

Chatterjee, Partha. 1993. *Nationalist Thought and the Colonial World: A Derivative Discourse.* Minneapolis: University of Minnesota Press.

———. 1994. *The Nation and Its Fragments: Colonial and Postcolonial Histories.* Princeton, NJ: Princeton University Press.

Chatterjee, Syantani. 2019. "The Labors of Failure: Labor, Toxicity, and Belonging in Mumbai." *International Labor and Working-Class History* 95: 49–75.

Cieraad, Irene. 1999. "Introduction: Anthropology at Home." In *At Home: An Anthropology of Domestic Space*, edited by Irene Cieraad, 1–12. Syracuse, NY: Syracuse University Press.

Cohn, Bernard. 1987. *An Anthropologist among the Historians and Other Essays.* New York: Oxford University Press.

Coleman, Leo. 2017. *A Moral Technology: Electrification as Political Ritual in New Delhi.* Ithaca, NY: Cornell University Press.

Collier, Jane, and Sylvia Yanagisako. 1987. *Gender and Kinship: Essays toward a Unified Analysis.* Palo Alto, CA: Stanford University Press.

Collier, Stephen J. 2011. *Post-Soviet Social: Neoliberalism, Social Modernity, Biopolitics.* Princeton, NJ: Princeton University Press.

Constable, Nicole. 2009. "The Commodification of Intimacy: Marriage, Sex, and Reproductive Labor." *Annual Reviews of Anthropology* 38: 49–64.

Corwin, Julia E., and Vinay Gidwani. 2021. "Repair Work as Care: On Maintaining the Planet in the Capitalocene." *Antipode*: 1–20.

Cowen, Deborah. 2020. "Following the Infrastructures of Empire: Notes on Cities, Settler Colonialism, and Method." *Urban Geography* 41 (4): 469–86.

Crang, Mike, Alex Hughes, Nicky Gregson, Lucy Norris, and Farid Ahamed. 2013. "Rethinking Governance and Value in Commodity Chains through Global Recycling Networks." *Transactions of the Institute of British Geographers* 38 (1): 12–24.

Daniel, E. Valentine. 1984. *Fluid Signs: Being a Person the Tamil Way.* Berkeley: University of California Press.

Das, Veena. 1998. "Wittgenstein and Anthropology." *Annual Reviews of Anthropology* 27: 171–95.

———. 2006. *Life and Words: Violence and the Descent into the Ordinary.* Berkeley: University of California Press.

———. 2010. "Engaging the Life of the Other: Love and Everyday Life." In *Ordinary Ethics: Anthropology, Language, and Action*, 376–99. New York: Fordham University Press.

———. 2015. *Afflictions: Health, Disease, Poverty.* New York: Fordham University Press.

Das, Veena, and Deborah Poole. 2004. *Anthropology in the Margins of the State*. Santa Fe, NM: School of American Research Press.

Das, Veena, and Shalini Randeria. 2015. "Politics of the Urban Poor: Aesthetics, Ethics, Volatility, Precarity: An Introduction to Supplement 11." *Current Anthropology* 56 (S11): S3–14.

De Munck, Victor C. 1996. "Love and Marriage in a Sri Lankan Muslim Community: Toward a Reevaluation of Dravidian Marriage Practices." *American Ethnologist* 23 (4): 698–716.

Deleuze, Gilles, and Felix Guattari. 1987. *A Thousand Plateaus: Capitalism and Schizophrenia*. Minneapolis: University of Minnesota Press.

Denning, Michael. 2010. "Wageless Life." *New Left Review* 66 (Nov–Dec): 79–97.

Dickey, Sara. 2000. "Permeable Homes: Domestic Service, Household Space, and the Vulnerability of Class Boundaries in Urban India." *American Ethnologist* 27 (2): 462–89.

Doherty, Jacob. 2019. "Filthy Flourishing: Para-Sites, Animal Infrastructure, and the Waste Frontier in Kampala." *Current Anthropology* 60 (S20): S321–32.

Douglas, Mary. 2002. *Purity and Danger: An Analysis of Concepts of Pollution and Taboo*. London: Routledge and Kegan Paul.

Dumont, Louis. 1980. *Homo Hierarchicus: The Caste System and Its Implications*. Chicago: University of Chicago Press.

Dutt, Yashica. 2019. *Coming Out as Dalit: A Memoir*. New Delhi: Aleph Book Company.

Eglar, Zekiya. 2010. *A Punjabi Village in Pakistan: Perspectives on Community, Land, and Economy*. Oxford: Oxford University Press.

Elinoff, Eli. 2016. "A House Is More than a House: Aesthetic Politics in a Northeastern Thai Railway Settlement." *Journal of the Royal Anthropological Institute* 22 (3): 610–32.

Elyachar, Julia. 2005. *Markets of Dispossession: NGOs, Economic Development, and the State in Cairo*. Politics, History, and Culture. Durham, NC: Duke University Press.

———. 2012. "Next Practices: Knowledge, Infrastructure, and Public Goods at the Bottom of the Pyramid." *Public Culture* 24 (1): 109–29.

Engineering Planning and Management Consultants. 1996. *Data Collection for Preparation of National Study on Privatisation of Solid Waste Management in Eights Selected Cities of Pakistan*. Lahore: Engineering Planning and Management Consultants.

Ercelawn, Aly, and Muhammad Nauman. 2004. "Unfree Labour in South Asia: Debt Bondage at Brick Kilns in Pakistan." *Economic and Political Weekly* 39 (22): 2235–42.

Falahi, Masood Alam. 2007. *Hindustan Mein Zaat-Paat Aur Musalman*. New Delhi: Al-Qazi.

———. 2020. "Sir Syed Ahmad Khan and His Justification for Ashraf Hegemony." *Pasmanda Democracy* (blog). May 9, 2020. https://pasmandademocracy.com/caste-religion/masood/sir-syed-ahmad-khan-and-his-justification-for-ashraf-hegemony/.

Feldman, Ilana. 2008. *Governing Gaza: Bureaucracy, Authority, and the Work of Rule, 1917–1967*. Durham, NC: Duke University Press.

Fennell, Catherine. 2015. *Last Project Standing: Civics and Sympathy in Post-Welfare Chicago*. Minneapolis: University of Minnesota Press.

Ferguson, James, and Akhil Gupta. 2002. "Spatializing States: Toward an Ethnography of Neoliberal Governmentality." *American Ethnologist* 29 (4): 981–1002.

Finkelstein, Maura. 2019. *The Archive of Loss: Lively Ruination in Mill Land Mumbai.* Durham, NC: Duke University Press.

Fischer, Michael M. J. 2003. *Emergent Forms of Life and the Anthropological Voice.* Durham, NC: Duke University Press.

Fortunati, Leopoldina. 1995. *The Arcane of Reproduction: Housework, Prostitution, Labor and Capital.* Brooklyn, NY: Autonomedia.

Foucault, Michel. 1991. "Governmentality." In *The Foucault Effect: Studies in Governmentality with Two Lectures by and an Interview with Michel Foucault,* edited by Graham Burchell, Colin Gordon, and Peter Miller, 87–104. London: Harvester Wheatsheaf.

———. 2007. *Security, Territory, Population: Lectures at the Collège de France, 1977–78.* New York: Palgrave Macmillan.

Fox, Richard G. 1984. "Urban Class and Communal Consciousness in Colonial Punjab: The Genesis of India's Intermediate Regime." *Modern Asian Studies* 18 (3): 459–89.

———. 1985. *Lions of the Punjab: Culture in the Making.* Berkeley: University of California Press.

Fredericks, Rosalind. 2018. *Garbage Citizenship: Vital Infrastructures of Labor in Dakar, Senegal.* Durham, NC: Duke University Press.

Freitag, Sandria B. 1991. "Introduction." *South Asia: Journal of South Asian Studies* 14 (1): 1–13.

Frystad, Kathinka. 2003. "Master-Servant Relations and the Domestic Reproduction of Caste in Northern India." *Ethnos* 68 (1): 73–94.

Fuller, Christopher John. 1996. "Introduction: Caste Today." In *Caste Today,* edited by C. J. Fuller, 1–31. New Delhi: Oxford University Press.

Fuller, Christopher John, and Veronique Benei, eds. 2009. *The Everyday State and Society in Modern India.* New Delhi: Social Science Press.

Fuller, Christopher John, and Haripriya Narasimhan. 2014. *Tamil Brahmans: The Making of a Middle-Class Caste.* Chicago: University of Chicago Press.

Gandy, Matthew. 1994. *Recycling and the Politics of Urban Waste.* New York: St. Martin's.

Gazdar, Haris. 2007. "Class, Caste or Race: Veils over Social Oppression in Pakistan." *Economic and Political Weekly* 42 (2): 86–88.

Gazdar, Haris, and Hussain Bux Mallah. 2012. "Class, Caste and Housing in Rural Pakistani Punjab: The Untold Story of the Five Marla Scheme." *Contributions to Indian Sociology* 46 (3): 311–36.

Ghertner, D. Asher. 2015. *Rule by Aesthetics: World-Class City Making in Delhi.* Oxford: Oxford University Press.

Gibson-Graham, J. K. 2006. *The End of Capitalism (As We Knew It): A Feminist Critique of Political Economy.* Minneapolis: University of Minnesota Press.

Gidwani, Vinay. 2008. *Capital, Interrupted: Agrarian Development and the Politics of Work in India.* Minneapolis: University of Minnesota Press.

———. 2013. "Value Struggles: Waste Work and Urban Ecology in Delhi." In *Ecologies of Urbanism in India: Metropolitan Civility and Sustainability*, edited by Anne Rademacher and K. Sivaramakrishnan, 169–200. Hong Kong: Hong Kong University Press.

———. 2015. "The Work of Waste: Inside India's Infra-Economy." *Transactions of the Institute of British Geographers* 40 (4): 575–95.

———. 2018. "Abstract and Concrete Labor in the Age of Informality." In *Handbook on the Geographies of Power*, edited by Mat Coleman and John Agnew, 164–77. Cheltenham, UK: Edward Elgar.

Gidwani, Vinay, and Sunil Kumar. 2019. "Time, Space, and the Subaltern: The Matter of Labor in Delhi's Grey Economy." In *Subaltern Geographies*, edited by Tariq Jazeel and Stephen Legg, 142–66. Athens: University of Georgia Press.

Gidwani, Vinay, and Rajyashree N. Reddy. 2011. "The Afterlives of 'Waste': Notes from India for a Minor History of Capitalist Surplus." *Antipode* 43 (5): 1625–58.

Gidwani, Vinay, and Joel Wainwright. 2014. "On Capital, Not-Capital, and Development: After Kalyan Sanyal." *Economic and Political Weekly* 49 (34): 40–47.

Gill, Kaveri. 2009. *Of Poverty and Plastic: Scavenging and Scrap Trading Entrepreneurs in India's Urban Informal Economy*. New Delhi: Oxford University Press.

Gill, Navyug. 2019. "Limits of Conversion: Caste, Labor, and the Question of Emancipation in Colonial Panjab." *Journal of Asian Studies* 78 (1): 3–22.

Gille, Zsuzsa. 2007. *From the Cult of Waste to the Trash Heap of History: The Politics of Waste in Socialist and Postsocialist Hungary*. Bloomington: Indiana University Press.

Gilmartin, David. 1988. *Empire and Islam: Punjab and the Making of Pakistan*. Berkeley: University of California Press.

———. 1994a. "Biraderi and Bureaucracy: The Politics of Muslim Kinship Solidarity in 20th Century Punjab." *International Journal of Punjab Studies* 1 (1): 1–29.

———. 1994b. "Scientific Empire and Imperial Science: Colonialism and Irrigation Technology in the Indus Basin." *Journal of Asian Studies* 53 (4): 1127–49.

———. 1998. "Partition, Pakistan, and South Asian History: In Search of a Narrative." *Journal of Asian Studies* 57 (4): 1068–95.

———. 2020. *Blood and Water: The Indus River Basin in Modern History*. Berkeley: University of California Press.

Glenn, Evelyn Nakano. 1992. "From Servitude to Service Work: Historical Continuities in the Racial Division of Paid Reproductive Labor." *Signs: Journal of Women in Culture and Society* 18 (1): 1–43.

Glover, William. 2005. "Objects, Models, and Exemplary Works: Educating Sentiment in Colonial India." *Journal of Asian Studies* 64 (3): 539–66.

———. 2007. "Construing Urban Space as 'Public' in Colonial India: Some Notes from Punjab." *Journal of Punjab Studies* 14 (2): 211–24.

———. 2008. *Making Lahore Modern: Constructing and Imagining a Colonial City*. Minneapolis: University of Minnesota Press.

Goswami, Manu. 2004. *Producing India: From Colonial Economy to National Space*. Chicago: University of Chicago Press.

Government of Punjab. 1876. *Lahore Scheme for Water and Drainage*. Lahore: Superintendent of Government Printing.

———. 1884. *The Panjab Municipal Act.* Lahore: Superintendent of Government Printing.

———. 1895. *Gazetteer of Sialkot District.* Lahore: Civil and Military Gazette Press.

———. 1924. *Lahore Main Drainage Scheme "D".* Lahore: Superintendent of Government Printing.

———. 1931. *Report on the Affairs of the Municipal Committee of Lahore.* Lahore: Superintendent of Government Printing.

———. 1945. *Annual Administration Report of the Lahore Improvement Trust.* Lahore: Dinmuhammadi Press.

———. 1952. *Annual Health Report of the Punjab.* Lahore: Superintendent of Government Printing.

———. 2006. *Gazetteer of the Lahore District.* Lahore: Sang-e-Meel.

———. 2013 [1908]. *Imperial Gazetteer of India, Provincial Series: Punjab.* Vol. 1. Lahore: Sang-e-Meel.

Govindrajan, Radhika. 2018. *Animal Intimacies: Interspecies Relatedness in India's Central Himalayas.* Chicago: University of Chicago Press.

Greeson, Emma, Stefan Laser, and Olli Pyyhtinen. 2020. "Dis/Assembling Value: Lessons from Waste Valuation Practices." *Valuation Studies* 7 (2): 151–66.

Gregory, Chris A. 2012. "On Money Debt and Morality: Some Reflections on the Contribution of Economic Anthropology." *Social Anthropology* 20 (4): 380–96.

Gregson, Nicky, Mike Crang, Sara Fuller, and Helen Holmes. 2015. "Interrogating the Circular Economy: The Moral Economy of Resource Recovery in the EU." *Economy and Society* 44 (2): 218–43.

Grewal, Reeta. 2009. *Colonialism and Urbanization in India: The Punjab Region.* New Delhi: Manohar.

Guerin, Isabelle. 2014. "Juggling with Debt, Social Ties, and Values: The Everyday Use of Microcredit in Rural South India." *Current Anthropology* 55 (S9): S40–50.

Guerin, Isabelle, Bert d'Espallier, and Govindan Venkatasubramanian. 2013. "Debt in Rural South India: Fragmentation, Social Regulation and Discrimination." *Journal of Development Studies* 49 (9): 1155–71.

Gupta, Akhil. 2012. *Red Tape: Bureaucracy, Structural Violence, and Poverty in India.* Durham, NC: Duke University Press.

Guru, Gopal. 1995. "Dalit Women Talk Differently." *Economic and Political Weekly* 30 (41/42): 2548–50.

Guyer, Jane I. 2004. *Marginal Gains: Monetary Transactions in Atlantic Africa.* Chicago: University of Chicago Press.

Hall, Derek, Philip Hirsch, and Tania M. Li. 2011. *Powers of Exclusion: Land Dilemmas in Southeast Asia.* Honolulu: University of Hawai'i Press.

Hamlin, Christopher. 1998. *Public Health and Social Justice in the Age of Chadwick: Britain, 1800–1854.* Cambridge: Cambridge University Press.

Han, Clara. 2018. "Precarity, Precariousness, and Vulnerability." *Annual Reviews of Anthropology* 47: 331–43.

Hansen, Thomas Blom, and Finn Stepputat. 2001. "Introduction" In *States of Imagination:*

Ethnographic Explorations of the Postcolonial State, edited by Thomas Blom Hansen and Finn Stepputat, 1–38. Durham, NC: Duke University Press.

Harding, Christopher. 2008. *Religious Transformation in South Asia. The Meanings of Conversion in Colonial Punjab*. Oxford: Oxford University Press.

Harms, Erik. 2013. "Eviction Time in the New Saigon: Temporalities of Displacement in the Rubble of Development." *Cultural Anthropology* 28 (2): 344–68.

Harrison, Mark. 1994. *Public Health in British India: Anglo-Indian Preventive Medicine, 1859–1914*. Cambridge: Cambridge University Press.

Harriss-White, Barbara. 1999. *Agricultural Markets from Theory to Practice: Field Experience in Developing Countries*. New York: St. Martin's.

———. 2003. *India Working: Essays on Society and Economy*. Cambridge: Cambridge University Press.

Hart, Keith. 1985. "The Informal Economy." *Cambridge Anthropology* 10 (2): 54–58.

Harvey, David. 2012. *Rebel Cities: From the Right to the City to the Urban Revolution*. New York: Verso.

Hasan, Arif. 2010. "Migration, Small Towns and Social Transformations in Pakistan." *Environment and Urbanization* 22 (1): 33–50.

———. 2015. "Land Contestation in Karachi and the Impact on Housing and Urban Development." *Environment and Urbanization* 27 (1): 217–30.

Hasan, Arif, and Hamza Arif. 2018. *Pakistan: The Causes and Repercussions of the Housing Crisis*. London: International Institute for Environment and Development.

Hecht, Gabrielle. 2018. "Interscalar Vehicles for an African Anthropocene: On Waste, Temporality, and Violence." *Cultural Anthropology* 33 (1): 109–41.

Herod, Andrew, Graham Pickren, Al Rainnie, and Susan McGrath-Champ. 2013. "Waste, Commodity Fetishism and the Ongoingness of Economic Life." *Area* 45 (3): 376–82.

Herzfeld, Michael. 2005. *Cultural Intimacy: Social Poetics in the Nation-State*. New York: Routledge.

Herzig, Rebecca, and Banu Subramaniam. 2017. "Labor in the Age of 'Bio-Everything.'" *Radical History Review* 2017 (127): 103–24.

Hird, Myra J. 2012. "Knowing Waste: Towards an Inhuman Epistemology." *Social Epistemology* 26 (3–4): 453–69.

Hird, Myra J., Scott Lougheed, R. Kerry Rowe, and Cassandra Kuyvenhoven. 2014. "Making Waste Management Public (or Falling Back to Sleep)." *Social Studies of Science* 44 (3): 441–65.

Holston, James. 1991. "Autoconstruction in Working-Class Brazil." *Cultural Anthropology* 6 (4): 447–65.

Howell, Philip. 2000. "Prostitution and Racialised Sexuality: The Regulation of Prostitution in Britain and the British Empire before the Contagious Diseases Acts." *Environment and Planning D: Society and Space* 18 (3): 321–39.

Hull, Matthew. 2012. *Government of Paper: The Materiality of Bureaucracy in Urban Pakistan*. Berkeley: University of California Press.

Human Rights Commission of Pakistan. 2019. *State of Human Rights in 2018*. Lahore: Humans Rights Commission of Pakistan.

Hussain, Ghulam. 2019b. "Understanding Hegemony of Caste in Political Islam and Sufism in Sindh, Pakistan." *Journal of Asian and African Studies* 54 (5): 716–45.

———. 2020. "'Dalits Are in India, Not in Pakistan': Exploring the Discursive Bases of the Denial of Dalitness under the Ashrafia Hegemony." *Journal of Asian and African Studies* 55 (1): 17–43.

Ibbetson, Denzil. 1916. *Panjab Castes*. Lahore: Superintendent of Government Printing.

Imran, Muhammad. 2010. *Institutional Barriers to Sustainable Urban Transport in Pakistan*. Karachi: Oxford University Press.

International Labor Organization. 2018. "Informal Economy in Pakistan." https://www.ilo .org/islamabad/areasofwork/informal-economy/lang—en/index.htm.

Jalal, Ayesha. 1994. *The Sole Spokesman: Jinnah, the Muslim League and the Demand for Pakistan*. Cambridge: Cambridge University Press.

Jan, Muhammad Ali. 2019. "The Complexity of Exchange: Wheat Markets, Petty-Commodity Producers and the Emergence of Commercial Capital in Colonial Punjab." *Journal of Agrarian Change* 19 (2): 225–48.

Javed, Nasir, and Sana Riaz. 2020. "Issues in Urban Planning and Policy: The Case Study of Lahore, Pakistan." In *New Urban Agenda in Asia-Pacific*, edited by Bharat Dahiya and Ashok Das, 117–62. Singapore: Springer.

Javed, Umair. 2019. "Ascending the Power Structure: Bazaar Traders in Urban Punjab." In *New Perspectives on Pakistan's Political Economy: State, Class and Social Change*, edited by Matthew McCartney and S. Akbar Zaidi, 199–215. New Delhi: Cambridge University Press.

Javid, Hassan. 2011. "Class, Power, and Patronage: Landowners and Politics in Punjab." *History and Anthropology* 22 (3): 337–69.

———. 2015. "Elections, Bureaucracy, and the Law: The Reproduction of Landed Power in Post-Colonial Punjab." In *State and Nation-Building in Pakistan*, edited by Roger D. Long, Yunus Samad, and Gurharpal Singh, 53–77. New York: Routledge.

Javid, Hassan, and Nicolas Martin. 2020. "Democracy and Discrimination: Comparing Caste-Based Politics in Indian and Pakistani Punjab." *South Asia: Journal of South Asian Studies* 43 (1): 136–51.

Jegathesan, Mythri. 2018. "Claiming Ūr: Home, Investment, and Decolonial Desires on Sri Lanka's Tea Plantations." *Anthropological Quarterly* 91 (2): 635–70.

Jinnah, Muhammad Ali. 1947. "Inaugural Address to Pakistan Constituent Assembly." In *Pakistan Movement Historical Documents*, 542–47. Karachi: Paradise Subscription Agency.

Jodhka, Surinder S. 2002. "Caste and Untouchability in Rural Punjab." *Economic and Political Weekly* 37 (19) 1813–23.

Johnson, Ryan, and Amna Khalid. 2012. "Introduction." In *Public Health in the British Empire: Intermediaries, Subordinates, and the Practice of Public Health, 1850–1960*, edited by Ryan Johnson and Amna Khalid, 1–31. New York: Routledge.

Joyce, Patrick. 2003. *The Rule of Freedom: Liberalism and the Modern City*. New York: Verso.

Kar, Sohini. 2017. "Relative Indemnity: Risk, Insurance, and Kinship in Indian Microfinance." *Journal of the Royal Anthropological Institute* 23 (2): 302–19.

Kaviraj, Sudipta. 1997. "Filth and the Public Sphere: Concepts and Practices about Space in Calcutta." *Public Culture* 10 (1): 83–113.

Keane, Webb. 2003. "Semiotics and the Social Analysis of Material Things." *Language & Communication* 23 (3): 409–25.

Kerr, Ian. 1980. "Urbanization and Colonial Rule in the 19th-Century India Lahore and Amritsar, 1849–1881." *Panjab Past and Present* 24 (1): 210–25.

Khalid, Amna. 2012. "'Unscientific and Insanitary': Hereditary Sweepers and Customary Rights in the United Provinces." In *Public Health in the British Empire: Intermediaries, Subordinates, and the Practice of Public Health, 1850–1960*, edited by Ryan Johnson and Amna Khalid, 51–70. New York: Routledge.

Khan, Naveeda. 2006. "Flaws in the Flow: Roads and Their Modernity in Pakistan." *Social Text* 24 (4): 87–113.

———. 2012. *Muslim Becoming: Aspiration and Skepticism in Pakistan*. Durham, NC: Duke University Press.

Kidambi, Prashant. 2007. *The Making of an Indian Metropolis: Colonial Governance and Public Culture in Bombay, 1890–1920*. Aldershot, UK: Ashgate.

Kornberg, Dana. 2019. "From Balmikis to Bengalis: The 'Casteification' of Muslims in Delhi's Informal Garbage Economy." *Economic and Political Weekly* 54 (47): 48–54.

Koselleck, Reinhart. 2004. *Futures Past: On the Semantics of Historical Time*. New York: Columbia University Press.

Kristeva, Julia. 1982. *Powers of Horror: An Essay on Abjection*. New York: Columbia University Press.

Krupa, Christopher, and David Nugent. 2015. "Off-Centered States: Rethinking State Theory Through an Andean Lens." In *State Theory and Andean Politics: New Approaches to the Study of Rule*, edited by Christopher Krupa and David Nugent, 1–31. Philadelphia: University of Pennsylvania Press.

Lahore Development Authority. 1980. *Lahore Urban Development and Traffic Study, Vol 1*. Lahore: Lahore Urban Development.

Lambek, Michael. 2001. "The Value of Coins in a Sakalava Polity: Money, Death, and Historicity in Mahajanga, Madagascar." *Comparative Studies in Society and History* 43 (4): 735–62.

Larkin, Brian. 2008. *Signal and Noise: Media, Infrastructure, and Urban Culture in Nigeria*. Durham, NC: Duke University Press.

———. 2013. "The Politics and Poetics of Infrastructure." *Annual Reviews of Anthropology* 42: 327–43.

Latif, Syed Muhammad. 2005 [1892]. *Lahore: Its History, Architectural Remains and Antiquities*. Lahore: Sang-e-Meel.

Latour, Bruno. 2005. *Reassembling the Social: An Introduction to Actor-Network-Theory*. Oxford: Oxford University Press.

Lee, Joel. 2017. "Odor and Order: How Caste Is Inscribed in Space and Sensoria." *Comparative Studies of South Asia, Africa and the Middle East* 37 (3): 470–90.

———. 2021. "Disgust and Untouchability: Towards an Affective Theory of Caste." *South Asian History and Culture* 12 (2–3): 310–27.

Legg, Stephen. 2009. "Governing Prostitution in Colonial Delhi: From Cantonment Regulations to International Hygiene (1864–1939)." *Social History* 34 (4): 447–67.

Lelyveld, David. N.d. "Ashraf – Keyword." SOAS. https://www.soas.ac.uk/south-asia-institute/keywords/file24799.pdf.

Lepawsky, Josh, and Mostaem Billah. 2011. "Making Chains That (Un)Make Things: Waste–Value Relations and the Bangladeshi Rubbish Electronics Industry." *Geografiska Annaler: Series B, Human Geography* 93 (2): 121–39.

Lepawsky, Josh, and Charles Mather. 2011. "From Beginnings and Endings to Boundaries and Edges: Rethinking Circulation and Exchange through Electronic Waste." *Area* 43 (3): 242–49.

Liboiron, Max, and Josh Lepawsky. 2022. *Discard Studies: Wasting, Systems, and Power.* Cambridge, MA: MIT Press.

Liboiron, Max. 2014. "Solutions to Waste and the Problem of Scalar Mismatches." *Discard Studies* (blog). https://discardstudies.com/2014/02/10/solutions-to-waste-and-the-problem-of-scalar-mismatches/.

———. 2021. *Pollution Is Colonialism.* Durham, NC: Duke University Press.

Low, Setha M., and Neil Smith, eds. 2006. *The Politics of Public Space.* New York: Routledge.

Majeed, Asma, Syeda Adila Batool, Muhammad Nawaz Chaudhry, and Rana Aatif Siddique. 2017. "Scavenging Demeanor in Bahawalpur, Pakistan: Social and Health Perspective." *Journal of Material Cycles and Waste Management* 19 (2): 815–26.

Malhotra, Anshu. 2002. *Gender, Caste, and Religious Identities: Restructuring Class in Colonial Punjab.* Delhi: Oxford University Press.

Maqsood, Ammara. 2017. *The New Pakistani Middle Class.* Cambridge, MA: Harvard University Press.

Marriott, McKim. 1968. "Caste Ranking and Food Transactions: A Matrix Analysis." In *Structure and Change in Indian Society*, edited by Milton Singer and Bernard S. Cohn, 133–71. Chicago: Aldine.

Marriott, McKim, and Ronald Inden. 1977. "Toward an Ethnosociology of South Asian Caste Systems." In *The New Wind: Changing Identities in South Asia*, edited by Kenneth David, 227–38. Chicago: Aldine.

Martin, Nicolas. 2009. "Politics, Patronage, and Debt Bondage in the Pakistani Punjab." PhD thesis, London School of Economics and Political Science.

———. 2016. *Politics, Landlords and Islam in Pakistan.* Abingdon, UK: Routledge.

Marx, Karl. 1977. *Capital: A Critique of Political Economy.* Vol. 1. New York: Vintage Books.

Masselos, Jim. 1982. "Jobs and Jobbery: The Sweeper in Bombay under the Raj." *Indian Economic & Social History Review* 19 (2): 101–39.

Maurer, Bill. 2006. "The Anthropology of Money." *Annual Reviews of Anthropology* 35: 15–36.

———. 2012. "Payment: Forms and Functions of Value Transfer in Contemporary Society." *Cambridge Journal of Anthropology* 30 (2): 15–35.

Mauss, Marcel. 2000. *The Gift: The Form and Reason for Exchange in Archaic Societies.* New York: W. W. Norton.

Mazzarella, William. 2004. "Culture, Globalization, Mediation." *Annual Reviews of Anthropology* 33: 345–67.

Mehta, Uday Singh. 1999. *Liberalism and Empire: A Study in Nineteenth-Century British Liberal Thought.* Chicago: University of Chicago Press.

Mies, Maria. 1998. *Patriarchy and Accumulation on a World Scale: Women in the International Division of Labour.* London: Palgrave MacMillan.

Millar, Kathleen. 2008. "Making Trash into Treasure: Struggles for Autonomy on a Brazilian Garbage Dump." *Anthropology of Work Review* 29 (2): 25–34.

———. 2014. "The Precarious Present: Wageless Labor and Disrupted Life in Rio de Janeiro, Brazil." *Cultural Anthropology* 29 (1): 32–53.

———. 2018. *Reclaiming the Discarded: Life and Labor on Rio's Garbage Dump.* Durham, NC: Duke University Press.

———. 2020. Garbage as Racialization. *Anthropology and Humanism* 45 (1): 4–24.

Miller, Daniel. 2001. *Home Possessions: Material Culture behind Closed Doors.* Oxford: Berg.

Mills, Charles W. 2014. *The Racial Contract.* Ithaca, NY: Cornell University Press.

Mitchell, Timothy. 1991. "The Limits of the State: Beyond Statist Approaches and Their Critics." *American Political Science Review* 85 (1): 77–96.

———. 1999. "Society, Economy, and the State Effect." In *State/Culture: State Formation after the Cultural Turn,* edited by George Steinmetz, 76–97. Ithaca, NY: Cornell University Press.

Mitra, Durba. 2021. "'Surplus Woman': Female Sexuality and the Concept of Endogamy." *Journal of Asian Studies* 80 (1): 3–26.

Moatasim, Faiza. 2019. "Entitled Urbanism: Elite Informality and the Reimagining of a Planned Modern City." *Urban Studies* 56 (5): 1009–25.

Mody, Perveez. 2008. *The Intimate State: Love-Marriage and the Law in Delhi.* Delhi: Routledge.

Moore, James W. 2017. "The Capitalocene, Part I: On the Nature and Origins of Our Ecological Crisis." *Journal of Peasant Studies* 44 (3): 594–630.

———. 2018. "The Capitalocene Part II: Accumulation by Appropriation and the Centrality of Unpaid Work/Energy." *Journal of Peasant Studies* 45 (2): 237–79.

Mosse, David. 2012. *The Saint in the Banyan Tree: Christianity and Caste Society in India.* Berkeley: University of California Press.

Mughal, Muhammad Aurangzeb. 2015. "Domestic Space and Socio-Spatial Relationships in Rural Pakistan." *South Asia Research* 35 (2): 214–34.

Muniesa, Fabian, Yuval Millo, and Michel Callon, eds. 2007. *Market Devices.* Malden, MA: Blackwell.

Munir, Kamal A., Natalya Naqvi, and Adaner Usmani. 2015. "The Abject Condition of Labor in Pakistan." *International Labor and Working-Class History* 87: 174–83.

Murphy, Michelle. 2015. "Reproduction." In *Marxism and Feminism,* edited by Shahrzad Mojab, 287–304. London: Zed Books.

———. 2017. *The Economization of Life.* Durham, NC: Duke University Press.

Mustafa, Daanish. 2013. *Water Resource Management in a Vulnerable World: The Hydro-Hazardscapes of Climate Change.* New York: I. B. Tauris.

Nelms, Taylor C., Bill Maurer, Lana Swartz, and Scott Mainwaring. 2018. "Social Payments: Innovation, Trust, Bitcoin, and the Sharing Economy." *Theory, Culture & Society* 35 (3): 13–33.

Nguyen, Minh T. N. 2016. "Trading in Broken Things: Gendered Performances and Spatial Practices in a Northern Vietnamese Rural-Urban Waste Economy." *American Ethnologist* 43 (1): 116–29.

———. 2019. *Waste and Wealth: An Ethnography of Labor, Value, and Morality in a Vietnamese Recycling Economy*. New York: Oxford University Press.

O'Hare, Patrick. 2019. "'The Landfill Has Always Borne Fruit': Precarity, Formalisation and Dispossession among Uruguay's Waste Pickers." *Dialectical Anthropology* 43 (1): 31–44.

Oldenburg, Veena Talwar. 1984. *The Making of Colonial Lucknow, 1856–1877*. Princeton, NJ: Princeton University Press.

Orsini, Francesca. 2006. "Introduction." In *Love in South Asia: A Cultural History*, edited by Francesca Orsini. Cambridge: Cambridge University Press.

Osella, Caroline, and Filippo Osella. 1998. "Friendship and Flirting: Micro-Politics in Kerala, South India." *Journal of the Royal Anthropological Institute* 4 (2): 189–206.

Pandey, Gyanendra. 1984. "'Encounters and Calamities': The History of a North Indian Qasba in the Nineteenth Century." In *Subaltern Studies: Writings on South Asian History and Society*, edited by Ranajit Guha, Vol. 3. Delhi: Oxford University Press.

Parreas, Juno Salazar. 2016. "The Materiality of Intimacy in Wildlife Rehabilitation: Rethinking Ethical Capitalism through Embodied Encounters with Animals in Southeast Asia." *Positions: East Asia Cultures Critique* 24 (1): 97–127.

Parry, Jonathan P., and Maurice Bloch. 1989. "Introduction." In *Money and the Morality of Exchange*, edited by Jonathan P. Parry and Maurice Bloch, 1–32. Cambridge: Cambridge University Press.

Peebles, Gustav. 2010. "The Anthropology of Credit and Debt." *Annual Reviews of Anthropology* 39: 225–40.

Petryna, Adriana. 2013. *Life Exposed: Biological Citizens after Chernobyl*. Princeton, NJ: Princeton University Press.

Piliavsky, Anastasia. 2014. "Introduction." In *Patronage as Politics in South Asia*, edited by Anastasia Piliavsky, 1–35. Cambridge: Cambridge University Press.

Pinzur, David. 2016. "Making the Grade: Infrastructural Semiotics and Derivative Market Outcomes on the Chicago Board of Trade and New Orleans Cotton Exchange, 1856–1909." *Economy and Society* 45 (3–4): 431–53.

Platts, John T. 1884. *A Dictionary of Urdu, Classical Hindi, and English*. London: W. H. Allen & Co.

Povinelli, Elizabeth. 2006. *The Empire of Love: Toward a Theory of Intimacy, Genealogy, and Carnality*. Durham, NC: Duke University Press.

———. 2011. *Economies of Abandonment: Social Belonging and Endurance in Late Liberalism*. Durham, NC: Duke University Press.

———. 2016. *Geontologies: A Requiem to Late Liberalism*. Durham, NC: Duke University Press.

Prakash, Gyan. 1999. *Another Reason: Science and the Imagination of Modern India*. Princeton, NJ: Princeton University Press.

Prashad, Vijay. 1995. "Marks of Capital: Colonialism and the Sweepers of Delhi." *International Review of Social History* 40 (1): 1–30.

———. 2000. *Untouchable Freedom: A Social History of Dalit Community*. New York: Oxford University Press.

———. 2001. "The Technology of Sanitation in Colonial Delhi." *Modern Asian Studies* 35 (1): 113–55.

Qadeer, Mohammad A. 1983. *Urban Development in the Third World: Internal Dynamics of Lahore, Pakistan*. New York: Praeger.

Raheja, Natasha. 2022. "GOVERNING BY PROXIMITY: State Performance and Migrant Citizenship on the India-Pakistan Border." *Cultural Anthropology* 37 (3): 513–548.

Rajan, Kaushik Sunder. 2006. *Biocapital: The Constitution of Postgenomic Life*. Durham, NC: Duke University Press.

Rao, Anupama. 2005. "Introduction." In *Gender and Caste*, edited by Anupama Rao, 1–47. New York: Zed Books.

Rashid, Maria. 2020. *Dying to Serve: Militarism, Affect and the Politics of Sacrifice in the Pakistan Army*. Palo Alto, CA: Stanford University Press.

Reddy, Rajyashree N. 2015. "Producing Abjection: E-Waste Improvement Schemes and Informal Recyclers of Bangalore." *Geoforum* 62: 166–74.

Rege, Sharmila. 1998. "Dalit Women Talk Differently: A Critique of 'Difference' and towards a Dalit Feminist Standpoint Position." *Economic and Political Weekly* 33 (44): WS39–46.

Rehman, Nida. 2009. "From Artifact to Site: Understanding the Canal in the City of Gardens." PhD thesis, Massachusetts Institute of Technology.

———. 2014. "Description, Display and Distribution: Cultivating a Garden Identity in Late Nineteenth-Century Lahore." *Studies in the History of Gardens & Designed Landscapes* 34 (2): 176–86.

Rahman, Tariq. 2022. "Landscapes of Rizq: Mediating Worldly and Otherworldly in Lahore's Speculative Real Estate Market." *Economic Anthropology* 9 (2): 209–308.

Reno, Joshua. 2009. "Your Trash Is Someone's Treasure: The Politics of Value at a Michigan Landfill." *Journal of Material Culture* 14 (1): 29–46.

———. 2015. "Waste and Waste Management." *Annual Reviews of Anthropology* 44: 557–72.

———. 2016. *Waste Away: Working and Living with a North American Landfill*. Berkeley: University of California Press.

Resnick, Elana. 2021. "The Limits of Resilience: Managing Waste in the Racialized Anthropocene." *American Anthropologist* 123 (2): 222–36.

Ring, Laura A. 2006. *Zenana: Everyday Peace in a Karachi Apartment Building*. Bloomington: Indiana University Press.

Rizvi, Mubbashir. 2019. *The Ethics of Staying: Social Movements and Land Rights Politics in Pakistan*. Palo Alto, CA: Stanford University Press.

Roitman, Janet L. 1990. "The Politics of Informal Markets in Sub-Saharan Africa." *Journal of Modern African Studies* 28 (4): 671–96.

———. 2003. "Unsanctioned Wealth; or, the Productivity of Debt in Northern Cameroon." *Public Culture* 15 (2): 211–37.

Rose, Nikolas. 2009. *The Politics of Life Itself: Biomedicine, Power, and Subjectivity in the Twenty-First Century*. Princeton, NJ: Princeton University Press.

Roseberry, William. 1989. "Peasants and the World." In *Economic Anthropology*, edited by Stuart Plattner, 108–27. Palo Alto, CA: Stanford University Press.

Rouse, Shahnaz. 1988. "Agrarian Transformation in a Punjabi Village: Structural Change and Its Consequences." PhD diss., University of Wisconsin–Madison.

Roy, Ananya, and Nezar AlSayyad. 2004. "Urban Informality: Crossing Borders." In *Urban Informality: Transnational Perspectives from the Middle East, Latin America, and South Asia*, 1–6. Lanham, MD: Lexington Books.

Rutherford, Danilyn. 2009. "Sympathy, State Building, and the Experience of Empire." *Cultural Anthropology* 24 (1): 1–32.

Sanyal, Kalyan. 2007. *Rethinking Capitalist Development: Primitive Accumulation, Governmentality and Post-Colonial Capitalism*. New York: Routledge.

Sanyal, Kalyan, and Rajesh Bhattacharyya. 2009. "Beyond the Factory: Globalisation, Informalisation of Production and the New Locations of Labour." *Economic and Political Weekly* 44 (22): 35–44.

Sargent, Adam, and Gregory Duff Morton. 2019. "What Happened to the Wage?" *Anthropological Quarterly* 92 (3): 635–62.

Scott, James C. 1998. *Seeing Like a State: How Certain Schemes to Improve the Human Condition Have Failed*. New Haven, CT: Yale University Press.

Sharan, Awadhendra. 2006. "In the City, Out of Place: Environment and Modernity, Delhi 1860s to 1960s." *Economic and Political Weekly* 41 (47): 4905–11.

Sharma, Aradhana, and Akhil Gupta. 2009. "Introduction: Rethinking Theories of the State in an Age of Globalization." In *The Anthropology of the State: A Reader*, edited by Aradhana Sharma and Akhil Gupta, 1–41. Malden, MA: Blackwell.

Shehryar, Muhammad. 2014. *The Informal Economy of Pakistan*. Lahore: Lahore University of Management Sciences.

Shryock, Andrew. 2004. *Off Stage/On Display: Intimacy and Ethnography in the Age of Public Culture*. Palo Alto, CA: Stanford University Press.

Siddiqi, Ayesha. 2019. *In the Wake of Disaster: Islamists, the State and a Social Contract in Pakistan*. Cambridge: Cambridge University Press.

Siddiqui, Shaukat. 2015. *Khudā Kī Bastī*. Karachi: Raktab.

Simone, AbdouMaliq. 2004. "People as Infrastructure: Intersecting Fragments in Johannesburg." *Public Culture* 16 (3): 407–29.

———. 2019. "Maximum Exposure: Making Sense in the Background of Extensive Urbanization." *Environment and Planning D: Society and Space* 37 (6): 990–1006.

Singh, Bhrigupati. 2011. "Agonistic Intimacy and Moral Aspiration in Popular Hinduism: A Study in the Political Theology of the Neighbor." *American Ethnologist* 38 (3): 430–50.

Singha, Sara. 2015. "Dalit Christians and Caste Consciousness in Pakistan." PhD thesis, Georgetown University.

Solomon, Marisa. 2019. "'The Ghetto Is a Gold Mine': The Racialized Temporality of Betterment." *International Labor and Working-Class History* 95: 76–94.

Sreenath, Shreyas. 2020. "Black Spot: An Account of Caste, Contract, and Discards in 21st Century Bangalore." PhD diss., Emory University.

Stamatopoulou-Robbins, Sophia. 2019. *Waste Siege: The Life of Infrastructure in Palestine.* Palo Alto, CA: Stanford University Press.

Star, Susan Leigh. 1999. "The Ethnography of Infrastructure." *American Behavioral Scientist* 43 (3): 377–91.

Stoler, Ann Laura. 2002. *Carnal Knowledge and Imperial Power: Race and the Intimate in Colonial Rule.* Berkeley: University of California Press.

Streefland, Pieter. 1979. *The Sweepers of Slaughterhouse: Conflict and Survival in a Karachi Neighbourhood.* Assen, Netherlands: Van Gorcum.

Subramanian, Ajantha. 2019. *The Caste of Merit: Engineering Education in India.* Cambridge, MA: Harvard University Press.

Sullivan, Basil. 1929. *A Note for the Use of the Lahore Improvement Committee and of the Lahore Improvement Trust When Formed, with Special Reference to the City of Lahore inside the Walls.* Lahore: Superintendent of Government Printing.

Talbot, Ian. 1988. *Punjab and the Raj, 1849–1947.* New Delhi: Manohar.

Tassadiq, Fatima, 2022. "Producing dispossessed and humanitarian subjects: Land acquisition and compensation policies in Lahore, Pakistan." *PoLAR: Political and Legal Anthropology Review.*

Thiranagama, Sharika. 2018. "The Civility of Strangers? Caste, Ethnicity, and Living Together in Postwar Jaffna, Sri Lanka." *Anthropological Theory* 18 (2–3): 357–81.

Tsing, Anna Lowenhaupt. 2015. *The Mushroom at the End of the World: On the Possibility of Life in Capitalist Ruins.* Princeton, NJ: Princeton University Press.

Tuck, Eve. "Suspending Damage: A Letter to Communities." *Harvard Educational Review* 79 (3): 409–28.

Tuck, Eve, and K. Wayne Yang. "Unbecoming Claims: Pedagogies of Refusal in Qualitative Research." *Qualitative Inquiry* 20 (6): 811–18.

Turner, Terence. 2008. "Marxian Value Theory: An Anthropological Perspective." *Anthropological Theory* 8 (1): 43–56.

Viswanath, Rupa. 2014. *The Pariah Problem: Caste, Religion, and the Social in Modern India.* New York: Columbia University Press.

Von Schnitzler, Antina. 2016. *Democracy's Infrastructure: Techno-Politics and Protest after Apartheid.* Princeton, NJ: Princeton University Press.

Vora, Kalindi. 2015. *Life Support: Biocapital and the New History of Outsourced Labor.* Minneapolis: University of Minnesota Press.

Wakil, Parvez. 1972. "'Zat' and 'Qoum' in Punjabi Society: A Contribution to the Problem of Caste." *Sociologus* 22 (1): 38–48.

Walbridge, Linda S. 2003. *The Christians of Pakistan: The Passion of Bishop John Joseph.* London: Routledge.

Weber, Max. 1978. *Economy and Society: An Outline of Interpretive Sociology.* Vol. 1 and 2. Berkeley: University of California Press.

Weeks, Kathi. 2007. "Life within and against Work: Affective Labor, Feminist Critique, and Post-Fordist Politics." *Ephemera: Theory and Politics in Organization* 7 (1): 233–49.

———. 2011. *The Problem with Work: Feminism, Marxism, Antiwork Politics, and Postwork Imaginaries*. Durham, NC: Duke University Press.

Whitehead, Judy. 1995. "Modernising the Motherhood Archetype: Public Health Models and the Child Marriage Restraint Act of 1929." *Contributions to Indian Sociology* 29 (1–2): 187–209.

Wilson, Ara. 2004. *The Intimate Economies of Bangkok: Tomboys, Tycoons, and Avon Ladies in the Global City*. Berkeley: University of California Press.

World Bank. 1994. *Project Completion Report on Pakistan: Lahore Urban Development Project*. Washington, DC: World Bank.

Yengde, Suraj. 2019. *Caste Matters*. Gurgaon: Penguin Viking.

———. 2021. "Global Castes." *Ethnic and Racial Studies* 1–21.

Zaidi, S. Akbar. 2014. "Rethinking Pakistan's Political Economy: Class, State, Power, and Transition." *Economic and Political Weekly* 49 (5): 47–54.

Zaloom, Caitlin. 2003. "Ambiguous Numbers: Trading Technologies and Interpretation in Financial Markets." *American Ethnologist* 30 (2): 258–72.

Zelizer, Viviana A. 2005. *The Purchase of Intimacy*. Princeton, NJ: Princeton University Press.

Zhang, Amy. 2020. "Circularity and Enclosures: Metabolizing Waste with the Black Soldier Fly." *Cultural Anthropology* 35 (1): 74–103.

Zimring, Carl. 2015. *Clean and White: A History of Environmental Racism in the United States*. New York: New York University Press.

Zulfiqar, Ghazal Mir. 2018. "Dirt, Foreignness, and Surveillance: The Shifting Relations of Domestic Work in Pakistan." *Organization* 26 (3): 2–16.

Brand New Nation: Capitalist Dreams and Nationalist
Designs in Twenty-First-Century India
Ravinder Kaur (2020)

Partisan Aesthetics: Modern Art and India's Long Decolonization
Sanjukta Sunderason (2020)

Dying to Serve: the Pakistan Army
Maria Rashid (2020)

In the Name of the Nation: India and Its Northeast
Sanjib Baruah (2020)

Faithful Fighters: Identity and Power in the British Indian Army
Kate Imy (2019)

Paradoxes of the Popular: Crowd Politics in Bangladesh
Nusrat Sabina Chowdhury (2019)

The Ethics of Staying: Social Movements and Land
Rights Politics in Pakistan Mubbashir
A. Rizvi (2019)

Mafia Raj: The Rule of Bosses in South Asia
Lucia Michelutti, Ashraf Hoque, Nicolas Martin, David Picherit, Paul Rollier,
Arild Ruud and Clarinda Still (2018)

Elusive Lives: Gender, Autobiography, and the Self in Muslim South Asia
Siobhan Lambert-Hurley (2018)

Financializing Poverty: Labor and Risk in Indian Microfinance
Sohini Kar (2018)

Jinnealogy: Time, Islam, and Ecological Thought in the Medieval Ruins of Delhi
Anand Vivek Taneja (2017)

For a complete listing of titles in this series, visit the
Stanford University Press website, www.sup.org.

Printed and bound by CPI Group (UK) Ltd, Croydon, CR0 4YY

25/03/2025

14647335-0003